moholy-nagy

experiment in totality

moholy-nagy

experiment in totality

sibyl moholy-nagy

with an introduction by **walter gropius**

the m.i.t. press
massachusetts institute of technology
cambridge, massachusetts, and london, england

Grateful acknowledgment is given to the following collections for permission to reproduce paintings in their possession: Solomon R. Guggenheim Foundation (*Figs. 49, 58, 67*), Ida Bienert, Munich (*Fig. 62*), Daniel Crowley, Peoria, Illinois (*Fig. 68*), Mrs. Suzette Hamill-Zurcher, Lake Forest, Illinois (*Fig. 71*), The Art Institute of Chicago (*Fig. 77*) and Galerie Chalette, New York (*Fig. 7*). The photographs were provided through the courtesy of: F. Levstik, Jr., Lucia Moholy, Bartloucci, Pritchard of London, A. R. Sinsabaugh, Arthur Siegel, Hedrich-Blessing Studio, *The Saturday Evening Post*, The Art Institute of Chicago, and The School of Design Photo Workshop.

"—and she tried to imagine what the flame of a candle looks like after the candle is blown out, for she could not remember ever having seen such a thing."

Alice in Wonderland

introduction

by **walter gropius,** chairman, department of architecture, harvard university

When I first saw the manuscript of this book I felt a certain apprehension which, I think, was quite natural for one who is about to see the life and work of his close friend revealed to the public; a friend, moreover, whose activities were so intensely connected with one of the most decisive periods of my own life. But soon I felt reassured as I became acquainted with this splendid and honest account of Moholy-Nagy's development from early experiments to full maturity. Moholy was always in the public eye, yet most people saw only the more obvious milestones of achievement which crystallize into "news stories." The other story, the intimate and often bitter story of one man's struggle for fulfillment, has been up to now the precious possession of his friends and collaborators, and of his wife, who was certainly the most devoted.

Looking back today, the difficult, contradictory and confusing years between the two World Wars, which form the background for the greater part of this book, seem to have provided a pitifully short time for a generation which approached its artistic endeavors with the zeal and enthusiasm released by the political change in Central Europe. But it was a period inspired by constructive ideas not as yet subjected to the blight of frustration which overshadows the world today. Those were the years of Moholy's and my collaboration in the Bauhaus of Weimar and Dessau, the development of which was deeply influenced by Moholy, the fiery stimulator.

After the Nazi nightmare had caused us both to leave Germany, we saw each other again in England, and later in the United States where I was fortunate enough to secure his leadership for The New Bauhaus in Chicago, subsequently renamed the Institute of Design. As the Bauhaus principles had never been based on limited nationalistic concepts, its seeds could be transplanted and further developed in this country. Against heavy odds which might have discouraged a giant, Moholy managed to pull the Institute through difficult years, never losing his indomitable courage and confidence. And still he did not let himself become absorbed only in his educational work, extensive as it was, but simultaneously produced a wealth of art that embraces the whole range of the visual arts.

His greatest effort as an artist was devoted to the conquest of space. His genius ventured into all realms of science and art to unriddle the phenomena of space and light. In painting, sculpture and architecture, in theater and industrial design, in photography and film, advertising and typography, he incessantly strove to interpret space in its relation to time, that is, motion in space.

Constantly developing new ideas Moholy maintained an unbiased curiosity, from which originated his continually fresh point of view. With a shrewd sense of observation he investigated everything that came his way, taking nothing for granted, always applying his acute sense of the organic. His was the attitude of an unprejudiced, happy child at play, surprising us by the directness of his intuitive approach. Here I believe was the source of his priceless quality as an educator: his never-ceasing power to stimulate and fire others with his enthusiasm. What more can true education achieve than setting the student's mind in motion by that contagious magic?

Moholy has been successful simultaneously as thinker and artist, as writer and teacher. That would seem to be almost too vast a range for one man, but abundant versatility was uniquely his. With his power of imagination he kept this broad variety of interests in balance. His vision took brilliant shortcuts, synchronizing his observations into a consistent whole, for he was aware of the danger of today's overspecialization which so often leads to fallacies.

Moholy seems always to have been acutely conscious of the preciousness of time; he worked with dedicated zeal to realize his ideas as though driven by the recognition that the destructive tendencies of our time could be changed into constructive forces only by a universal, superhuman effort. He had convinced himself of the generative power of all art and he wanted to see that power liberated in each individual with whom he came in contact. He had molded himself into a world citizen who would not let his ever-broadening outlook be narrowed by national barriers. Thus, Moholy the artist finally became a moral leader, all his activities being controlled by his strong social responsibility.

This book, *Moholy-Nagy, Experiment in Totality*, is evidence of a new attitude in the contemplation and formation of our physical world.

WALTER GROPIUS

introduction
to the second edition

Laszlo Moholy-Nagy died in November 1946. My account of his life was written in 1948 and published in the Spring of 1950. It went out of print some three years later and for a dozen years was largely forgotten. When I received the first inquiries about a new edition I declined because I felt that the two premises on which the book had been written were no longer relevant.

Of these two premises, a personal and a historical one, the personal had been as primordial as death itself: the compulsive desire to hold in the abstract what had vanished in the flesh. If I did not give it meaning, the circumstantial evidence of Moholy's life as a man among men, lover, husband, father, friend, teacher, would be obliterated by time. Only much later did I face the truth that the driving force was the need to come to terms with what had happened to me while recounting what had happened in his personal relationships. And with this realization grew a strong reluctance to make public again what I had come to consider a personal dialogue. Although I had never intended to be a teacher, my growing awareness of Moholy's influence left me no alternative when I had to choose a profession in order to make a living. As I groped my way from a purely emotional afflatus to the documented knowledge of professional competence, this dialogue established step by step that which separated me from my source of inspiration and that which remained our basic identity. For almost thirty years Moholy had disciplined his most personal visions into a doctrine, universally applicable and socially relevant. I came to consider the isolation of the original personality as inherent in the creative process whose charges were at best received as a message by those who lead society. He was a Utopian, I a historian; he the vitalist and I the humanist. He was the originator who had to exclude all other criteria besides total contemporaneousness. I saw myself as the interpreter of the sum total of cul-

tural evolution whose values were judged by a timeless perma-
nence. What united us with steadily increasing conviction as my
mind matured was faith in man's salvation through image-making.
We were both committed to work with those who try to purify
"the mutable, caused and developing aspect of things." Moholy
had chosen art as catalyst of this imaginative intelligence, I
architecture. He believed that it would be technology that had
the power to raise a cosmos above the flat plain of expedient
purpose; I believed in structure. His reason for being a teacher
and mine for becoming one was ENTHEOS — enthusiasm — inspired by the godlike force of living. If no one had ever mentioned Moholy's name again and his paintings had survived nowhere except in my rooms, I would have been content that I
finally knew what his life had directed me to do. This first premise, hazily established in the biography, seemed twelve years
later too personal to justify restatement.

The second premise on which the book hinged was more objective, because it attempted to win a historical argument about the
validity of the Constructivist idea through the work of one of its
representatives. As many young Germans of the first emancipated
generation that matured during the early 1920's, I had protested
against an education that bored us blind with fine differentiations
between Classic allegoric and Medieval symbolic art, and between
the divine Germanic patriotism of a Wagner opera and the "art-
fremde" (alien) frivolity of an Offenbach libretto. The first atonal
music scores, abstract art exhibitions, expressionistic plays and
dances liberated us from the meaninglessness of archaic symbols,
the charades of a society that had ceased to exist with the defeats
of the First World War. Instead of convention there now was
being. The new arts gave body, participation, reality to the exuberance of hearing, seeing, and feeling which we had sought
to express ineptly in the German Youth Movement. Camps developed and heated combat. Those who chose Constructivism over
Expressionism broke more radically with German tradition, because they rejected the metaphysical message of art. Neither Malevitch's Suprematism or Mondrian's Neoplasticism would have
been considered Constructivism, as they are today, because they
used the structured image for metaphysical sermons. We con-

xii

quered a new visible world through our senses, permitted to love or reject where before we had been commanded to venerate. The joy to be exposed made even the most innocent inquiry after representational meaning in art a hideous crime.

My attempt to reconstruct Moholy's role in this visual revolution of the 1920's was written at the close of a unique, exceedingly brief moment in the history of European culture. Individual intention and collective response had converged to the almost possible, as they had once before, in the 13th century. The creative imagination of the artist had been alerted to such a degree to the universality of sense perception that he could project his constructed images with full integrity into the entire man-made environment. The total framework of his influence included painting, sculpture, architecture, the printed word, the kinetic picture, implements, machines, dance, poetry, theatre. Moholy's profusely misinterpreted and ridiculed axioms that "everyone is talented" and that "to the artist an ink-bottle label is as important as a painting or the planning of a town" referred to the perceptive potential of each designed object, not to their hierarchical order. The raw materials of all visual creation were the eternally present visual fundamental: line–color–texture–light, and the three dimensions of form, space, and movement. Everyone in possession of his senses could be a creative participant.

The medium by which perceptive intuition and the rigorous discipline of shaping became compatible was technology. Technelogos, the art of knowing how to make, fell naturally and historically into the realm of perceptive fundamentals. The first obsidian chisel gave birth to technology. Technology became the most subtle and demanding instrument of Constructivism. For the artist it verified scientifically what he had perceived emotionally; for the engineer it added the vast field of perceptive responses to the narrow limits of the laboratory experiment. The excellence of machine precision demanded by technology defined the contrast to industrialization and the mediocrity of mass mechanization.

By the time I had finished the biography, this experiment in totality had lasted one generation, from about 1918 to 1945, and it had come to an end. The emotional chaos and the personal tragedies of the Second World War and its causes found compensation in Abstract Expressionism, a deeply pessimistic isolationism of the heart. The academic barrier between the arcane realm of artistic vision and the fundamental perceptions of ordinary men was reerected. Painters whose works were x-ray records of personal disorders could no longer concern themselves with film, photography, industrial design and graphics. "Applied art" reverted back to being purely commercial, subservient to artificial obsolescence. In a parallel development, technology stopped being a creative tool and became purely the domain of industrial research concerned with competitive minimum standards. The creative engineer was soon to lose out to the idiot's brain, the computer. The dead hand of art history embalmed Constructivism in textbook indexes to which a reissue of my book would have merely added one more bibliographical reference.

In the mid-1960's there occurred a sudden change in attitude toward Constructivism in general and the work of Moholy-Nagy in particular. For some time the old oblivion and the new awareness existed side by side. In America it was impossible to interest any museum in a retrospective show as the 70th anniversary of his birth approached in 1965. In Europe several comprehensive exhibitions, among them three splendid shows on Light, Lissitzky, and Moholy-Nagy in Eindhoven, Holland, were already under way. By 1968 large surveys of Constructivism occupied publishers and museum directors, and the trend projected in the future. The gentle, withdrawn curator of the Busch-Reisinger Museum in Cambridge recorded with consternation that Moholy's Light Machine (Fig. 26) had become an object of inquisitive pilgrims who upset the museum routine; and I was tempted to establish domicile halfway between Europe and America at 39,000 feet height to escape an unmanageable correspondence with publishers, editors, art dealers, lecture committees, and an uninhibited horde of thesis students hoping to wrest from me that last undivulged secret of Moholy's life that would clinch a degree.

My decision to agree to a new edition of EXPERIMENT IN TOTALITY was only partly a reaction to this "popular demand." The stronger persuasion came from an awareness that my two original premises were no longer valid, or rather that they had merged into a new motivation of which I had known nothing before. An

xiv

absolute union between two people that has been destroyed by death can only be reconstructed as a different morphon, another *Gestalt*. The one who keeps living must accept a double identity which measures new experiences on mutually agreed standards but which in turn judges the validity of these standards by the force of new experiences. I had compressed an entire life cycle from naïve childhood through acquisitive adolescence toward productive maturity into the twenty years since my husband's death. The directive force that guided me through monstruous blunders and exhausting efforts to expand Moholy's work beyond his lifetime was an inexorable drift toward objectivation. My initial compulsion to save the human side from oblivion seemed now as irrelevant to Constructivism as say, the information that Karl Marx relished family picnics on Hampstead Heath where he sang Germon folksongs would be to Marxism. It mattered even less whether my teaching career was a case of metempsychosis or rather a question of survival, utilizing practical lessons well learned. The justification of the book lay elsewhere.

Physical life is a vessel which is weighed by its contents, the degree to which it sinks below the surface of appearances. The contents of the vessel I had tried to preserve was beyond dispersion because it transcended mere contemporaneousness. The oldest God of Sumer had invested human beginning with The Word — the ability of man to name things. Plato slew matter with the ineffable supremacy of The Idea. The Faustian ethos is grounded in the beginning of The Deed, and Descartes thought he was because he thought he thought. But it was Berkeley, standing at the threshold of our own time, who said:

"To be is to be perceived!" [1]

It was a statement of such shattering originality that it escaped the philosophical schools, but worked deeply in the *Zeitgeist* (from which, like all good philosophy, it had derived). Mankind in the aggregate loved life less and less by religious sanction and more and more as a manifestation of material well-being. As educators inherited the mandate of priesthood, they upheld concept [2] as the

---

[1] perceive = to obtain knowledge through the senses; to take cognizance of existence, character, or identity by means of the senses.

[2] concept = an idea comprehending the attributes of a logical species.

only valid source of life consciousness. There were philosophical revolutions against the dictatorship of analytical intellect: William James's *Pluralistic Universe,* and above all Henri Bergson's *Creative Evolution* from 1910. "Feeling absorbs the luminous nucleus of pure intellect by transcending it." — "Perception is proportionate to the power of choice. It lights up the zone of potentialities that surrounds the act."

Moholy had never read Bergson when he made "the unity of art and life" his basic premise, "adding to the politico-sociological a biological bill of rights. . . . Self-expression which on the highest level becomes art forms the opening wedge to that otherwise unreachable realm, the subconscious feelings. . . . Contemporary art tries to establish a new morality and a new ethics not hampered by metaphysical absolutes." [3]

His new morality sought a state of grace that was not divinely predestined but gradually attained through an emotional equilibrium between mind and matter, feeling and the senses. To be the shaper of a swirling cosmos of images, to provide emotional sustenance with "tumultuous transfigurations" of visible fundamentals, celebrated the permanent impermanence of man's ceaseless becoming. The artificial eternity in a picture frame or on a pedestal had to be replaced by the improbable possibility still resting undiscovered in the nature of materials, the flexibility of static laws, the incommensurables of mathematical relationships. A plastic sheet (Fig. 58), a lense diaphragm, an electronic impulse were as essential raw stuff as was a light reflection on a cloud formation, the grain of a wooden floor (Fig. 59), or the ancient stones of the Acropolis (Fig. 35). To love the material world not less but more was the impetus to creative technology.

It is generally assumed that the revival of Constructivism is "a return to machine art." Progressive depersonalization of Western culture, elimination of "the human element" by the robot dictatorship of remote-control systems, a boundless fascination with the interchangeable parts and sonic-kinetic combinations of electronic hardware, are inspiring OP art. If these motivational definitions are correct, then the claim that Constructivism is the father of this latest "movement" is false on two counts. Con-

[3] L. Moholy-Nagy, *Vision in Motion,* Chicago 1947.

structivist hardware was medium, not end. The technological competence that selected it was informed by an emotional image, much as an architect selects building materials and methods to achieve the design image of his mind. The first industrially finished metal surfaces which Moholy used for his paintings (Fig. 64) were selected because they widened space into a nonperspective depth. The much-publicized "telephone pictures" (Fig. 14) were not intended as "engineer-esthetic sensations," as one recent critic put it. They were offered as proof of "the creative spiritual process. The production process counts only insofar as it must express a maximum of technical competence, direct or indirect, manual or mechanical." [4] The Light Machine (Fig. 26) was not a piece of sculpture and was never exhibited in Moholy's lifetime as a work of art. It was a technologically precise motion machine whose controlled light and shadow effects were reflected in an abstract film composition called *Lightplay black–white–gray*.[5] The sequence of Plexiglas light modulators that emerged from Moholy's hands in the last years of his life needed no blinding bulb batteries nor the shock effect of stroboscopic vibration to equate a sublimation of materials and techniques with a sublimation of emotional responses. Perception had to feed the senses, not to brutalize them (Figs. 71, 72, 80, 81).

The other count by which an all-too facile ancestor worship is spurious has an ethical connotation, or, in more contemporary terms, a sociological one. A total Constructivist had to be a teacher, whether he accepted the avocation or not. The faith in every man's biological rights, in the perfectability of his perception toward a higher emotional existence, was an educational commitment. The artist, gifted with heightened powers of perception, selection, implementation, and sublimation of image-making, was a leader — not a prima donna but a leader. Moholy was agonizingly aware of the sacrifice involved in having a working community of disciples, of the exhausting investment in time, strength, and the loss of solitude for creative concentration. He accepted the sharing of his life as biological law because it was

---

[4] L. Moholy-Nagy, *Painting-Photography-Film*, Bauhaus Bücher No. 8, 1927; English Edition London 1968, Cambridge, Mass., 1969.

[5] Radim Films Inc., New York.

bios — the interaction of vital impulses, that stimulated man to work for his emotional fulfillment. In contrast to much false pretense in the contemporary art hierarchy, Moholy saw himself not as a guru but as a teacher, not as a prophet but as a searcher among searchers. The almost violent compassion with which he identified himself with the creative problems of his collaborators and students heightened his sense of responsibility for perfection. The highest attainment of selective craftsmanship was a faultless recognition of the phenomenal integrity of a material image. Each specific phenomenon was related by this responsibility of its maker to the multitude of other realizations born from a ceaseless probe into the nature of visual fundamentals.

The current interest of young people in Moholy's work seems to have no roots in a wave of Art and Technology foundations whose aim is "the esthetic contribution to technology, the upgrading of the new world of automation science through art." The membership of this latest branch of the industrial establishment is, in New York, fittingly domiciled in Automation House, and its membership middle-aged and arrived. They have nothing to say to a new generation that seems to recognize in Moholy's bio-technical matter the message of an inexhaustible cosmic energy he tried to decode. The precise dynamics of his floating forms in painting (Fig. 77), sculpture (Figs. 71, 72), exhibition design (Fig. 73), stage design (Fig. 19), and photography (Fig. 30) penetrates a boundless space of emotional liberation.

Perhaps it was too positive an axiom in a world view of deepening negativism, too optimistic and single-minded in assuming man's recognition of his emotional deprivation, too intolerant toward the salvations of the mind. Perhaps Moholy failed as a teacher where he offered no alternative to the tragedy of perceptive failure. The limitations of Moholy's message matter less than his impact. The simple narrative of this biography can be no more than a framework, a travel guide toward an understanding of a new vision — a vision in motion through the new dimension of space-time whose milestones are images shaped from man's emotional needs and fulfillments.

New York,   SIBYL MOHOLY-NAGY
August, 1968

contents

moholy-nagy

experiment in totality

1 With the last shot fired in World War I, the Age of Imperialism exploded. Revolutions of all shades, from the Bolshevist extreme to a bureaucratic Social Democracy, propelled Germans, Russians, and the peoples of the vast Austrian Empire into an age of collectivism for which they were not prepared. Apart from a handful of intellectual leaders who had nursed a Marxian theorem into political reality, a whole generation was straddling history. If they were to survive, they had to stake claims on unfamiliar ground and leave the roots of mind and soul behind. Teachers had to revise the patriotic clichés on "priceless heritage"; clergymen had to forget about the hallowed alliance of throne and altar and learn the humiliating dependence on private congregations; the feudal estates were broken up and became the responsibility of the former tenant farmer; industrialists had to court labor unions instead of potentates; and the titled army officer made way for the political commissar in the new armies. It was a chaotic era of clashing convictions, but in time man's inherent need for order cast life into a solid mold again, and by 1922 the revolution of yesterday had become the new *status quo*.

The only lasting evidence of the anguished transition survives in new art forms, and in a changed relationship between artist and society. Every overthrow of esthetic traditions has been characterized by bitter battles between iconographer and iconoclast, between the recognized interpreter and the anonymous prophet. What distinguished the breakup of 1918 from earlier revolutions was a strange reversal of effects. For the first time the artist was deprived not of his social acceptance but of his isolation. This social isolation had been a by-product of the Industrial Revolution, as typical and as pernicious as slums, mechanization, and unemployment. The new ruling class had been willing to glorify art with money if art was willing to glorify money with

1

art. But it became a travesty of creativeness. In less than a hundred years, the eclectics studded the Western Hemisphere with Hellenistic bank buildings and Renaissance mansions, their plazas and gardens populated by Roman monuments, and their walls papered with sensuous nudes and luscious still lifes.

The genuine creators among the artists to whom this new patronage tasted sour, withdrew into the art colonies where they survived in a purely ornamental function. In a century of perverted Darwinism, they were exempted from the struggle for economic survival. In exchange for the luxury of a creative conscience they could die as they pleased. The new society looked on coldly as their geniuses from Géricault to Van Gogh starved to death—the new martyrs of an undevout age. Montmartre, Schwabing, Bloomsbury, and Greenwich Village were expressions as typical of nineteenth century mentality as Wall Street, Lloyds of London, La Bourse, and *Das kaiserliche Berlin*. Art had become part of the "conspicuous waste" a successful capitalism could afford.

It was an ostracism, brutally ignorant of the creative process, but it had its rewards. It narrowed the field of artistic competition and secured highly professional standards. *L'art pour l'art* was valid in more than the accepted meaning of esthetic narcissism. It also expressed a mental inbreeding in which the artist lived and worked, succeeded or failed, through the artist. The great battles between Romanticists and Impressionists, between Cubism and Expressionism, were fought in attics and sidewalk cafés. The outside world was never drawn into the arena.

At the close of World War I, this carefully segregated artist colony was invaded by the Socialist partisans. No other revolution had ever before turned to art as a weapon. Reynolds and Gainsborough painted like Lebrun and Watteau in spite of 1688, and Jean Louis David glorified the gravediggers rather than the heroes of the French Revolution. When in 1918 the young generation demanded new symbols which would fly before them as the banner of a better social order, they turned to art to give form to this new vision. Neither the scientific analysis of color by the Impressionists, nor the intellectual form hypothesis of the Cubists, or the vivisection of the Expressionist soul seemed any longer

2

adequate for a continent where thousands died for a collective goal in street battles and political purges. Surrounded by the shambles of the triumvirate of state, church, and family, the need was for a new code of visual values. The violence of this demand killed portrait painting and *nature morte*. It spit in the face of the harmonious image which had hidden decay, deceit, and exploitation. The visual world had to be stripped of its anthropocentric symbols before new ones could be created. The battle cry was: "Back to the fundamentals." The imitative iconography of the old social order was denounced. Past fame became an indictment. The established artists had either to recant or to retire. The alternatives were obsolescence or revolution.

The burning zeal of those who chose revolution equaled that of the early Christian painters who had denied themselves the worldly beauty of antiquity to fight for a new spiritual order. The emotional appeal of familiar forms was consciously shunned by the rebels. Color, line, light, and the structure of materials were explored in their primordial purity, unadulterated by man and his perverted symbolism. The old techniques of *peinture* and *trompe l'oeil* gave way to an austere honesty of elemental vision. Art was declared free of representational associations, a remedy for the war-violated dignity of the individual, and a promise for the crushed expressional freedom of the worker. New vision and new society merged in a powerful alliance. Art as social action became interdenominational, interracial, and international, the common property of all awakened men. The goal was a nonhierarchical scale of values in which esthetic and economic gratification ranked equal with political freedom.

The artist colony was liquidated; the studio battles were carried into the assembly halls. Multitudes were to be taught in place of a few initiated apprentices. Canvas and plaster were supplemented by poster, pamphlet, photograph, film, and stage setting. The old society was to be attacked from within—with functional design for mass production and mass distribution, and with organic architecture that would serve the tenant instead of oppressing him. In a spirit of high optimism that characterized the European mind in the 1920's, it was assumed that designed

3

physical environment would produce designed social relationships. The basic nature and function of vision and material, demonstrated in an all-embracing revolution of design, would create a clean logic of social and biological relationships.

Those were the years of Malevich's and Lissitzky's designs for radio stations and airdromes, and of their philosophy of pure universal emotion, expressed through the "Suprematist straight." Mondrian and van Doesburg demonstrated the objective harmony of rectangle and primary color, and Gabo planned his Constructivist monument to the Industrial Revolution. Picasso and Léger designed settings for the Diaghilev Ballet; Eisenstein, Eggeling, and Duchamp blazed the way for experimental film art. Gropius designed a Total Theater and Le Corbusier the "City of Three Million People." Literature and typography, music and the dance joined the cultural revolution. Artists became teachers, and teachers had to be artists. The Beaux-Arts Academy was utterly destroyed. Where each creative act challenged the tradition of centuries, the whole world became a school.

The great drive lasted for ten years—"kindred spirits, bold, soaring, unwearied, and sublimely confident." By 1930 it had spent its force. The Fascist counterrevolution had been victorious. One by one the bastions of art in society were lost. The alliance between artist and worker was dissolved. The demand for creative liberation was drowned out by hour and wage disputes. No one mentioned the nonhierarchical scale of human values any longer. The word *Utopia* became an invective again, and the term *l'art décadent* started to crop up in print. The rout was almost universal. The great rebels recoiled from administrative pressure and political intimidation. They stopped teaching and tried to withdraw into the old ivory towers. But the artist colony had vanished, its spirit of noninvolvement refuted and its economic privilege invaded by the financial chaos of the bourgeois world. Caught in a disastrous depression, society could no longer afford to tolerate its detractors. The days were past when Victorians looked through tearful eyes at *La Bohème*. Art had shown its true face when it supported the specter of a proletarian revolution. New patronage had to be bought with an open renunciation of the new

4

vision, and most art complied. Modern design was eliminated from the political scene. The footlights went out in the experimental theaters. The Russian film giants of the days of "Potemkin" produced nationalistic eulogies, and the French avant-garde turned out potboilers for Hollywood. Italian Futurists brassily blared the *Giovinezza*; the original staff resigned from the German Bauhaus; Cubist sculptors produced cemetery statuary, and Surrealists painted perfume ads and arranged screen versions of the subconscious.

Those who did not comply—and there were numbers of them in all countries—worked in a social vacuum. They were no longer wanted as allies by the new labor bosses, and the liquidation of such revolutionary art groups as *"Der Sturm,"* *"MA," "Munka," "i 10," "Der Blaue Reiter," "De Stijl,"* and *"Broom,"* severed the contact even among each other. The only alternative to ideological sellout was the bitterness of complete isolation. Europe was fast becoming a no man's land of the arts where those who doubted their past labored to produce acceptable wares, and those who could not recant hid in fearful isolation.

There was a third group, however, a mere handful of men who drew from defeat and frustration the inspiration to become leaders. One of them was László Moholy-Nagy. Born on July 20, 1895, he grew up in the anachronistic feudalism of Hungary. His father had gambled away the large wheat farm in the southern part of the country, and disappeared in America. The boy was brought up by a grandmother who ruled her ancient estate as a true matriarch, and by a gentle poetic mother whose marital misfortune had turned her toward religion. When she returned with two of her children to her mother's house, after having been forced by family council to give her oldest boy to wealthy relatives in Germany, she knew she was an outcast. With the traditional illogic of all conventional groups the villagers scorned the woman because her husband didn't want her, but they also taunted the boy for having a no-good father who had abandoned his family. This ostracism tied László to his mother in a tender, long-lasting affection, and it made him fiercely ambitious to redeem his name.

When he was thirteen years old he wrote in his diary:

5

My soul knows that a time will come when people's scorn will hurt no more, when my head is high and my spirit free because my name is known to the world[1]

and he vowed to his mother, in a letter written in 1909, that it would be for her that he would achieve the unusual:

DEAR MOTHER:

I have so many things in my heart which would fill books if I were to try to tell them. But you and I know each other. We are one—but we are alone. This is your birthday, and I ask God that he may finally bring you security and independence from other's whims. You can stand before *Him* in great grace because you lived for your family, you gave joy. If only you would never be hurt again, your face not darkened by sorrow. I shall be great and good—I promise—and if I don't fulfill this promise you may take my life.

And in the bloody winter of 1917 on the cracking front in Galicia he wrote a verse in his notebook:

Not to be here—to be anywhere, where?
My mother's figure shines from far away.
When will I see her eyes again—eyes like stars?
O old desire, O old light, be mine.
Years passed—not years but centuries are gone
And all her sorrow passed from her to me.

He was a quiet child, an ardent learner, and a dreamer, but fiercely ambitious to do what he had decided best. An unjust or rash criticism either about himself or others would send him into furious outbursts which left him exhausted and—in his own words—"stupefied almost to a state of death." The hostile atmosphere around him gave him an insatiable hunger for acceptance that was not stilled in a lifetime, but it also robbed him of all illusions that success could be had for less than total effort.

I lived my childhood years in a terrible great quietness [he wrote in a diary which he kept between his 15th and 18th year]. Although the villagers didn't understand me, they sometimes seemed to think that I would be a leader one day. Our old coachman would look at me, half sadly, half proudly, and he would shake his head: "You're so different, young master,

[1] Quotations from Moholy's early literary efforts and letters have been translated from the Hungarian.

6

you're so different." But I didn't want to be only different; I wanted to be someone's ideal. Yet all during my school years I couldn't make it anything more. It was only that difference in me that separated me from everything else. Only my little brother Bandi feared me as he would a roaring waterfall.

The only male influence in László's youth was an uncle, Gusti Bacsi, a successful country lawyer who hated the Austrians and the Hapsburgs and loved Petöfi, the poet-hero of the abortive Hungarian Revolution of 1848. In contrast to the farmers and merchants, he was a man of the world, a bachelor, who had traveled widely, owned a large library in Hungarian, German and French, and who corresponded with many important men of his era. His influence upon the boy was profound. Through his uncle's eyes he came to identify the church-dominated peasantry with backwardness and stagnation, and the faraway culture of the industrial cities with progress and unlimited development.

László was ten years old when the uncle arranged for his first visit to Szeged, Hungary's second largest town. But the excursion was a failure. In his imagination the boy had identified this town—all towns—with the skyscrapers of New York, pictured in *Over Land and Sea,* the family magazine of the turn of the century. He threw himself down in the unpaved street and refused to open his eyes to look at the two-story wooden houses, the ancient churches, and the modest townspeople. After this visit the dream of the great industrial landscape grew stronger and more precise, and removed him farther from the native scene. By the time he was called up to fight in the First World War, the uncle had died and the Austro-Hungarian monarchy was fading out, its millennial structure crumbling under the impact of industrialization and the demand for home rule in the vassal states.

His training as an artillery officer brought László to Budapest. At the age of nineteen he discovered the culture of a big city, the love of women, and the supremacy of his own vision. A poem, dedicated "to Panna" and entitled "Love and the Dilettante Artist," is the first testimony of his dedication to light as a creative force, and the first intimation of his later life as a painter.

Little girl, you mean so well—
Hot kisses, the treasure of love—
A tired child, I fall into your lap.
Guard me well, little girl, guard my love.

I swam in the Danube this afternoon
And I forgot all about you.
Longing for the old ecstasy—light.
The waves rushed against each other
And my paper heart filled with wonder.
I was gazing at Buda.

How beautiful was Buda this afternoon,
Under a cover of light
A tender silken cover of green, a shroud of bluish mist.
Cap-like it leaped, glowingly, from spire to spire.

But the mood changed. War on the Russian Front was ferocious. In four bloody years Moholy grew up to be a man. He rarely spoke of his experiences, and when he mentioned war, it was with profound disgust. But there were, over the years, certain flashbacks, which shed light on the impact of this travesty of culture and civilization on the dreaming farm boy. Revulsion against the drinking orgies of his fellow officers made him an abstainer and a nonsmoker, and the wanton destruction of raw materials and machinery which could have served mankind made him conscious of values and preservation. He never forgot the helplessness and mute fury caused by the sadism of a superior officer who assigned the losers in a nightly chess game to patrol duties involving almost certain death, and throughout his life he shunned jokes and stag-party stories because they reminded him of the coarse companionship in dugouts and mess halls. After two years in the front lines, a snow-white streak divided his black hair; but he survived. Late in 1916, in a battle along the Isonzo River in Venezia Giulia, his whole battery was wiped out, he alone escaping, with a shattered thumb and a fast-spreading infection that kept him for months in military hospitals.

Up to this point his release from inner protest and isolation had been poetry—an ecstatic transfiguration of his violated ego into a higher state of harmonious universality.

This dedication and this fearful urge
To give, to bleed, to wrench the last creative breath

8

Fig. 1. Dying soldier, 1916. Grease crayon on paper.

> From sore and starving hearts—
> This is between the two of us—you smiling,
> I clawing with my nails the earth for her life-giving seed—

he wrote in 1914 in one of the poems that appeared in the avant-garde magazines that emulated the expressionist poet Ady. In the stench and isolation of a base hospital, surrounded by the crumbling morale of a failing army, he experienced the inadequacy of poetic escape. For the first time he felt compelled to analyze reality by recording its face. In innumerable sketches

9

Fig. 2. Barbed Landscape,
1917. Grease crayon on paper.

on postcards and fever charts, in notebooks, and later on field
orders and dossiers, he drew his fellow soldiers, and their entou-
rage of ragged starving civilians. There's a tubercular soldier,
reading the Bible, the bone structure of his emaciated skull bared
by sharp anatomical strokes. A prostitute lies on a blue spread,
the contours of her dress etched into the white paper, and the
same figure—in the nude—in an identical pose of incomplete
relaxation. Famished women, dying soldiers, one with a strange
cherubic face, tangled in a maze of barbed wire (Fig. 1), and
above all the landscape of war, under a sky that is outlined by
wild forbidding loops (Fig. 2).

Without art training or the guidance of conscious art
appreciation, he searched for contact with a visual world that was
far removed from the death struggle of Eastern Europe. A few
Van Gogh reproductions had found their way into Hungarian
magazines, and many years later, in "Abstract of an Artist,"
Moholy wrote:

> The analytical nature of his ink drawings taught me that line
> drawings ought not to be mixed with halftones; that one
> should try to express three-dimensional plastic quality by the
> unadulterated means of line. . . . In trying to express this
> three-dimensionality, I used auxiliary lines in places where
> ordinarily no lines are used. The result was a complicated
> network of a peculiar spatial quality applicable to new prob-
> lems. . . . I saw that this experiment with lines brought an
> emotional quality into the drawings which was entirely un-
> intentional and unexpected, and of which I had not been aware
> before. I tried to analyze bodies, faces, landscapes with my
> "lines," but the results slipped out of my hand, went beyond
> the analytical intention. The drawings became a rhythmically

10

articulated network of lines, *showing not so much objects as my excitement about them.*[2]

These line drawings were the exercises of a born painter who knows instinctively that art cannot grow without self-training.

Early in 1917 he had crystallized a philosophy of vision. He was twenty-one years old then, isolated from his fellow men, and suffering bitterly from his ill-treated wound. Between fever deliriums he wrote the creed of his life:

Learn to know the Light-design of your life.
You will find it different from chronology.
A different measure, called *Eternitas,*
Proud battle for the secrecy of order.

Space, time, material—are they one with Light?
Dependent on the Light that gives you life?
Idea of great magnitude that grows
Within your soul, poor creature, steers your way
As by an arm to latitudes
So utterly unknown to lightless eyes.

Search desperately—-what is Light as essence?
What is its substance, what its price?
I cannot kill my thirst nor even lessen it.
Space, time and system—essence or mere chaos.
Realities that seem eternal
For creatures not eternal, bound by death.

Light, ordering Light, where are you? Far away.
A luster that illuminates mere being.
Come over me, proud Light, fierce Light, burn deep,
Ferocious Light, spread through me, cleanse my eyes.

A dampish tomb, the earth will then collapse.
Dead worries rot in soon-forgotten graves,
Refuted sacraments impeding Light.

"Everything"—-you hear its hollow sound
If we maintain the nothingness of darkness.
"Nothingness"—you hear it roaring on
If "Everything" is us denied.
Precarious balance—time, material, space—
Resting on nothingness and meaning everything.

[2] L. Moholy-Nagy, *The New Vision* (New York, 1948).

11

But human brain, so pitifully small,
Pierced through the darkness of the void, and tied
Material, space and time to Light contours,
To Light eternal, Light the striding life.
And nothingness, so vainly measured out
In time and space, transforms the darkened man—
Light, total Light, creates the total man.

When the war was over and he returned to Budapest
he knew that he had to become a painter. It was a decision not
without inner conflict. On May 15, 1919 he wrote in his notebook:

> During the war, but more strongly even now, I feel my responsi-
> bility toward society. My conscience asks incessantly: is it
> right to become a painter in times of social revolution? May
> I claim for myself the privilege of art when all men are
> needed to solve the problems of sheer survival?
>
> Art and reality have had nothing in common during the last
> hundred years. The personal satisfaction of creating art has
> added nothing to the happiness of the masses.
>
> I have had many talks with men and women on my long train
> trips. I have seen what is needed beyond food. I have finally
> learned to grasp what is biological happiness in its complete
> meaning. And I know now that if I unfold my best talents in
> the way suited best to them—if I try to grasp the meaning of
> this, my life, sincerely and thoroughly—then I'm doing right
> in becoming a painter. It is my gift to project my vitality, my
> building power, through light, color, form. I can give *life* as
> a painter.

To please his mother, he finished his undergraduate
work in law at the University of Budapest, but it was done with
the left hand, so to speak. All his energies, the undivertible intensity of his mind and his senses, were concentrated upon visual
representation. At first he was intimidated by the apparent chaos
of revolutionary painting in 1918. He had found a hold in the
articulation of space through line, but the use of color was governed by more complex canons. There were the coloristic fantasies
of the Expressionists—Marc's blue horses, and the green-faced
figures of Chagall. The Cubists had devaluated color to mere
shadings, and the Purists used it in a raw, poster-like directness.
To find his bearings, Moholy copied the "solid" values of Renais-

12

Fig. 3. Bridges, 1919. Oil on canvas.

sance and Baroque painters. He produced dozens of nudes, portraits, landscapes. Later he tried to return to the vivid primary contrasts of slavic peasant art—brilliant reds and yellows, contrasted with deep blues or luminous yellows. Like the embroidery on the blouse of a Hungarian peasant, or the wreath of flowers painted around a cup or a bowl, the chromatic scale of Moholy's early paintings was simple and virile, inspired by and bound to a folk art which had been the only visual experience of his childhood. But the subject matter was alien, far removed from the mythological tales or the idyllic stylizations. The rigid triangles of iron construction and the swinging arches of bridges (Fig. 3), rise into the gaily colored areas. Mathematical numbers fly through the sky, and geometrical sections destroy any attempt at perspective illusion. The agony of a whole people, torn between the ageless tradition of decorative art and the new forms of a technological existence, is expressed in these paintings. The final decision would be between the reds, blues, and yellows of the Hungarian Plains or the geometric shapes of the industrial landscape. When Moholy finally broke through the confines of tradition, it was not a conscious decision dictated by esthetic considerations. It was an intuitive need for a solution, peculiar to him and to no one else, which expressed his profound inner transformation during the postwar chaos.

For more than four years in the trenches, Moholy had shared the collapse of a hopelessly decayed society. He had experienced on his own flesh the irresponsibility, exploitation, coercion, and brutality that had held his people under Austrian dominance for centuries. When Béla Kun broke the hateful ties and declared a Hungarian Soviet, Moholy together with many of his generation saw in him the messiah of a new world. With the flaming enthusiasm of youth he offered himself, his art, and his willingness to teach, to the Communist regime. But he was not accepted. The landholding status of his family made him suspect to the party heads, and his rank as an officer in the army aggravated this suspicion. Yet, the real basis of his nonacceptance was not political but artistic. Between him and the Communist Party stood his newly won assurance of nonrepresentational art as an essential revolutionary weapon. On March 21, 1920, living as an exile in

Vienna, he formulated this conflict in sentences which prove the growing maturity of his mind.

This is the bitter anniversary of the birth and death of the Hungarian Revolution, which died in infancy because to be able to live it had to have revolutionary content. Instead, it was born within unshakable nationalistic walls, attended by the faithlessness of the Social Democrats and the stifling dogmas of the bourgeoisie.

The leaders of this revolution, instead of solving the spiritual and material needs of the wanting masses, were busy with *historical* materialism, with neutral zones and national power. A heap of contradictions!

Under their poorly dyed red cover, the revolutionaries forgot the real meaning of a revolution. They forgot to promote the inner revolution of life. They forgot about culture. Their revolution is not a "revolutionary change." Their form of Communist economy does not mean a new system of production and distribution. It merely changes the powers of those who decide about production and distribution. This economic Communism is another form of capitalism, based on trusts, syndicates, state credit, patronage, and a hierarchy of unassailable state leaders.

A truly revolutionary new system would differ in all aspects from the familiar old pattern. It would eliminate first of all cagelike houses in slums, dead museums that glorify a false world picture, hospitals run for profit that kill patients with ignorance and greed and are actually morgues, the brothel parties of the high officials who buy women, the theaters and operas that stink of ethical foot-and-mouth disease, the constrictions upon creative opportunity in schools which reward only caste spirit.

The present Communist Party is still part of this bourgeois world and its able propagator. It blows a red tin trumpet while imitating the cult of the dead and base past under the deceptive name of "prolet cult." The present Communist system of economy might offer new opportunities to a number of men who can cleverly mix enterprise and politics, but it will never solve the deeper and most vital needs of survival.

Even though madness and reaction have followed this revolution, we hope for new human raw material, prepared in the

14

Fig. 4. Collage in red, yellow, and black on black paper, 1921.

right kind of school-kettles to build and maintain a society dedicated to a totally new culture.

To translate the full scope of his protest into visual symbols, Moholy needed a *tabula rasa*, a cleansing of all symbolic connotations reminiscent of the social order he had rejected. This was his discovery of the visual fundamentals—the colors, shapes, and interrelationships underlying all visual form.

> I discovered that composition is directed by an unconscious sense of order in regard to the relations of color, shape, position, and often by a geometrical correspondence of elements. . . . I eliminated the perspective employed in my former paintings. I simplified everything to geometrical shapes, flat unbroken colors: lemon yellow, vermilion, black, white—polar contrasts. . . . Color, which so far I had considered mainly for its illustrative possibilities, was transformed into a force loaded with potential space articulation, and full of emotional qualities.[3]

During his last months in Budapest, and nine obsessed and hungry months in Vienna, Moholy explored the space-articulating power of the colored form. The light and heavy qualities, and the advanc-

[3] "Abstract of an Artist," *op. cit.*

15

Fig. 5. Portrait: Reinhold Schairer, 1921. Grease crayon on paper.

ing and receding tension, inherent in certain shapes, colors, and surface textures, were registered in dozens of collages. He glued colored paper strips to backgrounds of varying tones, separating, or superimposing colored form elements. These collages afforded him "a rhythmical and emotional exultation as yet unmatched by the use of oil on canvas."[4] (Fig. 4). Later the superimpositions and parallelograms were repeated in water color, adding transparency as a new element to this new language of fundamentals. To attempt in 1920 a visual contact between artist and public by purely objective, noniconographic forms, was a declaration of independence which called for great courage in a young painter who felt himself unsupported by any recognized group. In a country as isolated from the Western World as Hungary, it severed all contacts with the artistic fraternity. Only a small fraction of political dreamers saw an inner connection between their goal of a clear functional society, and the abstract symbols of man's universe. His friends and relatives on the farms and in the small Hungarian

[4] *Ibid.*

16

towns who had reluctantly admired his severe portraits and line-scapes felt he was throwing away not only his time but financial success as well, and the Symbolists and Expressionists in the artist cafés of Budapest and Vienna, riding the vogue of the *"Brücke"* and *"Blaue Reiter"* movements, sneered at the "emotional barrenness" of the Constructivist approach. Realizing his total isolation, Moholy decided to break all the contacts of his youth. In January, 1921, he arrived in Berlin.

Being almost penniless, he had to work his way across eastern Germany as a letterer and sign painter. As soon as he had enough money for a railroad ticket, he would take a slow train to the next large town. On this journey he picked up a severe case of "flu" which was decimating the German population in the winter of 1920. Racked with fever he arrived at a Berlin hotel, and collapsed in the lobby when the clerk wouldn't take him in. A young pedagogue, Reinhold Schairer, found him there. He and his wife cared for the sick anonymous stranger as part of their rehabilitation work for veterans of the First World War. Without their devotion, Moholy would never have survived this crisis. His gratitude is expressed in his portrait of Doctor Schairer. It was his last representational drawing (Fig. 5).

After his recovery he found an empty attic in Berlin's western section, and with the help of some Quaker rations, estab-

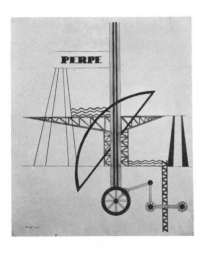

Fig. 6. Perpe, 1919. Gouache on white paper.

Fig. 7.   Collage and Watercolor, 1921.

lished himself as a painter who now tried to translate the form relationships of the collages and the superimpositions and transparencies of the water colors on canvas. "Perpe, 1919," a gouache composition on paper, and "Water Color, 1921" (Figs. 6, 7) indicate the full scope of the problem he had set for himself. The direction led from severe simplification of form in two-dimensional space, to the creation of visual depth through color transparencies.

> My transparent pictures around 1921 became completely freed from all elements reminiscent of nature. Their genesis was determined by a complete liberation from the necessity to record. I wanted to eliminate all factors which might disturb their clarity—in contrast for instance with Kandinsky's paintings which reminded me of an undersea world. My desire was to work with nothing but the peculiar characteristics of colors, with their pure relationships. I chose simple geometric forms as a step toward such objectivity. I see today that this was the logical continuation of the Cubist paintings I had admiringly studied.[5]

By 1922, Moholy had reached the first definite position in his life work. He had proved to himself the visual vitality and creative essentiality of pure color and form elements in any medium. His instinctive protest against the exclusion of creative individuality from the political program of the Hungarian Revolution *had* been justified. Through his new vision he felt himself intimately connected with the social reality of his time. Constructive design and reconstructed society were an inseparable

[5] "Abstract of an Artist," *op. cit.*

18

entity. It was a confirmation of elating certainty, and the teacher in him insisted on formulating what the painter had discovered.

Constructivism and the Proletariat[6]

Reality is the measure of human thinking. It is the means by which we orient ourselves in the Universe. The actuality of time—the reality of this century—determines what we can grasp and what we cannot yet understand.

And this reality of our century is technology: the invention, construction, and maintenance of machines. To be a user of machines is to be of the spirit of this century. It has replaced the transcendental spiritualism of past eras.

Everyone is equal before the machine. I can use it, so can you. It can crush me; the same can happen to you. There is no tradition in technology, no class-consciousness. Everybody can be the machine's master, or its slave.

This is the root of Socialism, the final liquidation of feudalism. It is the machine that woke up the proletariat. We have to eliminate the machine if we want to eliminate Socialism. But we know there is no such thing as turning back evolution. This is our century: technology, machine, Socialism. Make your peace with it; shoulder its task.

Because it is your task to carry revolution toward reformation, to create a new spirit that will fill the empty forms cast by the monstrous machine. Manufacture in itself doesn't make a better life. Look around: the people are not happy in spite of the machine. Well-being is caused by the spirit that animates technology; it is a socialism of the mind, a dedication to the spirit of the group. Only a proletariat awakened to this grasp of essential communality can be happy.

Who will teach them? Words are heavy, obscure. Their meaning is evasive to the untrained mind. Past traditions cling to their meanings. But there is art, the language of the senses.

Art crystallizes the emotions of an age; art is mirror and voice. The art of our time has to be fundamental, precise, all-inclusive. It is the art of Constructivism.

Constructivism is neither proletarian nor capitalistic. Constructivism is primordial, without class or ancestor. It expresses the pure form of nature—the direct color, the spatial rhythm, the equilibrium of form.

[6] Excerpts from an article in "MA," May, 1922. "MA" (meaning "Today") was a revolutionary Hungarian magazine, published between 1918 and 1925.

19

Fig. 8.   Market woman, ca. 1923.   Photographic negative.

The new world of the masses needs Constructivism because it needs fundamentals that are without deceit. Only the basic natural element, accessible to all senses, is revolutionary. It has never before been the property of civilized man.

In Constructivism, form and substance are one. Not substance and tendency, which are always being identified. Substance is essential, but tendency is intentional. Constructivism is pure substance. It is not confined to picture-frame and pedestal. It expands into industry and architecture, into objects and relationships. Constructivism is the socialism of vision.

And in the *Buch Neuer Künstler*, which he and his friend Ludwig Kassak published in 1922, the introduction proclaimed:

This is the hour to weigh the past heroes of destruction against the fanatics of construction. There has never been an epoch comparable to ours in which legions of awakened men set out in so many different directions in search for new form—in which so many men burn with a fanatical flame from which bursts the cry of a new birth: an epoch which creates simultaneously the fury of despair and the flaming pillar of positive fight.

Verbal expression didn't come easily to a painter of such obsessed vision. He needed help, the patient influence of a trained mind. This influence was Lucia, a young university woman whom Moholy met during his first year in Berlin. To the delirious sense-perception of his new vision she added her superior intelligence and the sober working discipline of a scholar. In collaboration with her, Moholy acquired the ability to think and express himself logically and intelligibly. She was not at home in the artist cafés or the smoke-filled studios. Through her and a circle of friends, Moholy became part of the movement for psycho-biological reform that spread through Germany after the First World War. Its program was based on the rules of the Persian Mazdaznan sect, prescribing exercises of Spartan rigor to attain self-control, and a strict vegetarianism permitting only the consumption of raw vegetables. Outdoor living with long hikes over the countryside carried him far away from his youth as an army officer and the nocturnal existence of a revolutionary. "Laci" and Lucia were poor, and the extreme frugality of their life emphasized the spiritual basis of their relationship. Their bond

21

was a shared vision of the totality of revolutionary design, and an unlimited willingness to work and to sacrifice for it.

It was during those long walks, on which he rediscovered landscape, that Moholy started to photograph. The basic elements of form, light, and color gradation, which he had stabilized in his paintings, gave to the human figure, to animal and plant a reality never previously observed. Shadows and textures expressed a pattern of design that corresponded to his own work (Fig. 8). At first Lucia was the apprentice of his perceptive interpretation. Later she added to this vision the systematic knowledge of the craftsman who learns his trade well, until she became one of the outstanding photographers of Europe. Their marriage lasted until 1929. By then the nursling of a new age had grown to be the mentor of the next generation. His alumnus days had passed, and from the comradeship he and Lucia had shared he turned to the complex relationships of manhood.

The other decisive influence upon Moholy during his first years in Berlin was Kurt Schwitters. The Hanoverian Dadaist had not been in Zürich in 1916 when Ball, Tzara, Arp, and Huelsenbeck founded the "Cabaret Voltaire." But the war-madness of European imperialism, and the venality of conformist artists, had aroused similar reactions in him. He developed his own form of Dadaism which he called MERZ.[7] Some of his poems were wordless sound-symphonies, composed of the rich vocality of vowels and consonants without literary meaning, like the notes of a music score. His prose was a cunningly disguised social satire. Through a seemingly childish pattern of repetition and banality, he achieved a highly sophisticated exposure of the petit bourgeois. But his strongest influence came from his pictures, the MERZ COLLAGES. Schwitters wrote in the first issue of his magazine *Merz*:

> In a piece of art it is only important that all parts are correlated to the whole. . . . In the relationship of a known and an unknown quantity, the unknown varies and modifies the

[7] The name was accidental and came from the four central letters of the word "*kom*MERZ*iell*," which had appeared on a scrap of newspaper in one of the MERZ collages.

22

Fig. 9.   Look before you leap, ca. 1922.   Photomontage.

known. It is irrelevant whether materials had any established value before they were used for producing a piece of art. They receive their evaluation through the creative process.

That is why I use discarded cogwheels, tissue paper, can tops, glass splinters, labels, and tickets. By being balanced against each other, these materials lose their characteristics—their personality poison. They are dematerialized and are only stuff for the painting which is a self-related entity. A significant art product has no longer an outward relationship to the material elements that formed it.

In *Vision in Motion*, more than twenty years later, Moholy paid homage to the genius of Kurt Schwitters by analyzing his importance for modern art. But in 1922 he was fascinated not by Schwitters' historical significance but by the bold humor of the Dadaists who attacked with ridicule where Moholy and his Mazdaznan friends had brandished weighty principles. Under Schwitters' influence, he turned to political collage and photomontage ridiculing the undefeated nationalism of the Germans, the senselessness of journalistic verbiage, and the shoddy authority of the police state (Fig. 9).

But of greater importance for Moholy's future work was Schwitters' preoccupation with typography. To "equalize contrasts and distribute the centers of gravity," as he had proclaimed in the first number of his *Merz* magazine, Schwitters— and with him most of the Dadaists—disassociated the letters of the alphabet from their familiar word context. Single vowels and consonants became compositional elements in many different art forms: in music for instance, as self-expressive sound associations in Schwitters' "Sonata in Primordial Sounds"; in the photogram by supplying an infinite variety of exact forms, overlying free forms and flowing textures; or in painting, where typographical elements added visual and chromatic associations to the two-dimensional plane. The letters F, N, and O worked into a collage or a canvas represented curved or angular forms, but they also produced an associative sound experience in the spectator who not only saw but also "heard" the picture. One of the most ingenious of these experiments is Moholy's canvas *"Gelbe Scheibe,* 1921 (Yellow Disc, 1921)"* in which the letters of the name *Moholy* are composed into a Constructivist entity (Fig. 10).

24

Fig. 10. Typographical painting spelling out MO- HOLY, 1921. Oil on bur- lap.

Schwitters dedicated a series of his brightest MERZ collages to Moholy, and he gave him the first copy of his famous *Anna Blume*, bound in a multicolored paper cover made by him- self, and inscribed: "To Moholy on the last day of the reduced streetcar tariff."

But although Moholy understood the liberating out- burst of the subconscious pandemonium in Dadaism, he never became part of it. His creative impetus came from different sources. He lacked the peculiar obsession of the frustrated revolu- tionary artist which feeds on the tension between self-indulgence and social accusation. He never could at the same time serve and ridicule the suprapersonal goal he had recognized as binding. He was unschizophrenic, and throughout his life he retained the sincerity of the child—dedicated, without irony.

After Schwitters' collages had opened Moholy's eyes to the *Gestalt* value of integrated symbolic elements, he discovered the *photogram*, a creation of pictorial compositions in black and white through the photographic printing process.

25

Fig. 11. PNEUMATIK, 1923. Photomontage as automobile-tire advertisement.

In spite of a long and bitter battle it has never been decided conclusively which photographer first put an object directly on light-sensitive paper in the secrecy of his darkroom and then exposed the arrangement to a flash of artificial light, "painting" in this manner the solid forms on the light-sensitive emulsion. Henry Fox Talbot, the English discoverer of photography, made a lace photogram around 1850, and it is certain that Christian Schad, a member of the Dadaist *Cabaret Voltaire* in 1916 created variations of the Dadaist collages in the photogramatic manner. He composed political posters, attacking the bourgeoisie, by putting cut-out letters, and free-form outlines on photographic paper, naming the results *Schadographs*, from his own name and quite unaware of the double meaning in the English language. A few years later the American Man Ray used the same method to produce abstract "light paintings." Like Schad, he named his *Rayograms* after himself, but it was Moholy who gave the process its lasting name. His designation *photogram* (or *fotogram*) is today generally accepted.

There was a direct connection between Moholy's photograms and the "rubbish" pictures of Schwitters. The Dadaist insistence upon the equal pictorial worth of all materials, which had been anticipated by the followers of Synthetic Cubism, suggested a search for photogram material in places where academic photographers refused to tread. Bathroom fixtures and bobby pins, chicken wire, a human head resting directly on the photographic paper, or a flower, etc., were the elements of these creative configurations. They could be combined with collages and drawings, and they could be purely pictorial or commercial (Fig. 11).

In 1923, for the catalogue of his first photographic exhibition, Moholy wrote:

> The concretization of light phenomena is peculiar to the photographic process and to no other technical invention. Cameraless photography (the making of photograms) rests on this. The photogram is a realization of spatial tension in black-white-gray. Through the elimination of pigment and texture it has a dematerialized effect. It is a writing with light, self-expressive through the contrasting relationship of deepest black and lightest white with a transitional modulation of the finest

grays. Although it is without representational content, the photogram is capable of evoking an immediate optical experience, based on our psycho-biological visual organization.

It was through the parallel exploration of photogram and photography that Moholy was able to arrive at clear definitions for both. The photogram was the creation of elemental optical relationships, and basically one with Constructivist painting. Photography was representation of symbolic form, bound by the associative content of plant, animal, structure, and man. In a widely reprinted article, "Isms and Art,"[8] which later was to constitute the basis for his book *Painting-Photography-Motion Picture*,[9] Moholy asserted that only a fetishistic adherence to Romantic handicraft traditions could challenge the supremacy of photographic representation over so-called realistic painting.

> The representation of either the object or the human being has been perfected to such a degree in photography that the interpretation through manual means—painting—seems indeed primitive. The battle between brush and camera becomes ridiculous if one realizes, through constant photographic practice, that all representation is interpretation—that the choice of object, segment, light, shadow, even the choice of soft or hard photographic paper, are highly creative "artistic" decisions. The danger of the photographic medium—including the motion picture—is not esthetic but social. It is the enormous power of mass-produced visual information that can enhance or debase human values. Brutal emotionalism, cheap sentimentality, and sensational distortion can, if they spread unchecked, trample to death man's newly won ability to see gradation and differentiation in the light-pattern of his world.

With this pronouncement, which he emphasized and amplified throughout his life, Moholy not only promoted the photographer to the position of teacher and social leader, but he also included him among the artists. In uncounted photographs Moholy explored man's socio-biological manifestations. He saw children and cats, old houses and the steel skeletons of mammoth factories, mountain lakes and the pavement patterns of city streets, with a camera eye that tried to be human before being realistic.

[8] *Vivos Voco*, Vol. V, No. 8/9 (Leipzig, 1925).
[9] Moholy-Nagy, *Malerei-Photography-Film* (Bauhaus Bücher, No. 8, Munich, 1927).

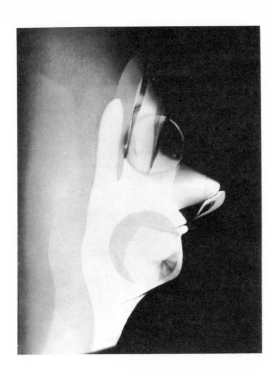

Fig. 12. Photogram (cameraless photo), showing Moholy lighting a cigarette, ca. 1922.

The artistic transfiguration of the insignificant object, first proclaimed by Schwitters, was supplemented by a structural analysis in the photogram that surpassed the Cubists with their limited capacity to break through the surface of appearances by means of paint and brush stroke (Fig. 12).

Photography had its influence upon Moholy's work as a painter. Other artists had used photography to record the style of their sculptures and easel paintings. Moholy reversed the process and painted his photographic experiences. His canvases from 1922 are photogramatic compositions, decisively influenced by the technical eye of the camera. The superimposition of planes, the activation of light, and the smooth, textureless handling of the surface are photographic in character (Fig. 13). They expressed his interest in the Russian predecessors of the Constructivists, the Suprematists, whose work had reached the West through the paintings of Kasimir Malevich and El Lissitzky. To express the supremacy of a pure, depersonalized emotion as the universal property of all men, Malevich and Lissitzky had reduced painterly effects to a minimum of individual *"peinture."* Moholy disliked the emotional symbolism of Malevich's titles:

29

Fig. 13. Painting, 1922. Oil on canvas. Spheres painted with spray gun.

"Emotion of the Mystical Will Rejected" or "Emotion of a Mystical Wave from the Universe," but he was deeply affected by the precise analysis of visual elements. Malevich's last painting, showing a white square on a white background, was for Moholy "the ideal screen for light and shadow effects which reflect the surrounding world in the painting. The manual picture is suppressed by the painterly possibilities of light projection."[9] It became his goal "to eliminate color (pigment) or at least to sublimate it to a point where the visual impact rests on the most essential medium —the direct light."[10]

The physical conditions of Moholy's life lent the right background to this art of austerity. Berlin had no heat and little light in the inflation winter of 1922.

"One gets frightfully spiritual on crackers and apple butter," Moholy said many years later looking at the funereal black of his canvases from that time. "My life acquired depth and substance during those years, but all the colored feathers were plucked from my wings. I had always liked to laugh, and I loved a good time. But we lived in a spirit of self-sacrifice, obsessed with the desire to submerge our egos into the collective whole."

As a climax to this self-effacing objectivity, Moholy painted three pictures by telephone. He had to prove to himself the supra-individualism of the Constructivist concept, the existence of objective visual values, independent of the artist's inspiration

[10] *Ibid.*

30

and his specific *peinture*. He dictated his painting to the foreman of a sign factory, using a color chart and an order blank of graph paper to specify the location of form elements and their exact hue. The transmitted sketch was executed in three different sizes to demonstrate through modifications of density and space relationships the importance of structure and its varying emotional impact (Fig. 14).

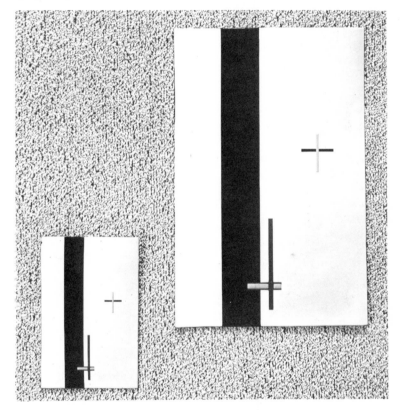

Fig. 14. Two compositions on baked enamel, ordered by telephone from color grid ("telephone pictures"), 1923.

When in the winter of 1922 the art gallery *Der Sturm*, under the brilliant leadership of Herwarth Walden, arranged for the first showing of Moholy's work, the obscurity of his existence was over. "Compositions of high appeal," wrote the famous *Vossische Zeitung*, "created with a powerful sense of form and a tender taste for hue and gradation." And the *Frankfurter Zeitung* said:

> It takes discipline to be modern. This is where the artistic and the arty part company. Moholy has the iron discipline of a scientist. Many men paint Constructivistic, but no one paints as he does. Don't talk about coldness, mechanization; this is sensuality refined to its most sublimated expression. It is emotion made world-wide and world-binding.

In the spring of 1923 Moholy-Nagy joined the faculty of the Bauhaus in Weimar.

2 In 1919 Walter Gropius had founded the *Staatliche Bauhaus* in Weimar, Germany

> with the specific objective of realizing a modern architecture which should be all-embracing in its scope. Within that sovereign federative union, the different "arts"—every branch of design, every form of technique—could be coordinated and find their appointed place.[1]

This philosophy had a natural affinity with the exuberant lines from the *Buch Neuer Künstler*:

> We must change—we must create, because movement means creation. Movement must be brought into equilibrium because only so can *form* be created. This new form is *architecture.*[2]

The Bauhaus was the catalyst for the visual revolution of the twentieth century. It tested the validity of each new concept on the reality of day-by-day existence. *The house* as the nucleus of man's growth became the measure by which to evaluate color and structure, space, light, form. Ideological clarification and creative effort, combined with manual-technological training, were focused on the central idea of *building* as man's basic constructive impulse. Pedagogically the Bauhaus program had a twofold aim:

> 1. The intellectual, manual and technological education of creative people for design work specifically related to building, and

> 2. The execution of practical research work related to building and furnishing, and the development of model types for industry and crafts.[3]

[1] Walter Gropius, *The New Architecture and the Bauhaus* (London & New York, 1937).

[2] Ludwig Kassak and L. Moholy-Nagy, *Buch Neuer Künstler*, activist magazine "MA," Vienna, 1922.

[3] Walter Gropius, "Bauhaus 1" (*Bauhaus Chronik* 1925-1926, quarterly publication of the *Staatliche Bauhaus*, Dessau, Germany).

33

Within the scope of this designed totality came the picture on the wall and the rug on the floor, the furniture for child and adult, and the utensils in the kitchen. Dance and dramatic arts were of equal importance with poetry and music. Man's shelter and the activities maintained within this shelter were considered the aggregate expression of man's cultural progress.

Gropius' appeal was convincing enough to induce some of the best men in modern art to join the Bauhaus faculty. Kandinsky, Klee, Feininger, Schlemmer, were at the height of their creative power when they became teachers. Other great names of European art and literature formed a group of active supporters. Oud, Mondrian, Giedion, Werfel, Einstein, and many others, declared their unanimity with the Bauhaus idea.

During the first three years of collaboration, the Bauhaus faculty were united by the common aim of constructing a design nucleus in which artist and craftsman ranked as equals. In their first proclamation they declared:

> Architects, sculptors, painters, we must all turn to the crafts. . . . Let us create a new guild of craftsmen, without class distinctions which raise an arrogant barrier between craftsman and artist. Together let us conceive and create the new building of the future which will embrace architecture and sculpture and painting in one unity and which will rise one day toward heaven from the hands of a million workers like the crystal symbol of a new faith.

By 1923 two radically different interpretations of this new faith had become evident. Johannes Itten, who taught visual analysis and the interrelationship of color and personality, led a group of fanatic individualists whose artistic convictions were those of German Expressionism. A dedication to metaphysical speculation and mystic rites produced form and color creations based on subconscious automatism and emotional introspection. In contrast to the Expressionists stood the Constructive objectivists whose aim was a form language based on geometric order and tensional equilibrium. Their inspiration came from Mondrian's Neoplasticism; their esthetic orientation rested on the universal functionality of a designed world.

34

For Gropius and his goal of an integrated archi-
tectonic vision, the predominance of the Expressionist element in
the Bauhaus faculty was a negative factor, and he decided to draw
stronger Constructivist forces into the orbit of the school. In 1923
he appointed Moholy-Nagy as master of the advanced foundation
course and the Metal Workshop. Although the student council had
supported Gropius' decision, the reaction of many Bauhaus members to Moholy's coming was negative. Paul Citroen, a student of
that time, has given a description of the divided feelings.

> None of us who had suggested Moholy, liked his Construc-
> tivism. This "Russian" trend, created outside the Bauhaus,
> with its exact, simulatively technical forms was disgusting to
> us who were devoted to the extremes of German Expressionism.
> But since Constructivism was the newest of the new, it was—
> so we figured—the cleverest move to overcome our aversion
> and, by supporting Gropius' choice of one of its creators, in-
> corporate this "newest" into the Bauhaus system.

> We were conscious of the danger of drawing into the inner
> circle the representative of an art form we basically negated.
> But it was only an experiment, something easily to be undone
> since Moholy was very young, and most probably inexperi-
> enced. So Moholy came to Weimar as "the champion of
> youth," as we labeled him in contrast to the "old" faculty
> members Kandinsky, Feininger, and Klee who were between
> forty and fifty-five.

The ensuing dilemma is convincingly illustrated in the
catalogue of the first big Bauhaus Exhibition. The expressionism
of Kandinsky, the dream world of Paul Klee, and the mysticism
of J. Itten, contrast strangely with Moholy's angular metal sculpture and his objectified canvases (Fig. 15).

The hopes of the "young" to find in Moholy a spokes-
man opposing the "old masters" were not fulfilled. Despite some
sharp brushes with Gropius, which were settled through their
common devotion to a great goal, a friendship developed which
lasted a lifetime. The impetuous, self-obsessed Hungarian was
attracted by the subtle taste and the restrained reasoning of the
older man. Moholy was well aware of his lack of formal art
education, and he was decided to overcome his handicap by an

unlimited willingness to learn. He admired in Gropius the solid knowledge and the critical mind he himself still lacked, and Gropius was stimulated and supported by the intuitive creativeness and the associative energy of his young adjutant. "Moholy was one of my most active colleagues in building up the Bauhaus," Walter Gropius wrote in his preface to the third edition of Moholy's *The New Vision.* "Much that was accomplished stands

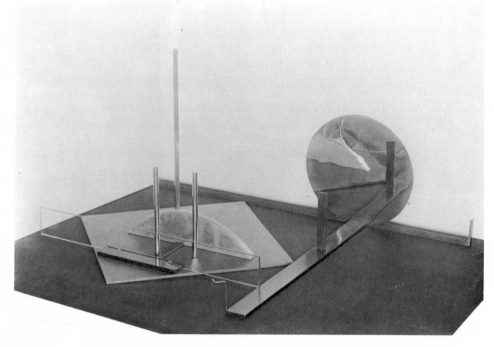

Fig. 15. Geometrical sculptural composition in glass and nickel on black wood base (Metallplastik), 1921/22.

to his credit. . . . He constantly developed new ideas. These proved as fruitful to the school as to his own development." And in an obituary note to the fourth edition of the same book he added:

We might well call the scope of his contribution "Leonardian," so versatile and colorful has it been. He was successful at once as a thinker and as an inventor, as a writer and as a teacher. . . . Constantly developing new ideas, he managed to keep himself in a state of unbiased curiosity from which a fresh point of view could originate. With a shrewd sense of observation he investigated everything that came his way, taking nothing for granted but using his acute sense for the organic.

The publication of the Bauhaus books was perhaps the most fruitful result of this friendship. Today these fourteen volumes are the only remaining proof of the united effort to integrate new visual values—embracing all art forms in all countries. They bear witness to the gigantic scope of actual work done, refuting all those who like to deride modern art for an abundance of verbalization and a lack of planned effort. But the main importance of this project did not rest with the subject matter presented. Progressive magazines and book publications were abundant in Europe between 1920 and 1930. The primary distinction of the Bauhaus books was their function as authentic textbooks, written by the creators of new forms and philosophies and not by disciples of disciples. Pictorial material, theoretical content, and typographical form were documents of a new, unified, visual education. They are the first—and to date the only—co-ordinated effort to relate the teaching of all visual disciplines to one integrating principle—architecture.

The typography was Moholy's job. Although he was a newcomer in the field, Gropius trusted his taste and his workmanship. In his own publication in the series, *Malerei—Photographie—Film*,[4] Moholy explained his interest in printing and layout:

A long-range influence, still overlooked today, comes from the work of the printer. It is his task to create international understanding with all it implies ethically and politically. The work of the printer is part of the foundation on which our world is built. But, with the newest mechanical aids at their disposal, most printers still have a "hand-type mentality," as if mass-distribution of mass-information could be ignored. The essential factor in typographical progress has to come not from form but from organization, not from new type faces but from the optical effectiveness of the page. For the really contemporary typographer the type face is not merely a means of conveying meaning, but an optical disposition of space

[4] See page 28.

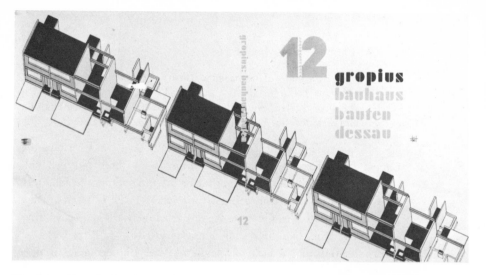

Fig. 16. Dust jacket for Bauhaus Book No. 12. Black and red on translucent tracing paper, 1925.

urging the reader to recognize the essentiality of clarity, brevity, and precision.

The Bauhaus books influenced two generations of progressive typographers and commercial artists; their wrappers became landmarks of jacket design (Fig. 16), and their texts served to annihilate the beaux-arts spirit. They also confirmed Moholy's ability in a new field in which he retained a lifelong interest. Yet, in the totality of the Bauhaus effort, the publications were only a supplementary task. The centers which radiated all strength and all creativeness were the workshops. In the spring of 1923 Moholy became head of the Metal Workshop and the Advanced Foundation Course.

The Metal Workshop had been under the guidance of Paul Klee, who, in the words of Xanti Schawinsky, turned out "spiritual samovars and intellectual doorknobs." Moholy saw a chance to create implements which would fill the urgent demand for good mass-production models and at the same time serve his obsession with the problems of light. Under his guidance the Metal Workshop of the Bauhaus produced a line of lighting fixtures which, still today, constitute the basic design of most modern lamps (Fig. 17). In a photomontage called "ME," Moholy has portrayed himself with his master students: Marcel Breuer, Hin Bredendieck, and others (Fig. 18).

The Preliminary or Foundation Course was the backbone of the Bauhaus program. Its purpose was the study of basic materials, of wood, glass, metal, fiber, and their workability by hand and tool. When Moholy joined the Bauhaus faculty in 1923 Joseph Albers had already established a curriculum that combined the exploration of property values with simple functional construction methods. The accent was on activation of the senses. Moholy expanded this course into a second semester where the basic knowledge of matter and method, acquired earlier, was applied to the inventive creation of form. Experiment, the free play of intuition and material knowledge, was valued higher than the finished result. "Education by process" became the motto of the Foundation Course.

Fig. 17. Lamp design, metal workshop, Bauhaus, Dessau, 1925.

But Moholy's peculiar impact upon the Bauhaus community was due less to his pedagogical skill, which was still in its beginnings, than to his personality, to his obsessed drive toward total identification. In an obituary note, Paul Citroen wrote:

> Like a strong eager dog, Moholy burst into the Bauhaus circle, ferreting out with unfailing scent the still unsolved, still tradition-bound problems in order to attack them. The most conspicuous difference between him and the older teachers was a lack of the typically German dignity and remoteness prevalent among the older "Masters" as all Bauhaus teachers were called. He never asked what was the impression

39

Fig. 18.   Photocollage ME, Bauhaus, Dessau, showing Moholy (top, wearing glasses) and master students, 1925.

he made, or whether what he had to suggest would affect anyone's ego. He knew neither toga nor cothurnus in his relationship to students, and when first he was often mistaken for a
student, he was delighted.

We who had been already several years at the Bauhaus were
often sceptical of so much innovation, aware of intrigues,
jealousies, personal advantages; and we certainly never did
any work if there was the slightest danger that anyone else
might get credit for it. Moholy was totally uninfluenced by
these modifications of our enthusiasm. There never lived anyone more devoted to an objective cause. His high opinion of
the importance of the Bauhaus remained unimpaired, and he
devoted himself to it with such fervor that we started to discuss
his possible collapse. But as a newcomer he got no credit.
Many of us used him for our own advantage and burdened
him with tasks we ourselves should have solved. But, with
the smiling enthusiasm of a child, Moholy accepted all demands, and his vitality seemed unlimited.

It was equally important for Moholy to help organize
a "Bauhaus Fest"—the annual fancy-dress ball which had become
nationally famous—to design settings for the Bauhaus Ballet, or
to hit the road in an attempt to collect money for an expansion
of the Bauhaus program. Life and work in Weimar and Dessau
fused to such an extent that the word *leisure* dropped out of
Moholy's vocabulary. The processes of living, from eating and
sleeping to a streetcar ride or a business meeting, were as much
part of his work as giving a lecture or painting a picture. The
mere fact of existence implied a continuous process of growth, in
which positive and negative factors were analyzed through observation and experimentation, and added to his creative stock.

Years later in New York, the former head of the
largest publishing house in Berlin, recounted Moholy's visit to him
in 1926.

"His German was abominable, and he had to make up
for missing adjectives with expressive gestures. I disliked modern
art and I had agreed to give the poor fellow a few minutes only
to please one of my art editors. But I became fascinated by
Moholy's performance. Under his arm he carried a folder of
clippings culled from my own publications. Using a red pencil,
he showed me how layout, color scheme, and illustrations could

have been a million times more effective. He criticized my desk lamp—smilingly but cunningly—and he promised me a hundred years of healthy existence if only I'd sit in a functional chair and read by functional light. The most striking feature was Moholy's obvious enjoyment of his mission. He had neither the meekness nor the forced cockiness of the typical money-raiser. In the end I made out a check that was much higher than I myself had planned."

As we stepped into the elevator of the small New York hotel where the one-time newspaper magnate lived as a refugee from Hitler, Moholy reminisced wistfully.

"It's a good thing to know the art of camouflage. God, how much hurt pride and self-conscious embarrassment I've covered up with shows like that. No one had to overcome greater handicaps in asking help than I. That was what made me so determined to be a success."

The productive freedom, the atmosphere of creative equality, and the glamour of international recognition outweighed the friction which sparked incessantly among a group comprised of some of the most creative men of an era. Much of this friction resulted from charges of artistic plagiarism, leveled against Moholy by some of his colleagues. He was accused of taking someone else's concept and developing it into a new form, a new theory, a new workshop exercise. But there was nothing less comprehensible to him than the tight grip on an idea. Throughout his life he flung projects and suggestions into the arena, not caring whether anyone else would claim them. He lent carefully compiled lantern slides, his vast collection of prints and clippings, even his own manuscripts, to any friend who had to make a speech or wanted to write a book. The willingness to share creative experience seemed to him particularly important in teaching. Integrated design had accepted the whole world as its field of action. The few men who took up this challenge were dependent on spiritual solidarity for success. Gropius' attempt to co-ordinate in the Bauhaus faculty all efforts toward a realization of the design totality seemed to Moholy the ideal state of unified diversity. The hunt for epigoni, the pastime of so many art critics, only aroused his contempt, which he formulated in an open letter to one of the most powerful art editors of his day.

WEIMAR, July 1, 1924   STAATLICHES BAUHAUS

Mr. Paul Westheim
Editor
Das Kunstblatt
Berlin

DEAR MR. WESTHEIM:

In the last number of your *Kunstblatt,* Alfred Kemeny takes issue with an article by Paul F. Schmidt in which I am characterized as a representative of Suprematism. Kemeny uses this classification, which, by the way, was used by Schmidt without my knowledge, to accuse me of eclecticism, plagiarism, and self-promotion under false creative pretenses. He analyzes my "sterility," the lack of "economy" and precision in my work, and the "general incompetency of my artistic efforts." But this is irrelevant to what I have to say.

Kemeny was once my closest friend and co-fighter in the days of the Hungarian MA movement. For purely personal reasons he has become a bitter enemy who vents his anger through public denunciation of my painting. Returning from a visit to Russia only two years ago, in 1922, he wrote that only the work of Peri and myself among the young generation could compare with the maximum achievement of Russian art.

But I am totally uninterested in whether or not Mr. Kemeny questions my originality; whether he or anyone else labels me Suprematist, Constructivist, Functionalist, etc. Many years ago, at the very beginning of my life as an artist, some comrades and I warned in an article in "MA" against these catchwords. Classifications are born by accident, through a journalistic quip or a bourgeois invective. The living force of artistic development changes the meaning of the term without giving the artist a chance to protest his false identity.

Kemeny states that I have "contributed nothing to the task of finding for our time a visual expression commensurate with its technological and economic urgencies." It is not for me to decide this, nor am I interested in the decision. My work at the Bauhaus is concerned with translating my concept of contemporaneousness into form and word. This is so big a task that it leaves me no time to worry about its interpretation from without. Whatever the quality of my oil paintings and my

43

sculptures might be, I am satisfied that I am given the privilege
—rare to anyone—to translate revolution into material reality.
Compared to this task, the fiddling of Kemeny and others
about priorities is quite irrelevant. A few years from now the
selective principle of quality will decide upon our endeavors,
and no catchwords or personal enmities will influence this
selection.

Sincerely yours,

MOHOLY-NAGY[5]

The inner certainty of these lines was not conceit. It
was the acceptance of work as the supreme gratification of man.
Moholy had learned to work, and all that he achieved in later
years he achieved through effort. No artist held less to a mystical
belief in the automatic self-revelation of the genius. When he
had learned English, he adopted for art Edison's definition of
genius, "one per cent inspiration and ninety-nine per cent perspira-
tion," as one of his favorite sayings.

The most important contribution the Bauhaus years
made to Moholy's development was his acceptance of teaching as
a life task. The contact with young people and the vitality of the
creative group lessened the frantic search of his Berlin years.
The zest of living productively and collectively erased "the terrible
great quietness" of his childhood and the horrors of war; and it
liberated him from the faddish prejudices against a full enjoyment of life that had narrowed the minds of his early German
companions. He discovered the unity of doing and being, the
organic oneness of living soundly and producing creatively. This
became the keynote of his teaching program.

> From his biological being every man derives energies which
> he can develop into creative work. *Everyone is talented.* Every
> human being is open to sense impressions, to tone, color, touch,
> space experience, etc. The structure of a life is predetermined
> in these sensibilities. One has to live "right" to retain the
> alertness of these native abilities.
>
> But only art—creation through the senses—can develop these
> dormant, native faculties toward creative action. Art is the
> grindstone of the senses, the co-ordinating psycho-biological
> factor. The teacher who has come to a full realization of the

[5] All quotations from letters and manuscripts dating from 1922 to 1941
were written in German and have been translated by the author.

44

organic oneness and the harmonious sense rhythm of life should have a tongue of fire to expound his happiness.[6]

But, together with this biological impetus and the inner satisfaction of giving guidance, Moholy discovered the depleting effects of teaching. Little has ever been written about the psychological dilemma inherent in art instruction. It is taken for granted that all knowledge and inspiration can be shared, and that security against the hazards of an artist's existence can be guaranteed by a paid position. As Moholy became an experienced teacher he discovered that the creative process lent itself poorly to the inevitable routine of the classroom, that it often died of verbalization. It became his conviction that art itself cannot be taught, because young people look for absolutes whereas the artist maintains a precarious equilibrium between self-assertion and self-rejection. Even the teaching of the fundamentals of integrated design, derived from a socio-biological understanding of human needs, demanded from the artist-teacher a total dedication which needed the sustenance of the creative community and the unlimited confidence of the students. Many years later in America Moholy warned against the destruction of native talent in the "resident artist" who is expected to dissect his soul fourteen hours a week under the strict supervision of the Trustees. To teach a new concept successfully, he told his graduates, called for a deep respect for the artist's integrity in any school administration, and a high state of self-renunciation in the artist himself, which can only be maintained by a profound love for youth.

This contrast between the humanist who thinks in terms of relationships, and the specialist who thinks in terms of isolated problems, emerged slowly in the late 1920's. The synthesis of art and technology on which rested the Bauhaus program was slowly destroyed by a cancerous growth of the technological cells. Political reaction joined forces with technocratic utilitarianism, demanding that state-endowed education serve no other purpose than the training of specialists. Under the leadership of Hannes Meyer, an architect, a group of Bauhaus masters denounced the original concept of an integrated education where process and experiment ranked supreme over specialized skill.

[6] Moholy-Nagy, *Vom Material zur Architektur* (Bauhaus Bücher, No. 14, Munich, 1928), published in English under the title *The New Vision*.

45

Since this change in pedagogical conviction corresponded to a change in the political climate of Germany, foreshadowing totalitarianism, the opposition group found ready support among some of the politicians upon whose vote depended the Bauhaus budget.

The pressure brought upon Walter Gropius became more and more powerful. The alternatives were abandoning his lifework or consenting to a compromise which would level off the summit of integrative effort to a flat technological expediency. On January 13, 1928, he resigned as head of the German Bauhaus. On January 17 Moholy declared his complete accord and resigned too, followed by Herbert Bayer, Marcel Breuer, and Xanti Schawinsky. In a letter, addressed to the *Meisterrat* of the Bauhaus, Moholy formulated his reasons for resigning his position. It is a statement that in twenty-odd years has lost nothing of its validity for the acute problem of endowed education.

> For the Bauhaus begins now a time of stabilization conditioned by the length of its existence. As a consequence of the growing scarcity of money, it is demanded that it be productive, efficient—today more than ever.
>
> Even though human and pedagogical considerations are not eliminated intentionally, they suffer because of this stabilization. Among the students, this reorientation is noticeable in their increased demand for technical skill and practical training above anything else.
>
> Basically one can't object if human power wants to measure itself on the object, the trade. This belongs essentially to the Bauhaus program. But one must see the danger of losing equilibrium, and meet it. As soon as creating an object becomes a specialty, and work becomes trade, the process of education loses all vitality. There must be room for teaching the basic ideas which keep human content alert and vital. For this we fought and for this we exhausted ourselves. I can no longer keep up with the stronger and stronger tendency toward trade specialization in the workshops.
>
> We are now in danger of becoming what we as revolutionaries opposed: a vocational training school which evaluates only the final achievement and overlooks the development of the whole man. For him there remains no time, no money, no space, no concession.

46

I can't afford a continuation on this specialized, purely objective and efficient basis—either productively or humanly. I trained myself in five years for a specialty, the Metal Workshop, but I could do this only by also giving all my human reserves. I shall have to resign if this demand for specialization becomes more intense. The spirit of construction for which I and others gave all we had—and gave it gladly—has been replaced by a tendency toward application. My realm was the construction of school and man. Under a program of increased technology I can continue only if I have a technical expert as my aide. For economic reasons this will never be possible. There is always money for only one of the two. I exerted great effort over these years to make the expert unnecessary. I can't give more than I gave so far; therefore I have to relinquish my place to him. I am infinitely sad about this. It is a turn toward the negative—away from the original, the consciously willed, character of the Bauhaus.

The school today swims no longer against the current. It tries to fall in line. This is what weakens the power of the unit. Community spirit is replaced by individual competition, and the question arises whether the existence of a creative group is only possible on the basis of opposition to the *status quo*. It remains to be seen how efficient will be the decision to work only for efficient results. Perhaps there will be a new fruitful period. Perhaps it is the beginning of the end.

It *was* the beginning of the end. During the following four years different men tried to save the Bauhaus by compromising with the growing political opposition. A last attempt by Ludwig Mies van der Rohe to continue it as a private school in Berlin failed when the Hitler regime wiped it out as a "center of *Kulturbolschewismus.*"

In the fall of 1928 Moholy returned to Berlin. He was no longer anonymous as when he had first pleaded with a hotel clerk for a bed, but he also was no longer without scars and the consciousness of defeat. The great illusion of a creative union between government and education was destroyed. From now on the realization of an integrated life concept depended on the individual fighting power of those who believed in it. As a member of the visionary group that had mapped total design as a future principle of living, Moholy had been a contributor, not a leader.

47

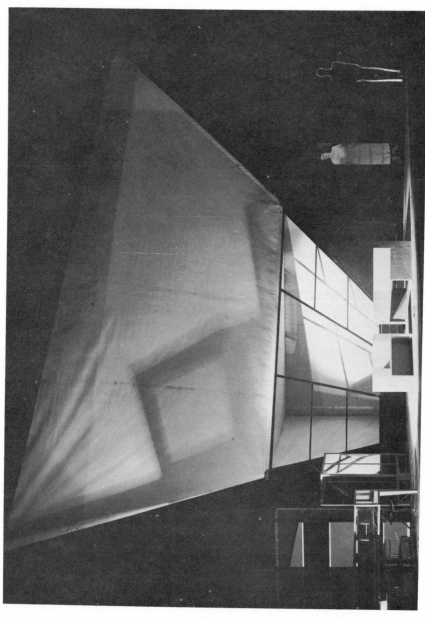

Fig. 19. Stage Setting for "The Tales of Hoffmann," State Opera, Berlin, 1929.

The dimensions of his inner stature became apparent only after all supports were gone and he had to choose between retreat and attack. In testing the needs of a civilization that seemed to have abandoned all creative hope, he discovered its potentialities. As he faced his times artistically, emotionally, and politically, he became a contemporary in the deepest meaning of the word. Somewhere between 1928 and 1929 Moholy sensed that his integrity had to be preserved not through social retreat but through total involvement and identification.

The State of Prussia maintained two opera theaters in Berlin: the classical house *Unter Den Linden*, and the *Krolloper*, *l'enfant terrible* of the operatic art. A trio of unusual talent worked at the latter: Otto Klemperer, the conductor; Ernst Legal, the producer; and Hans Curjel, the manager. Early in 1929 they hired Moholy to design their settings. None of them quite realized what this appointment would entail, although a quip of Legal's indicated some suspicions about his new designer:

"I'm supposed to believe I'm walking a dog," he said, "when it's actually a lion."

The first task assigned to Moholy was the scenery for Offenbach's *Tales of Hoffmann*. The spectator who came to lose himself in the sweetness of the "Barcarole," and to revel in a papier-mâché image of the Canale Grande, found his conservative pleasures persiflaged by an unremittingly modern scene (Fig. 19). Instead of barges there were stainless steel folding cots for the romantic couples to recline on, pulled out of the bare wall at the musical cue of the conductor. Instead of a neon-lit sky studded with bulb stars, a tapered white ceiling led into a deep perspective from which Hoffmann's rococo figures emerged in costumes which contrasted the clownish tuxedo of Antonia's father with the futuristic mobility of his daughter's gown (Fig. 20).

Moholy's *Hoffmann* was the event of the opera season, arousing an equal amount of enthusiastic support and fierce denunciation. In an interview for the *Musikalische Monatshefte*, Moholy wrote:

> Grand opera is dead, but much of its music cannot die. Let us shed the monstrous decorations that smell of glue and mold and will not fool a small child into an illusion of fairyland.

49

Fig. 20. Antonia. Figurine from "The Tales of Hoffmann," State Opera, Berlin, 1929.

Let us test the staying power of so-called great music by having fun with its trappings. If we insist on grand opera, let us see it as contemporaries.

But after designs for Mozart's *Marriage of Figaro* he felt his optimism crumble. In 1930 he wrote:

Grand opera and Total Theater don't blend. One can't dress obsolete content with modern design. One could, but the guardians of tradition won't let us. As long as writer, composer, and producer do not work as a creative unit to create theater art, all efforts at a theater revival will be wasted in feeble compromises.

After one more setting for the *Krolloper*, Hindemith's *Hin und Zurück* (Figs. 21, 22), Moholy saw a chance for the collaborative effort he had wanted. *The Merchant of Berlin* was a social drama written by Walter Mehring and produced by Erwin Piscator who was the director of a "political theater" in Berlin. The play used the German inflation of 1923 as a dramatic motif. A small Jewish speculator, desperately determined to provide a life of luxury for his tubercular daughter, teams up with nationalistic armament profiteers. In a frantic succession of finance maneuvers, they wring the last pennies from the starving masses, comforting them with the prospect of a new armament boom. In the end the Jew is ruined by his titled friends who ride into political power on their illegal profits. The equally senseless death of those killed in battle and those starved to death by the speculators is symbolized by the "Unknown Soldier" whose corpse is

50

Fig. 21. Sketches for figurine and painted backdrop for the operetta "Hin und Zurück" (back and forth) by Paul Hindemith, State Opera, Berlin, 1930.

swept into the garbage bin together with billions of worthless inflation money.

Moholy's scenery was an experiment of great boldness. The tragic proletarian level, the tragicomic middle-class level, and the grotesque militaristic-capitalistic level were represented by three platforms, moving vertically on the stage. The different levels merged and separated, rose and fell, while endless conveyor belts carried men and objects in incessant motion. Neon signs glared into the face of the little Jew, wandering through Berlin in search of profit, and the Potsdam militarists were harassed by shrieking choruses of the starving unemployed, by enormous projections of

51

Fig. 22. Stage setting for "The Tales of Hoffmann," Barcarole Scene, State Opera, Berlin, 1929. Overlapping of scaffolding and projection.

statistics and slogans, and by advancing and receding background units of slums and barracks.

The curtain had not yet fallen when one of the most violent theater battles in Berlin's history broke loose. Nationalists and Socialists in the audience attacked each other with fists and boots, slinging verbal mud which appeared in the next day's papers. Unanimity between Left and Right was only restored when it came to the stage settings. There the outcry against "intellectual decadence" and "technological mania" had all hues, from the crimson of the Social Democrats to the black-white-red of the Nationalists.

Moholy was stunned. He could not understand why the public was so unprepared for a presentation which was much less extraordinary than, for instance, Schlemmer's Bauhaus Ballets, or some of the settings presented by the experimental theaters in Munich, Frankfort, and Stuttgart. The Bauhaus had missed no opportunity to demonstrate that

> drama remains mere literature if an event or an impending event—no matter how imaginative—is formulated and enacted without a creative form peculiar to the stage. Only if the tensions inherent in the most constructive use of stage effects have been co-ordinated in a dynamic relatedness of action can we talk of stage technique.[7]

Walter Gropius had published his powerful appeal for a "Total Theater," demanding for

> the universal producer a great light-and-space keyboard, so impersonal and variable that it confines him nowhere and remains flexible to all visions of his imagination. . . . The Total Theater must be a mobilization of all spatial means to rouse the spectator from his intellectual apathy, to assault and overwhelm him, coerce him into participation in the play.[8]

New designs for theaters had been widely publicized, exposing the audience to projections on ceilings and walls, with U-shaped or circular stages, and with technical equipment ranging from percussion orchestras to apparatus for the inclusion of scent sensations into the stage effects. The question raised by the scan-

[7] Schlemmer and Moholy-Nagy, *Die Bühne des Bauhauses* (*The Stage of the Bauhaus, Bauhaus Bücher*, No. 4, 1924).

[8] Walter Gropius, *Theaterbau* (*Reale Accademia D'Italia*, No. XII, 1934).

dal of *The Merchant of Berlin* was why all these suggestions and realizations had had no effect on the public taste. The answer propelled Moholy from a merely revolutionary into a social consciousness. It revealed to him the basic cause for the sociological failure of the whole visual revolution.

The defenders of the new vision were guilty of an asocial isolation and a nonevolutionary abruptness. Their greatest shortcoming was a lack of feeling for organic transition. Theoretically Moholy had found convincing words against sophistication when he wrote in *Die Bühne des Bauhauses*:

> It is well to remember that the supposedly illiterate masses— in spite of their academic "backwardness"—usually formulate the healthiest instincts and preferences. Creative comprehension of the genuine, and not the synthetic, needs remains our permanent task.

It was on the definition of the genuine and the synthetic that the new theater art foundered. The experimental ballets and the persiflaged grand operas, performed before small select groups, had been successful because they appealed to intellectual curiosity. They were one more manifestation of a new pattern of relative value in color and form. They never affected the masses. But the dramatic spectacle—half drama, half comedy—is an essential part of European life. The existence of municipal theaters in the smallest provincial towns testifies to the eminent place it holds in the social pattern. It is in the theater that the people find their illusionary paradises. The acceptance of a play by the spectator depends on the right balance between sufficient realism to permit self-projection, and a glorification of suffering distinctly not his own.

In *The Merchant of Berlin* the traumatic agony of civic existence, the shame of exploited gullibility, and the secret hope for economic recovery by means of another world war, were exposed with stark realism. The familiar trappings of heroism and national pride were thrown into the ash can. The protest of the Berlin audience was self-defense.

If the co-ordination between actor and machine had functioned according to Moholy's demand that "in the Total Theater man is no longer central as in the traditional theater, but

54

Fig. 23. Stage setting for "Madame Butterfly," State Opera, Berlin, 1931. Stationary foreground props, varied from scene to scene by varying background projection from glass slides on curved stage horizon.

he must be used as a representational means of equal value beside the new forms of light, space, motion, and tone,"[9] perhaps the audience would have been intimidated by the crushing power of this new symbolism. As it was, Moholy proved his own point that "in this concentration of mechanical eccentricities man has no longer any place." The inadequacy of the human voice against the roaring stage apparatus, the awkwardness of the human figure, dwarfed and flattened out by the assault of light beacons, mechanical motion, and cacophonous sound, seemed to refute the new dramatic vision. The union between man and machine stood accused. Reactionary zealots had a rare day of triumph.

Moholy did one more stage setting the following year, a lovely light-play to the gentle score of *Madame Butterfly*. The mechanical experiments had been abandoned. He had decided to plead for visual revolution with the subtle means of kinetic light, the dramatic distortion of restless shadows, and the emotional excitement of transparency and translucency (Fig. 23). The only reminders of "Total Theater" and "mechanical eccentricity" were the costumes, which were orgies of pure color, and whims of line and form. But the fast-spreading political reorientation had al-

[9] *Die Bühne des Bauhauses.*

55

ready changed public opinion from defensive criticism to political assault, and even this score of finest values was denounced as "cultural Bolshevism."

The famous twenties had come to an end, and the high spirit of creation sank into a coma, pathetically close to death. Much energy had been wasted, and the goal of an integrated visual and social world had not been realized. But there had never been a decade more generously permitting man to dream in public. Many of these visions had not endured, but they had isolated agents which could never be destroyed. New architecture had established functional and esthetic standards; in painting and sculpture the self-expressive reality of color, form, space, and motion had been proven; and the educational philosophy of the Bauhaus had restored man—the fractional tool of industrial revolution—as master of art, science, and technology. It will remain the honor of the German Republic that it sheltered these forces and provided the means and the environment to formulate a new covenant between the creative individual and society.

3 *Madame Butterfly* was still playing in the Kroll Opera House when I took over the scenario office of a large motion-picture company in Berlin. In a thickening atmosphere of nationalistic isolation, the level of the Tobis production was above that of the average commercial firm. In leaving my previous engagement with the State Theater in Darmstadt, Hesse, I hoped that the international character of Tobis would save it from a Fascist mentality. But in shrewd anticipation of future developments, the Dutch and Belgian stockholders suddenly sold out their interest to I. G. Farben, which acted as spearhead for Herman Göring's planned consolidation of Germany's industry under Nazi rule. This transaction, involving millions of marks, emphasized a sense of impending disaster spreading slowly among German progressives.

Hitler's power, which had been a provincial buffoonery, acquired an unexpected reality in 1931. At the time of the Tobis stock transfer, millions of unemployed men started to join his private army, the SA, or the "Storm Troopers." Newspapers and radio commentators became increasingly sympathetic to the new *Weltanschauung.* Big industry picked up the scent of a potential rearmament boom, and economists spared no mental acrobatics to reconcile Hitler's threatened liquidation of capital interest with the mouth-watering promise of annihilation of the labor unions. Life started to be obscured by miasmic clouds of cowardice and treachery.

Among my colleagues at the motion-picture syndicate was Saul Levinson, who had made a name for himself by producing newsreels, short subjects, and educational films of high artistic quality. But the transfer of the company's stock had weakened his spine. He knew that the zeal of Joseph Goebbels for *Volksaufklärung* would cost him his neck if he did not prove his

57

loyalty to the future *Führer*. Like many others he tried to save his skin by frantic attempts to hang new convictions on an undesirable family tree.

One day in the winter of 1931 he called me over the house phone.

"I'm in a fix, Peech, and you have to help me. Some guy is down here in the projection room; unpronounceable name but supposedly famous. Has some photographs with him which look like so many darkroom accidents to me. Wants to run off some experimental film. But you know the situation. With the new stockholders in control we can't show *Kulturbolschewismus* any longer. I don't want to be the one to tell him, though. The State Theater boys sent him. They still count. He might be an insider for all I know. Tell you what. I'll scram and you look at his stuff; then throw him out, gently but firmly. I don't want his type around here any more."

When I got to the projection room, a man was sketching on the back of an envelope, explaining something to Levinson, who was watching the door instead of the paper. The visitor was medium-sized, and carefully dressed. He had a streak of white through his very black hair, and the simple features of a peasant, open blue eyes, high cheekbones, a heavy jaw, and a full mouth. But his hands were small, narrow, and very sensitive. He smiled at me as if he had met me many times.

"I'm so glad you could come. You are the scenario editor, aren't you?" he said, giving me a strange sensation of being his guest. "You'll be interested in this project." He handed me a sheaf of typewritten pages. "But we'll first look at the light-play. After you've seen it you'll recognize the idea."

The strong *r*'s and the soft *s*'s of his Hungarian accent gave his speech a musical rhythm.

"As I explained to this gentleman—"

Levinson winked at me, pointing his right thumb over his shoulder to remind me of the kickout I was to apply.

"I'm so sorry I have to leave, Professor. It was a great privilege." Levinson bowed affectedly to emphasize the irony of his words. But the man, to whom I hadn't been introduced, smiled without suspicion.

58

After Levinson had left, he returned to his sketch. It represented two plate-glass mirrors mounted on an open truck. A film camera was directed at each mirror. As the truck was driving through the streets of Berlin, each camera would photograph the happenings of a single day—between dawn and dusk. City life would be reflected, distorted, broken up, concentrated, through the medium of the mirrors.

"We could tilt them at times," he said, using the plural as if it were I who would be with him on the truck. "Or we could use one flat and one concave surface."

He searched his pockets for another piece of paper, and produced a calling card on which he drew a concave and a convex refraction scheme. As he handed the card to me, explaining how the mirage would work, I saw the name LÁSZLÓ MOHOLY-NAGY.

"Oh, it's you; you're Moholy-Nagy," I said, and his face, which had been serious in its intense concentration, lighted.

"You know my name? How nice"—as if everyone with an interest in modern art did not know who he was. But it was not an affected delight. It was genuine surprise, the joy of a child at being recognized. He never lost it, and even the incredulous intonation remained unchanged to the end of his life. "You really know my name?" floated gaily through the darkened hospital room during his last sickness fifteen years later, when an orderly turned out to be a former student of Black Mountain College.

I had known his name for ten years, I told him. In 1921 my conservative father had warned his daughters to stay away from a subversive art show called "*Der Sturm*," which was "polluting" the academic tradition of my native Dresden. The grave old man, a great architect and trustee of the Art Academy, had been particularly peeved by Moholy's collages, which he called "the cutouts of a child." Of course I had lost no time in seeing the forbidden show, and I had retained a vivid memory, not so much of specific paintings, but of a symphony of floating, merging, speaking elements of form.

The tone in which I told my reminiscences must have been full of the superiority which my generation felt toward the academic backwardness of their elders. To us they were worth only a contemptuous laugh, which I expected to share with this man whose work had been so ignorantly attacked. But Moholy-Nagy reacted differently.

"I could make your father understand a collage," he said. "I'm sure I could. If I had a chance to explain the basic idea to him—the overlying planes, and the relationship of color and texture—"

He crossed his spread fingers in the form of a grill, a gesture which I later came to accept as the most characteristic expression of his drive toward integration. I was touched by his demonstrative zeal, which, at that moment, was focused on my absent and old-fashioned father—as if it mattered whether or not he understood a collage. As I looked into Moholy's eyes, dark blue and startlingly direct, I realized half-consciously that for him everyone mattered. My supercilious mockery was as incomprehensible to him as Levinson's sarcastic reverence had been a few minutes earlier. Until now, I had never met a total teacher.

The operator in the projection room announced that he was ready and I saw the first version of "Light-Play Black-White-Gray," an abstract film which now has become famous in Europe and America. The patterns created by moving discs and rotating cylinders, by the solid black of dark metal and the transparencies of luminous plastic sheets, were totally new to my eyes, accustomed only to the obviousness of commercial film production. All I could do was *see*; I could not be objective, critical. But objectivity was what Moholy wanted. He was not interested in passive admiration; he did not even want the satisfaction of consent. This man whom I had never met before wanted my collaboration, and he wanted it then and there. He pressed another calling card and a pencil into my hand and urged me to take notes. The light-play ran its course. When it was over and I was unable to make a single negative comment, Moholy was disappointed.

"I was sure you'd have something to say." The tone in which he spoke made me feel absurdly guilty.

He called for the operator who had projected the film, and asked his impression. Nussbaum was a typical Berliner—quick-witted and cynical.

60

"Well, Professor," he started out, "my eyesight mustn't be any longer what it used to be. All I could make out were shaking rods and rolling balls with a few window panes thrown in. Not that I want to be critical, but. . . ."

"Yes, but?" Moholy interrupted eagerly, disregarding the sarcasm.

Nussbaum was stumped. No one ever asked his opinion and he hadn't cared about what he was asked to show.

"You projected the film," Moholy urged him on. "You see films all day long. You know more about it than I do. Your judgment would mean much to me."

He smiled with the same intensity that had touched me when I had first come into the projection room. It now touched tough Nussbaum. His quick tongue was stuck.

"That glass sheet with the holes . . ." he muttered.

"Yes?"

"—pretty," said Nussbaum, smiling with infinite relief because he had remembered some detail.

"All right, pretty. But what wasn't pretty?"

"Well, hard to look at the reflections on those polished disks."

Nussbaum spoke slowly, amusing to listen to after the tempo of his usual speech.

"Hard on the eyes," he concluded.

"Very interesting." Moholy made notes on his card. "Let's go over it again. Perhaps we can cut it."

"But Professor!" Nussbaum looked at his watch and so did I.

"It won't take more than ten minutes," Moholy smiled. "If we stand here debating it'll take much longer. This time, please, record your impressions," he said to me.

His features and his voice expressed a mixture of pleading gentleness and stubborn, almost threatening insistence which I later came to admire as the most successful coercion toward unconditional surrender.

When Moholy left late that afternoon we had seen the film three times. Between us Nussbaum and I had a dozen calling cards filled with scribbled comments, and a new word—*light-*

display—had been added to our vocabulary. Without knowing it, we had become collaborators and we had started to understand that, to a total worker, everybody mattered as a collaborator.

A few days later I went to Moholy's studio to return a film manuscript which he had urged me to read. The face of the young man who took me in the elevator to the top floor of the studio building on the *Kaiserdamm* reflected intense concentration. He was Gyorgy Kepes, a Hungarian painter who had come to work with Moholy a few years earlier. His reticence, and the perpetual solemnity of his mien, seemed to contrast strangely with Moholy's enthusiastic eloquence and outgoing cordiality. In time I came to understand their partnership. It was founded on their common devotion to *seeing* as a philosophy of life. Their differences of temperament and social orientation, often aggravated by their furious Hungarian egos, were settled through a deep mutual understanding about the fitness of demonstrative means. It was a matter of common emphasis and common taste. Later, in their American years, they added to this unifying vision the dedication to teaching. On behalf of the shared responsibility for the future of universal design they formed a team which lasted for twelve years. It added much to the visual pedagogy of our time.

Moholy's studio in 1931 looked like a relief chart of the landscape of design. There was almost no furniture; floor space was needed as a work area. From strings, extended across one corner of the room, long strips of film hung like spaghetti. It was a travelogue, ready to be cut and printed, which Moholy had brought back from Finland. Over another part of the floor was spread out a sequence of sketches—covers for the fashionable magazine *Die Neue Linie*, which frequently displayed Moholy's and Kepes' designs (Fig. 24). Typewritten pages of a lecture on photography, cut into strips and put together like a jigsaw puzzle, were lying somewhere else; and set up on a tripod was a camera aimed at a multitude of colored pins which were stuck in a white sheet on the wall. For hours I literally walked through projects in advertising, typography, film, and photography. I was not asked to be an interested visitor. As in the film projection room, I was asked to participate, to contribute. The typewritten puzzle of

62

Fig. 24. Cover page for periodical "Die Neue Linie," 1930. Photomontage.

the lecture was assigned to me first; later I held a polished metal sheet to supply highlights on a pile of woolen fabrics to be photographed for a clothing ad (Fig. 25). When suppertime came, we picked up some bread, cold meat, fruit, and cold tea from a wall cupboard. None of us seemed to think of going out to dinner.

When finally Kepes had left and it was time for me to go too, I realized that something I had expected to find was missing. There wasn't a painting in the studio, no sculpture, not even a sketch. For ten years I had thought of Moholy as a painter —one of the great four of the Bauhaus: Kandinsky, Klee, Feininger, Moholy-Nagy. Where were his paintings?

After I had asked him, there was the embarrassed silence that follows a tactless question. Then:

"I don't paint anymore."

I looked over the multitude of projects in the studio. "You have no time just now?"

"There's always time for painting," he said brusquely,

63

Fig. 25. Multicolored labels for textile industry, used in varying sizes for price tags, advertising, store decorations.

and the strange contradiction to his previous statement made it impossible to continue the conversation.

When Moholy next called for me at my office, he took me to the worker's district near Berlin's *Alexanderplatz*. We climbed dark stairs until we reached a dingy office with a roll-top desk and an archaic typewriter. Moholy told me to wait, and while I stared into the light of a bare bulb I wondered why I did not resent this strange companion who, like a magnetic force, constantly changed my direction. In the two weeks I had known him I had edited several articles written in his picturesque but non-literary German; I had spent many tiresome hours posing for a magazine title-page which was to show only the silhouette of a woman's body against a glaring backdrop of light, and I had broken dates and appointments to be in Moholy's studio at supper-time, loaded down with packages of cold meat, fruit, and pastry.

"You can come in now," said a wispy little man from a door.

In the center of a workshop stood a construction— half sculpture and half machine—a combination of chromium, glass, wire, and rods, in which I recognized the forms of the light-display film. As it turned slowly, invisible lights flared up and turned off, producing gigantic shadows on the walls and the ceiling (Fig. 26).

"This is beautiful," I gasped. "It's magnificent. It is—" and suddenly I saw the difference between concept and reality, "it is almost as beautiful as the film."

64

Fig. 26. Light machine, Mobile interplay of chromed and glass parts as projection instrument for the abstract film "Light Play Black-White-Gray," 1925/30.

Moholy smiled. His whole face expanded with happiness.

"There, did you hear?" he said to the little man.

"Hear what?"

"That the reflection is more powerful than the original, that I was right making a film?"

"Film, tsszz," hissed the man, and it was quite obvious that this was the continuation of an old argument. "But the craftsmanship, the precision, where does that show in your blasted film?"

He took me by the arm.

"Here, Lady, just take a look. See how that clears?" A small black ball rolled softly down a slanting rail passing through a rotating sphere.

"And the grills? Have you noticed the grills?" There was a sequence of chromium grills, their mesh formed by a variety of wire patterns.

"The light reflects differently in every one of them. See?"

He started the machine again and the light played dramatically on the metal.

"Film, my eye!" he repeated. "Craftsmanship—that's what matters!"

"We've been working on the machine for almost ten years," Moholy said as we went down the stairs. "I pay him whenever I've some money, but it has cost him more in time and materials than I'll ever be able to repay. He's a wonderful fellow. He's as obsessed by motion as I am by light."

All during dinner we talked about the light machine, which acquired human importance. Moholy explained its genesis by drawing on a sequence of calling cards his experiments, from the almost archaic wood sculpture he had done in 1921 to the floating glass construction in the center of the light machine, foreshadowing his later work with plexiglass. The *Lichtrequisit* had been exhibited in the room Moholy designed for the International Building Exhibition in Paris in 1930, and now he planned to synchronize its motions with a musical score.

66

"I'm so happy you understand," he said. "This is a wonderful day for me. You don't know what it means to me that you saw it."

I did not know yet either. In future years, on our wanderings through Europe and America, I would come to consider the light-display machine the problem child of my household because it refused to pass custom authorities the normal way. When it finally came to rest in Chicago it had been declared a mixing machine, a fountain, a display rack for various metal alloys and a robot, and it had caused me more trouble than a dozen children. But on that first evening of our acquaintance I admired it, without reserve.

"You'll write a music score," Moholy suggested, "and I'll compose the movements. Then we make another light-display film, this time with a sound track."

"I can't write music," I said soberly. "I never have."

"Of course you can." Moholy brushed over the table cloth. "Of course you're musical. I can hear it in your voice."

"All I do is listen to music," I tried to modify his enthusiasm.

"You wouldn't want to listen if you didn't have the inner need to re-create what you hear. That proves your musicality. Do you have another hour or two? Good, I'll show you that you're musical."

We went to a Hungarian restaurant where a gypsy band played dance music.

"You know czardas?"

"No, I've never danced it."

"You will," he said, beaming.

"Left and left—right and right." His voice was as intense as if he were speaking an invocation. "Hands on my shoulders. Left and left. Now jump."

From a slow square-dance rhythm we changed to faster and faster tempi. My hair came undone, my belt fell to the floor. An earring followed, but we didn't stop. I had never felt such an obsession for dancing, never had had a partner so obsessed. When we finally left the floor we were both drunk and we'd had no wine.

67

In the weeks that followed I saw the multiplicity of Moholy's life—his work for the textile trade and the fireproof glass industry, his posters, pamphlets, advertisements. With his friend, Herbert Bayer, he designed a settlement exhibition, the *Gehag*, demonstrating the urgent need for communal living. He set type for trade publications, arranged window displays, and worked on a sound film, engraving linear shapes on film negative. When he played it back on a sound projector he achieved a coincidence of tone and line that had never been demonstrated before. "I can play your profile," he would say to a friend, sketching the outline of the face in his notebook. "I wonder how your nose will sound."

But I never saw him paint, and we never talked about painting.

Each visit to his studio was filled with participation in the task most urgent at that particular time. It was like being inducted as a recruit. Perhaps I was also courted, but it was a courtship without precedent. It spoke through tasks assigned and slow confidences and shared convictions. If it was love, it was the most complete objectification of sentiment. It fitted the deckhand philosophy I had gained from a previous marriage, which had failed; and it also answered my contempt for the glamorous extravagances of the "roaring twenties."

Moholy's unremitting devotion to his work seemed hard to reconcile with his well-known friendship with one of the prettiest, most elegant young actresses of the Berlin stage. Her temperament and performance seemed rather incompatible with this total identification of life and task. Yet her picture appeared in many of Moholy's photographs and designs, his telephone conversations with her were of the charming politeness so peculiar to Austrians and Hungarians, and he usually called for her at night at the theater. He had mentioned a wife before. Was he divorced? I would have liked to know more about his personal relationships but I never asked the questions so much on my mind. In spite of his boyish enthusiasm and his radiant charm in contact with others, there was an element of remoteness, an ascetic dedication in Moholy's character which rejected curiosity. It removed him from gossip and left his private life undiscussed, but it also removed him from close friendships. Even for those who loved him, he ever retained a touch of unworldliness.

The idea of the film "Reflected Image," which he had tried to sell to Levinson that first afternoon we met, slowly took shape. I tried to work out a scenario in order to get some structure into the mirror-shots of the city. But the traditional rhythm of morning, noon, and night; of awakening, activity, and relaxation, seemed too trite.

"I'm not thinking in chronological terms," Moholy finally said. "At least not in the accepted sense. The rhythm of this film has to come from the light—it has to have a light-chronology."

He crossed his spread fingers to form the grill I had seen in the projection room.

"Light beams overlap as they cross through dense air; they're blocked, diffracted, condensed. The different angles of the entering light indicate time. The rotation of light from east to west modulates the visible world. Shadows and reflexes register a constantly changing relationship of solids and perforations. Come, I want to show you something."

Moholy had to move his bed in the small attic room adjoining his studio to get into a storage vault. As I watched him open the door and saw tiers of stacked canvases, I felt intense expectation. What I would have taken for granted—seeing the work of a painter in his studio—had acquired unusual significance through Moholy's statement that he had given up painting. He searched for a long time in the storage space and then brought out two pieces: a canvas and a small plastic. The plastic—a yellowish celluloid sheet—had been painted on the surface and on the construction board underneath the translucent material. It showed the characteristic Constructivist cross in a balanced tonality of gray and red (Fig. 27). As the light from a floor lamp struck the surface, the strong reflections changed the colors completely, almost dissolving them where the light was strong, and toning them down to fine gradations farther away from the light source. But it was the canvas that fascinated me most (Fig. 28). A white transparent disk floated over crossed beams of a radiant red, a

69

Fig. 27. First transparent painting, 1923. Oil on galalith sheet. Painted forms on surface, underside, and white wood background of composition.

warm auburn, and a deep black. I was not aware that Moholy slowly moved the floor lamp from left to right. I saw the disk advance out of the flat surface, setting the different tone values of the beam in slow motion. Suddenly I understood the meaning of a light-chronology. The advancing and receding white of the disk and the colors of the beams were moved by light. The shaded hues of the celluloid picture, controlled by opaqueness and translucency, had made it clear to me. This was the dramatic motif of the film "Reflected Image."

"Why don't you paint anymore?" I asked, feeling reproachful in a personal sort of way.

"Because art dies of stagnation." Moholy turned the pictures to the wall. "We're through with stagnant art."

"Who's we?"

"The original Bauhaus group." He lay down on his cot, hands clasped under his thick black hair. "We gave ten years of our lives to clarify the premises. Now that the means have been discovered and the solutions anticipated, there's a viciously ignorant publicity machine to separate us from the people. Their native instinct for organic values in design is systematically destroyed by an identification of revolutionary art with subversive politics. As if the art of living sensitively were not everyone's privilege."

"The more reason to paint," I said, but he shook his head.

"Art has to have a social reality," he stressed the word social, "expressing a socio-biological need that cannot be

70

Fig. 28. "A 17," 1923. Oil on canvas.

gratified in any other way. There were many who understood this as long as we were permitted to teach."

He smiled, looking up at the ceiling.

"Children and very simple people: workers, women, those who are not afraid to seem what they are. They haven't heard yet what art is supposed to be. They always respond to pure color harmonies and basic formal contrasts."

He jumped up and moved his cot again. He dove into the storage vault and came up with a large black portfolio.

"Here it is." He held a photogram against the light, showing a spiral, a disk, and an oval on a deep black background (Fig. 29).

"There was a kid, and you know what he said? He said: 'I never knew what night looks like.' It was the contrast between the white undefined form and the solid blackness that

71

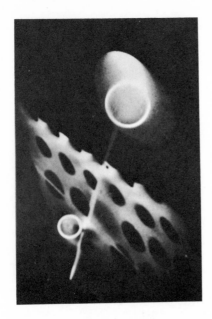

Fig. 29.   Photogram, ca. 1926.

had made the emotional experience of night clear to him. That's what I mean by a spontaneous need for art."

One night we stood on the top platform of the Berlin Radio tower. Below was an intricate pattern of light and darkness, the flashing bands of trains and automobile headlights; above were the airfield beacons in the sky. Moholy must have seen it a hundred times. He lived only a few blocks away, and he had done some fine photographs from the platform on which we stood (Fig. 30). But his enthusiasm was that of a surprised child.

"This is it—almost—this is almost painting with light."

The engine of a train puffed thick, white clouds into the night; the billowy denseness was rifted by streaks of glowing sparks.

"I've always wanted to do just this—to project light and color on clouds or on curtains of falling water. People would respond to it with a new excitement which is not aroused by two-dimensional paintings. Color would be plastic—"

His face was glowing, and at the same time relaxed in the freedom of expression.

"You've never stopped painting," I said. "You can't escape being a total painter."

"I know—but I didn't think anyone else knew." There

72

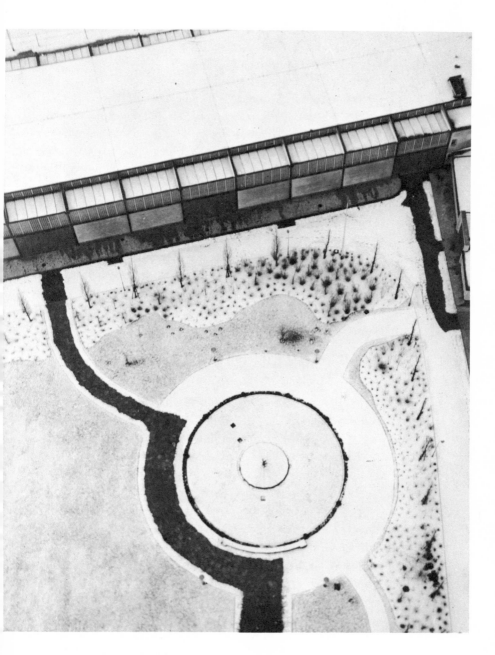

Fig. 30. "From the Radio Tower," 1928. Photograph.

was a flash of great warmth as he looked at me, and then his face closed up. "It's no use—all the lights have been blown out. We're all going blind from isolation."

"You have a friend." I mentioned the young actress whose companion he was. "And you had a wife."

"Women!" He flipped his left hand contemptuously through the air. "They're only part—they never are all. A good teacher—that was my wife. Her mind was like a beacon, lighting up my own emotional chaos. She taught me to think. All the discipline I have today I owe her. But it wasn't enough. I learned to remain alone with my emotions. And there's the good mistress —beautiful, relaxing to the point of stupor. But it's like drinking. It only lasts through the intoxication. Afterward the isolation is only more bitter. No woman understands totality in a man. It's eternal self-reference: their ego, their looks, their careers—"

He stopped for a moment.

"There's no patience in women. They can't let a man grow."

He clamped his hand on my shoulders.

"If only I knew what you are. I can't make you out." And after a silence:

"—If I talked, would you listen, and if I painted again, would you look?"

He let go of me. Slowly he walked to the opposite side of the platform. When I turned his face toward me I saw that he cried.

The film "Reflected Image" was never made. To shoot street scenes from a truck we needed a special permit from the Bureau of Public Safety. But the nationalist gangs roaming the streets of Berlin had already terrorized the authorities to a point where they dreaded any demonstration that might provoke curiosity. There had been too many bloody riots between Hitler's still illegal SS men and organized labor, fighting a hopeless battle against totalitarianism which would wipe out the rights of the worker. The project was rejected as dangerous to public security.

74

Fig. 31.   La Sarraz, 1930.

But we cheated the police nevertheless. For weeks we roamed the slum districts of Berlin, and Moholy shot the documentary film "Berlin Still Life." While "Marseille," the earliest of Moholy's documentary films, and "Light-Play Black-White-Gray" had emphasized light and dark contrasts, "Berlin Still Life" had a horizontal-vertical planar organization. Like the backdrops on an eerie stage, the shoddy tenements rise between man and man, leading into depths of ever increasing misery. In a human chaos of decay and disorder, the clean functional forms of machinery and the pleasant patterns of tracks and pavements acquire a ridiculous precision. Motion and countermotion of men and vehicles are deprived of any sensible direction by the towering blackness of backyard walls and defaced fences, symbolizing more powerfully than direct action the grim atmosphere of economic depression and political defeatism.

Through a coincidence it became known in my company that I worked with "an independent film producer," as Moholy was styled in the accusation. I was fired, but my position had become untenable anyway. The political demarcation lines started to become visible across all trades and all classes. I also had learned that knowing Moholy was a full-time occupation. When summer came and he left for a vacation in Switzerland I realized for the first time that the six months of our active collaboration had isolated me completely from my former world. I had started to live on a different plane.

Summer vacation in Switzerland was an annual occurrence in Moholy's life. He had found more understanding for his work and his problems among Swiss people than anywhere else. The friendship with Siegfried and Carola Giedion had added immensely to his knowledge of the historical and the philosophical elements in art. Many of his pictures had been bought by Swiss collectors. His summer visits always started in *La Sarraz,* a medieval castle near Lausanne where Madame de Mandrot maintained, each summer, open house for a select group of European artists. Women were not admitted to the circle, and the guests were asked to come without wives or sweethearts. This monastic arrangement was to provide an opportunity for concentrated creative work,

Fig. 32. Moholy-Nagy at "La Sarraz," 1932. Photograph by G. Augsburg.

and for exchange of ideas, undisturbed by sex competition and
the petty jealousies of women. Moholy was devoted to *La Sarraz*.
He loved the surrounding country, the exquisite French food, the
company of men of his own drive and convictions. Some of his
best pictures had originated during these vacations (Figs. 31, 32).
This particular trip in the summer of 1932 seemed no different

76

from those of earlier years. But a letter dated July 29, 1932, shows the significant psychological changes in the spiritual climate of the times:

DEAR SIBYL:

I have been here for two weeks and still I can't settle down to work. And it seems that no one else really can. There is something in the atmosphere that makes this different from other summers. Perhaps I have outgrown this rather artificial society of men. But I think it is something else. We are all so busy finding a new orientation in the political decisions of Europe that the easy group-spirit is gone. It is quite funny to watch us. When we're among ourselves there is much political talk—often quite violent and full of nationalistic animosities. G.A. the other day denounced me bitterly and stupidly for remaining in Germany, adding that I could do so only because Germans and Hungarians were equally fascistic at heart. And K., with whom I share a room and with whom I have worked so closely year after year, accused me of cowardice and lack of character because I am not a member of the Communist Party.

Then we go downstairs where Madame presides over the table and we all behave like schoolboys. We pretend not to have a worry in the world and that we are the "carefree artists" Madame wants us to be. Last night we made figures from bread dough and bombarded each other with bread-balls. Someone suggested we come in costume, and we all tried to look as silly as possible. Later Madame selected one or the other to drive her to Lausanne for an evening of entertainment. She is quite old by now and has arthritis but we all pretend to enjoy her company immensely. It has always been this way. And I used to like it. The difference this year is that patronage suddenly seems to taste sour. Perhaps we are all more conscious of getting old and that is a lonely business.

I went to Lausanne with S.G. [Siegfried Giedion] to see Corbusier's new house. We had a wonderful time, as always, speaking plainly and openly about the implications of the political situation for international cooperation among architects, and of the manifestations of social planning and individuality in modern architecture—Corbusier versus the English MARS group, for instance. When it was time to go back to *La Sarraz* it seemed almost ridiculous. It was as if everyone there were anxiously pledged to hide his true personality.

77

When Moholy returned to Berlin at the end of the summer he was much gentler, much more open to being loved than before. It was as if the experience of *La Sarraz,* the failing international camaraderie of the arts, had confirmed our union. For a while, at least, he gave himself without the suspicious fear that the surrender would be exploited. For the first time he did not try to hide the magnitude of his involvement, and showed no resentment that he loved so much.

In a spirit of defiance against the world without, and of confidence in the world which we had discovered within ourselves, we decided to make a film we'd call "Gypsies." It was a project Moholy had planned for a long time. Gypsies had been the romantic element in his Hungarian childhood. Their way of life was regulated by a primitive rhythm of child-bearing and dying, youth and age, ruling and obeying, independent of Western civilization. It was almost too late to record this ancient nomadic culture. Automobile and radio had reduced the horse-traders and fiddlers to utter poverty, and the still hypothetical race laws of the National Socialists were poised to exterminate these "non-Aryans" in Germany the day the Republic fell. Europe's great vagabonds were disappearing fast, and Moholy decided on a last record.

I was reluctant to face the great risk of making a film completely on our own. I urged Moholy to find first a distributor who would advance the production costs. As we pooled our financial reserves to buy material, I voiced my concern.

"As an amateur you haven't a chance. The commercial producers have a monopoly on distribution. The number of independent theater-owners who might be willing to show an experimental film is decimated each week by a new law or a new tax. We'll have to find a company that is "in" with the chain-theater owners. Without it we won't even get to first base, because censorship and tax-office work hand in hand with the big industry to keep people like us off the market. They'll demand so many changes before giving us a tax-free educational rating that we'll be bankrupt long before we have complied. And there's no hope for a sound track. The war between the different sound systems has driven all but the two largest patents from the market. And their royalties are far beyond our means if we have to pay it all from our own pockets."

But my professional wisdom made no impression whatsoever.

"I know," Moholy said. "I've been through all this with my other films, with "Marseille" and "Light-Play." I've lost plenty of money. But it has taught me only that the fight has to go on. Who will work on problems of focus and motion, cutting, simultaneity and all that, if it is not ourselves? Most of the old avant-garde is gone, swallowed by industry or silenced by their own discouragement: René Clair, Picabia, Léger, Cavalcanti, Feyder, Renoir, Man Ray. I and perhaps Albrecht Victor Blum and Hans Richter are the only ones left. But I won't force it on you. If you feel you'd rather—"

He smiled at me, and I knew I'd make this film even if I had to starve.

The Gypsies were a sorry lot, indigent, neglected demoralized, and defiant. It would take a miracle to produce even a spark of the proverbial fire in them—or gifts and bribes beyond our means. The old superstition that making an image of a person foreshadows his death was still alive among them and they were hostile to our attempts to film them or their children. We talked it over with the chieftains, who, next to the ruling matriarch, decide the fate of their group. A few of them seemed willing to take a chance with the images but they had their price, either in cash or in goods. Since the costs of raw film, developing, and printing would take all we had, I found myself begging my friends and acquaintances for highly colored clothes, costume jewelry, silk slippers, candy, and wine. This was during the depression. It didn't surprise me when most of them smiled thinly at my story of the Gypsies, and hinted that they thought either that I was down to my last blouse or that I must have decided to go into the used-clothing business. To continue my collections took more nerve than I actually had. When I told Moholy of my embarrassment, he was unimpressed.

"You'll have to find your own scale of values," he said coldly. "You must decide what is more important to you: the opinion of your friends, or the work with me. Once you have made your choice there's no such thing as being embarrassed."

I appeared each day at the Gypsy camp, loaded with what the canvass among Berlin's society had yielded: a feather hat, a doll, an iced cake, or some cans of food. But even if the adults gave in to our bribes, they still tried to protect their children from the evil eye of the camera. And it was the children in whom Moholy was particularly interested. Their features were still undistorted by the adult struggle for survival. They were like ethnological flashbacks to the original Gypsies who had come from the highlands of Asia. Their songs and dances, which they had learned from their grandmothers, were still free from artificiality.

Among the tribes was a Jewish girl from Palestine who had married a Gypsy. Her intellectual superiority to the rest of the women was quite obvious. She attached herself to Moholy with an open admiration, being our helper and informer. Moholy's total collaboration principle worked miracles with her. When we had finished our work and were leaving the camp she broke down and cried bitterly. Perhaps she knew that we had been her last contact with a free world, and she may have anticipated the long march to the gas chambers in Auschwitz and Buchenwald.

But while we worked she was happy. With great cunning she persuaded the men of her clan into a card game, in the beer garden of a distant inn. Then she alarmed the wives about the high stakes and losses, sending them after their menfolk to break up the gambling. This gave us time to film the small children doing an ancient reel. We had just started taking pictures of the adolescents of the camp, engrossed in a strange game of swinging long black ribbons in a rhythmical dance, when the mothers returned. Screaming, they drove their youngsters back into the wagons, where they barricaded themselves, throwing sticks and wood chunks at us. Moholy was fascinated by their wild faces, and with a total disregard for the flying missiles he went on filming. I feared for his skull, his eyeglasses, his camera, but he stood his ground until the film was spent. He was pale and silent on the way home but he didn't mention the incident.

When we returned to the camp next day it was deserted. The doors and windows of the gaily painted wagons were closed.

80

Fig. 33. Roofs in Helsinki. Photo superimposition.

Only a small boy, who had been playing with a dog, scurried toward his home-wagon when we entered the sandy circle. As Moholy focused his camera at him a sharp whistle stopped him. On the top of one of the adjoining brick houses stood a Gypsy, pointing a gun.

"Leave or be dead," he said in the impressive Gypsy lingo.

Moholy looked around. The windows of the wagons were open now, filled with the tense faces of men, women, and children. This was the chance for a panorama shot of the Gypsy community he had been waiting for. Forgetting the man on the roof, he started to move his camera slowly from window to window. There was a whizzing sound. A bullet streaked only a hand's-width from his shoulder and struck the sand. A few women shrieked and disappeared into the wagon. Moholy went on with his pictures. The man on the roof seemed dismayed. He filled the air with such a detonation of profanity that Moholy took the camera from his eyes and looked up, smiling admiringly. Whenever he detected a Hungarian word in the polyglot blast—and there were obviously many of them—he repeated it with relish, the strength of his voice matching that of his opponent. All faces had reappeared at the windows, laughing now as they watched the contest. Swiftly Moholy took up his camera again but the man on the roof was just as fast. He shot again, this time striking a wooden bucket which splintered noisily. A minute later there was a click in the camera, indicating that all the film in the magazine had been exposed. Unhurriedly, Moholy put his camera back in

81

its leather case and walked across the yard to the footpath where I waited with the car. I noticed how white he looked as we drove away. A few minutes later I had to stop because he became sick.

"Why didn't you leave when you saw the man on the roof meant business?" I asked, feeling annoyed at his bravura and irritated by my own agonizing fear. "Do you really think those film shots are more important than your life?"

"No, I don't think so," Moholy said slowly. "I stayed because I was afraid. I'm easily afraid, that's why I always stay. It's the only way of getting over it." He pointed to the white strand in his hair. "I got that in the Battle of the Isonzo during the war. Our dugout was undermined by the enemy and we expected to be blown up any minute. The married men in my unit cursed me for not withdrawing, even though I had no orders. From the floor I heard the Italians drill through the rock, and behind my back I heard the men loosen the safety catches on their guns. I've never been so afraid since. I was half-unconscious from fear, but I had to remain until I got orders. I'm not ashamed that I'm afraid. I am no hero." He smiled. "I'm no hero at all, and I hate danger. But I have learned to deal with myself."

It was a principle that carried him through many extraordinary situations. When he shot night scenes of "The New Architecture in the London Zoo," he had to balance himself, for a particular perspective, on the iron rods of a lion cage. The animal inside was incensed at the floodlights and the commotion and took enormous leaps trying to catch Moholy's ankles through the bars. Another time, a cornice on the roof of the India House in London had seemed the only spot from which to take pictures of a parade in the street below. Moholy usually became dizzy at unprotected heights. From my safe place on the center of the roof I saw him sway precariously, closing his eyes, and biting his lips before he took a firm hold on the camera and started to shoot. He had never been able to stand the sea, but many scenes in "Life of the Lobster" were taken in a raging storm from a tiny ketch, five miles off the Surrey coast; and the portraits of the fish-mongers of Billingsgate in "The Street Markets of London" were paid for by the enraged men with a bombardment of ice chunks.

82

He often got sick after these experiences, but he showed neither pride in his stamina nor shame in his weakness. Slowly I came to understand that he took danger and discomfort as part of the total reality from which he never wanted to escape. As the years went by, this pragmatic endurance of life became one of the keys to his character and his success.

The making of the Gypsy film opened a completely new vista for me. I had been raised on the two standard laws of film-making: maximum light and sharp focus, to achieve pictorial effects. Moholy was consciously "unartistic." He felt an almost religious obligation to "camera truth," demonstrated through interpretive means peculiar only to the movie camera. These means, constantly misused or neglected in commercial film production, were the recording of motion through rhythmic changes in the focus, and the interpretation of depth in space through dark-light gradations. While I watched him, not without protest, shoot rolls and rolls of precious film in gray light or murky interiors, he explained why, in spite of their technical perfection and physical glamour, Hollywood films appear flat compared with the human depth of the cheap Continental productions.

"All human life has its shadow. Without it, it stops being human. But the typical studio lighting—this insane cross-fire of illumination—creates a shadowless world that is without appeal because it is unfamiliar. How rarely does one actually see in sharp focus! There is an interplay of advancing and receding form in every movement—the unit that moves and the unit remaining static. One of them is always "out of focus." And from the corners of our eyes we are conscious of shadowy objects and anticipated faces. The invariably sharp focus of the commercial camera takes none of this into account. Vision becomes two-dimensional, and therefore uninteresting" (Fig. 33).

This principle of relative focus was effectively demonstrated in one of the Gypsy scenes. Our Jewish friend had again come to our help and had started a blazing battle between her sister-in-law and the camp midwife. Any conventional camera would have focused on the faces of the contestants, their changing expressions, the blows and clinches. Moholy started the scene by a quick succession of blurred images above the heads of the

83

fighters—slanting wagon roofs, tottering chimneys on the adjoining buildings, swaying tree tops. When fists and flying hair came into focus, the momentum of the fight had been established and the actual details were almost irrelevant.

Today only a reduced, commercialized copy of the film survives, but its production was an experience that could not be evaluated in material returns. We sat through many nights cutting the negative, and I came to understand the principle of time and space interpenetration. The sequence of the film was determined not only by chronological routine because the life of a community is not always a series of logical actions. The unifying element which demonstrated a peculiar visual pattern in a peculiar physical environment was the group impetus toward spontaneous action resulting from common stimuli. Sunlight when the cooking kettle was set up in the windbreak of the wagon wall; driving rain while man and beast huddled against the wagon window, watching hopefully for a passing of the clouds; sound, the fiddle or the zither, and the magnetic drive toward each other, crystallizing finally into a dance.

All the obstacles to commercial distribution which I had so glibly predicted were surpassed by reality. A young Hungarian had written a brilliant musical score. When the recording was finished a court decision declared our sound system illegal and the sound track had to be destroyed. The picture never passed the censor. The first objection was that it had been made by a foreigner who did not belong to the German Film Chamber. We changed the title and I appeared as producer but it was rejected again as showing German social conditions in an unfavorable light. Without complaint Moholy buried his last hope for creative work in Germany. His world had become very abstract.

4 Many of Moholy's friends in France, Holland, and England urged him to leave Germany, but emigration was a difficult decision to make. He felt a deep loyalty to the country that had given him creative maturity and artistic recognition. It was one of the great tragedies of his life that the political events after 1933 clashed so violently with this feeling of gratitude. He defended German inventiveness, craftsmanship, and devotion to duty, and he liked to quote Goethe, who once had said in patriotic despair: "What is it that makes one German such good company and a crowd of them an assembly of asses?" In addition to this faith in the German potential, there was in Moholy as in all of us a furious defiance against a gang of criminals who pretended to represent a people of seventy million. This defiance compelled him to help friends and strangers who had been politically active and were now persecuted. They came to him for shelter and financial aid. They slept in his bed, in the bathtub, in the storage vault, and one was housed for weeks hidden behind paintings in the attic. The constant tension of hope for the passing of disaster, and the creeping suspicion of total defeat, wore Moholy's nerves thin and paralyzed his creative power. Like Sisyphus he labored each day to roll the stone of his courage uphill, only to see it crash down again with monotonous regularity.

A week after the burning of the Reichstag in March, 1933, an association of progressive intellectuals called a meeting. Carl von Ossietzky, editor of the political magazine *Weltbühne* and Europe's greatest pacifist, had just been released from jail where he had served a sentence for defamation of the German army. He was to address the group. When Ossietzky mounted the rostrum he looked appallingly ill. It would have been thought impossible that he could survive another five years of prison torture. By his side was Erich Mühsam, who had fought many battles with him, a bearded husky man of fierce vitality.

"By police orders I have been restricted to twenty minutes," Ossietzky put his watch before him. "So let me be short and direct. I foresee times of unparalleled hardship and terror which can be visualized only by those of us who know the jails of our opponents. There will be oppression, dispersion, death. But the task remains unalterable—the task to oppose war and to defend the dignity of man. You will understand that I cannot specify our actions. I wish to close this meeting without police interference."

He made a sweeping gesture toward the doors which were guarded by heavily armed police.

"But let me tell you that there can be no escape from carrying on. Whatever may happen to every single one of you, there has to be, before you fall, someone to take up your particular banner of political, intellectual, artistic, freedom. Men are weak. The mortality rate of conviction and character is tremendous. Soon you will be the only ones left. It is up to you to preserve the unity of spiritual and political freedom."

He turned to his friend with a sad smile of resigned wisdom.

"We have been offered many opportunities to go abroad. But we have decided to stay. We want to remain the German conscience within its borders."

Two years later Mühsam was slaughtered in a concentration camp. Carl von Ossietzky died in 1938 of tuberculosis, a few months after the award of the Nobel Peace Prize had forced his release from Dachau.

As we left the meeting, Moholy was constantly wiping his glasses, clouded with the tears he tried to suppress.

"When he speaks, he must smell the prison walls, the rotten food, he must hear the frightened voices," Moholy said as we talked about Ossietzky in a small café. "How can he do it? How can anyone decide on this conscious self-sacrifice and remain human?"

Into the café had come two men, one a well-known composer who had written the score for the ill-fated *Merchant of Berlin,* and the other the drama critic for the *Rote Fahne,* a Communist newspaper.

86

"Mind if we sit down?" said the composer, and after he had ordered coffee and cigarettes: "How did you like the meeting, Moholy? Pretty grim, wasn't it?"

"Pretty grim and pretty final," said Moholy.

The usually beaming baby-face of the composer had a new expression of scorn that night.

"Tough times for esthetes," he said provocatively.

"Whom do you mean by esthetes?"

"Artists, individualists, the precious soloists of action."

"You mean Ossietzky?"

"Yes, and others like him."

"Ossietzky precious!" Moholy exclaimed bitterly. "He is giving his life, and he has given, already, his health and his freedom. He didn't ask for isolation tonight. He asked us to fight."

The composer whistled sharply through his teeth.

"And how are you going to do it? Fight a well-organized opponent like the Nazis, I mean?"

"Each according to his means," said Moholy. "You with your music, I with my art—"

"Art," snapped the man from the *Rote Fahne*. "Art for the dandies or art for the people?"

"That is a meaningless phrase." Moholy was impatient. "If art is genuine it is creative revolution, regardless of who looks at it."

"And perhaps regardless of who makes it—a comrade or a traitor? What a joke!"

The composer gulped his coffee, then he leaned across the table, his face close to Moholy's.

"Well, this may be my last chance, so let me tell you one thing. It is you and your kind who sold revolutionary art down the river and it is you who deliver guys like that poor idiot Ossietzky to the gallows. With your decadence and your precious experimentation you have destroyed the confidence of the masses in artists and writers. Because you fooled them they don't believe in art any more. They won't lift a hand for you when the great battle comes, and it's at the door now. And when we've won," he had the gleam of the victor in his eyes, "they'll gladly see you hang. There's no place for you in a proletarian state." He paused, hoping—it seemed—for an argument. "Go where you belong before they cut your throat—to the capitalists who finance Hindenburg and Brühning, Hitler and the Bauhaus; better still, join the long-haired martyrs who make death a show business. But don't dare to use the word revolution again. It makes me sick."

He took his coffee and motioned his friend to follow him to another table.

We didn't talk on our way home, but Moholy asked me up to his studio that night. His face was calm now, neither pained as when he had listened to Ossietzky nor infuriated as during his talk in the café. While I made tea he started to draw on typewriter paper. There were circles, a multitude of large and small rings, floating unrelatedly through space. He tried charcoal and the circles became balls, rolling over sheet after sheet which he flung on the gray linoleum floor. Later he took his colored chalks from the drafting table across the room.

"I'll go now," I said reluctantly, afraid to break the spell for which I had hoped so long.

"Oh no," he said with emphatic protest. "You don't go—not now." And after he had taken some tea: "Do you know Dürer's woodcut of St. Hieronymus? He has a lion under his desk while he works. You're my lion."

He went back to his work and slowly an interplay of colored forms appeared on the paper, circles and rectangles on varied backgrounds of red, brown, yellow. It was long past midnight when he pulled a sheet of water-color paper from a drawer. He used compass and ruler now, slowly dipping the crow's quill into India ink, wiping it clean, dipping, trying the thickness of the stroke on scratch paper. Spheres, wide connecting bands, finely engraved shading lines appeared almost simultaneously. At four in the morning he left the studio to get water from the bathroom. At his return he saw me in coat and hat, and his expression was almost of shock.

"But you can't go now. I told you, you can't! Don't you see?" Helplessly he looked at me, at his work, and at me again. "Don't you see that I need you?"

88

By dawn a pattern of ordered spheres had been created, related to each other by beams of light and fields of tension, a moving universe whose motion was sustained by the interdependence of all its worlds (Fig. 34).

Fig. 34. Water Color, 1932.

A few weeks later I knew that I was expecting a child. Although events since Hitler's rise to power in January, 1933, had made it quite clear that we were defeated, and that the frontal attack of National Socialism aimed at physical destruction of its opponents, I was winged with happiness. But Moholy reacted differently.

"An artist should be free," he said brusquely. "He can't be tied down by a family. Least of all now. I don't want a child."

"But you'll have one." For the first time during our life together his opinion didn't seem to matter. "I want this child."

89

"Then it's your responsibility. Don't count on me. This is no time for anything that needs stability."

"Don't worry. I won't need your help." I felt a magnificent confidence in my ability to raise a child unaided. "But one day I'll make you love it," I added with a flash of intuition, "because it's your child and it will be intelligent and beautiful."

In 1922 in a youthful burst of world challenge Moholy had written:

> We only consider a man a hero and worthy of our interest and our admiration who is qualified by nature and education to fulfill his hierarchical function without losing the powerful, original, and integrative impetus of the creative individual.

In 1933 there were few men left to qualify under this definition. The powerful, original, and integrative individuals were fighting a forlorn battle, cut off from their hierarchical function by a concentration camp legislation, and from contact with each other by weakhearted traitors in their midst. It was a matter of spiritual survival to reaffirm ideological bonds with friends and co-fighters outside the sick German culture. In the summer of 1933 Moholy left Berlin to attend the fourth congress of CIAM.[1] It is with great indebtedness to Dr. Siegfried Giedion that his account of this gathering is added to this book.

Moholy-Nagy and CIAM travel to Greece.
> At a meeting in the studio of Le Corbusier in Paris in April, 1933, I had to inform my friends that the country which had invited us to hold our fourth congress within its borders had suddenly withdrawn the invitation.

> What should we do? Our different groups had completed the analysis of thirty-two cities according to common measurements and principles. This material was to form the basis of our next meeting. Marcel Breuer, who participated in the meeting at Le Corbusier's, suggested holding the fourth congress not on dry land but on a ship. Le Corbusier telephoned Christian Zervos, editor of the *Cahier D'Art*, and a few hours later we had the assurance of the Greek steamship line *Neptos* that the "SS Patria II" would be at our disposal.

[1] *Congrès Internationaux d'Architecture Moderne.*

90

The congress would be held between July 29 and August 13, 1933, while we crossed the Mediterranean from Marseilles to Athens and back.

Moholy met us in Zürich to drive with me, my wife, and a secretary through France. The trip through the Alps and Provence was a harmonious beginning of our venture. Moholy had agreed to make a film about the congress. He also sat together with Le Corbusier, Jean Bardovici, the publisher of *Architecture Vivante*, Otto Neurath, the originator of the visual statistics, and the Swiss architect Steiger in the commission which would publish the findings of the Congress.[2]

One of the great difficulties of our culture rests with the fact that we have lost our common vocabulary. When representatives of science and art, philosophers, architects, or historians meet, there exists no basis for mutual consent but rather a morbid fear that any definite formulations might be misinterpreted or misused by opposition groups.

It is the significance of the CIAM that it tries to avoid this alienation by selecting its members in a manner so far employed only by the academies. Ever since its inception in 1927, the guiding principle in this selection has been not traditional but progressive. CIAM is governed by complexity of talents and variety of personalities, working toward an equilibrium of individual and collective thought.

The creative intensity of personal contacts, based on diversity of character and unity of goal, never produced better results than at the fourth congress. The staterooms and cabins of the "SS Patria II" changed into conference chambers. In smooth weather the meetings were held on deck, and town plans were mounted in the open air. The reorganization of thirty-two cities was discussed from many different viewpoints. Since identical signs, colors, and scales had been employed, the plan of London could be discussed in the same terms as that of Como, Detroit, or Stockholm. When we stepped on land again we had drawn universally valid conclusions which were formulated in the "*Charte d'Athènes*, 1933." It supplied directives for contemporary town-planning which in the meantime have become widely accepted.

[2] The outbreak of the war in Europe delayed this publication, which finally was added to the book by J. L. Sert, *Can Our Cities Survive* (Harvard University Press, 1941).

Fig. 35.   Acropolis, 1933.

It seemed incomprehensible in many quarters that we as the most outspoken representatives of modern architecture had chosen Greece as our meeting place. It was interpreted as an attempt to escape.

"In selecting Greece as the destination of our trip," I said in my opening address, "we do not try to escape from the chaos threatening Europe. We aim rather at combining with an opportunity for undisturbed deliberations a moment of concentration and contemplation to face the decisive problems which have started to crystallize in our subconscious mind."

These problems of the subconscious became fully clear only after the congress was over. They were a development of the purely functional tendencies in architecture toward a greater inclusiveness of other elements, esthetic, social, biologic. The full evaluation of this new, independent platform had been helped immeasurably through the contact with the past and our Hellenic heritage.

"I never realized," Moholy said as we stood on the hill of the Acropolis, "how deeply we are still moved by the Greek world, though in a totally different, more fundamental, way than was the nineteenth century." I was reminded of a sentence he had written ten years earlier in the German magazine *Der Sturm*: "We must replace the static interpretation of classical art with the dynamic interpretation of classical universality."

Nothing had diminished this concept. The broken pieces of the columns around us looked as if the Pentelian marble had cracked yesterday. Silently, Moholy and I absorbed the totality of this sacred area, the arrangement of the buildings which was without rigidity, almost accidental, yet cunningly calculated in floor-plan and detail. It was a perfect fusion of mathematical precision and organic freedom. There was no danger that the design of capitals or columns would ever move us to imitation. What touched us deeply was the immediacy of formed expression, the overt contrast between the planned maximum solution of architecture, and the structure of the primordial rock ledge (Fig. 35).

My memory went back to other rock ledges—Belle Île en Mer, an island off the coast of Brittany. I had spent my first vacation with Moholy there in 1925. I remembered the long conversations in the isolated hotel where we had first clarified what had to be achieved in our time. I remember Moholy taking a photograph of the terrace from a window high above it which annulled the perspective as it forced objects and proportions into the two-dimensional plane. No interesting motif—this concrete slab, a railing, a few chairs, a round table. But it was a completely new beginning. The camera had never been used like that before.

Passing through the Gulf of Corinth in the early dawn, we understood that Greek sculpture had not come about by co-incidence. Never before had we seen such perfect whitish-gray contours as those of Parnassus, of Helikon and Kithairon. As the boat anchored at Corinth, the quality of Greek light suddenly revealed itself. Water can be transparent anywhere; but here the sun had a power of penetration which transfigured even the bronze tone of the boat's screw. Greece was explained to us by light, materials, and the perfect realization of visualized form.

All his life Moholy had concentrated on giving expression to the intangible quality of light in his paintings. Color and pigment were secondary compared to the language of light which nowhere was more articulate than in Greece. Here the light had the power to clarify, modify, and enhance. Whether it was the boat screw in the water, accentuated into a luminous apparition, a precipice surmounted by the columns of the Parthenon, or olive trees against the white reflections of the houses, it was always the coincidence of light and structure that gave intensity to the world of vision. It is only what lies prepared within ourselves that is revealed to us in the nature of materials. For Moholy it was *light* that he absorbed in the phenomenon Greece.

These were experiences which we rarely expressed in words. They gave atmosphere to our community, and they reached a climax on a cruise to the Greek islands which a few of us undertook on the few days which were without group work. The "yacht" at our disposal was a converted English coal barge. The men slept on mattresses on deck because the only cabin was reserved for the women in the party. It was a colorful group—all in all about twenty. Léger, Moholy, Kurt Seligmann, Le Corbusier and his brother, the musician Jeanneret, Christian Zervos of the *Cahier d'Arts*, Van Eesteren, the Dutch city planner, Swiss architects, a famous French surgeon, poets, writers.

As we approached the Isle of Aegina, we dived headon into the water, Le Corbusier being the first one. We climbed to the temples of the Aeginates, the cool predecessors of the Parthenon. They were the first island monuments we saw, magnificently in scale with the proportions of the small isle, and yet—in all their simplicity—dominant over the landscape and the vast sea. Corbusier drew in his blue sketchbook, and Van Eesteren commented on "the wisdom of the cultural landscape." But in general it was a silent and emphatic immersion into the material form.

At sunrise we anchored in the harbor of Santorin, its mountains rising like glacier caps above the steep rock walls. As we came close, it struck Moholy how organically the house forms melted into each other, children playing on the flat roof of the adjoining house, and yet each unit commanding a free view of the sea through the steep decline of the street.

During the last night of this Odyssey the weather changed and the storm finally became a gale. We tied ourselves to the bunks as the sea swamped the deck. The small boat could no longer be steered. To avoid capsizing, it had to be left to the storm to decide its course. Through the roaring wind I could hear Fernand Léger's agonized curses as he paid his tribute to Poseidon; and in the bunk above me Le Corbusier repeated calmly, steadily through the night: *"Ne me crachez pas dessus."* In the morning we landed at Cape Sunnion. At noon we rejoined the Congress in Athens. If the former coal barge had sunk during the storm that night, a decisive chapter of contemporary art history would have come to a close.

In 1933 we still had the faith of the 1920's when the colors of the painters had been more radiant, and their beliefs more positive than ever before or after. This radiance expressed the confidence of our generation which felt called upon to heal the breach between the inner and the outer reality. We knew we were the ones to define what had to be done in town planning, architecture, and the arts. We saw the road clearly before us toward a final goal, and we did not want to admit that we stood already in the shadow of a world tragedy that would mutilate us and our time.

● ●

In October, 1933, our daughter Hattula was born. It had been a difficult summer for me. Moholy was away for four months, and I was faced with the need to accumulate funds for the obligation which I had promised to meet alone. I went back to my old job as a film scenario writer. The firm I had chosen

Fig. 36. Hattula, 1933. Film strip.

was financed by Catholic politicians who hoped for a comeback after the downfall of the National Socialists. But within a few months, they were forced into bankruptcy by fiercely anticlerical measures which banned all religious pictures from German movie theaters. I turned to newspaper reporting for juvenile and domestic court trials. Hiding my equatorial waistline under a ridiculous Victorian cloak which I had discovered in a secondhand clothing shop, I listened day in and day out to evidence of marriages "gone wrong" and children who hadn't turned out so well. It lent a depressing note to the last months of my pregnancy.

Moholy was stunned by his daughter. For the first time in his life he forgot about himself. The baby's reaction to light and sound, changes in color and movement, were revelations to him. He engaged in a running battle with a succession of nurses who objected violently to his disregard of schedule and routine. Whenever he could find time he continued a film started the day after his daughter's birth. At midnight or at seven o'clock in the morning he attacked the bassinet with his camera or he carried the child into the snow or balanced her on a window sill to get better light and more interesting shadows. Hattula was the most recorded child in Europe, and Moholy's friends came to dread his inevitable reach into his breast-pocket for the latest series of baby pictures (Fig. 36). It all came to a climax when I resumed my customary "open house" gatherings.

The men and women who came on these Sunday nights were actors, dancers, writers, painters, and musicians. The crumbling of their world of uninhibited freedom and radical political convictions, the increasing alienation of their audiences, and

96

the distrust in each other's integrity and character under Nazi pressure, had aggravated their tendencies toward esoteric talk and liquor. They were a nocturnal lot, far removed from the lullaby of normalcy. That night Moholy showed his latest film experiment—the ABC's scratched into a sound track. Played back it produced a strange tone sequence, a third dimension, so to speak, to the written and spoken alphabet. It was a good moment for me to disappear to feed the baby, unnoticed by our highstrung visitors. But I hadn't reckoned on the pile of overclothes on my bed. In shorter and shorter intervals dancers, actors, writers rushed into the bedroom, grabbed their coats, and, with a horrified look at the suckling infant, raced out of the room. It was a silent panorama of faces petrified by indignation and embarrassment. When I returned to the studio Moholy had just finished showing the film of his daughter's progress. To make sure that no detail of her personality and of our loving care was overlooked, he had run it twice. When he turned on the lights everyone had left. He was totally unmoved by the exodus of our guests and he would have been content to show the film a third time to himself. But Sergei Eisenstein, Russian director of "Potemkin" and other famous revolutionary films, was still there. He had dropped in that afternoon between trains en route from America to Moscow. He was sitting on the floor, propped against the projection tripod, and it wasn't clear whether he had remained out of inertia or friendship.

"Why do you go back to Russia?" I asked him. He had been working with Upton Sinclair on a film about Mexican peons which had displeased his government. "Aren't you afraid that you'll be put on trial?"

"Of course I'm afraid," he said, uncorking another bottle of brandy.

"And you go back?"

"Yes, I'm going back. A man can't live without a country."

"Oh, come on," said Moholy, slightly contemptuous about his friend's remark, which sounded patriotic in a shopworn way. "For an artist there's no such thing as *his* country."

Eisenstein gave him a long look. He had blue eyes of an extraordinary expressiveness. His face was drawn. For a man of forty he looked old. All his life-energy was concentrated in the intensity of his eyes.

"You're a child," he said in his heavy accent. "You know nothing. You'll remain in Germany?"

"I—I don't think so," Moholy admitted reluctantly.

Eisenstein drank, staring into his glass between sips.

"Another country—all right. You work, earn money, eat, sleep. Politically you don't count. No voice. You're mute. You read papers. Your country suffers, there are great decisions, victories, defeats. But you're an exile. No voice. You're mute." He wiped his mouth with the back of his hand. "The very name of your country becomes an insult—Russian, German, Hungarian, whatever you are. You hide it, you don't admit it any more. Afraid —you're afraid to lose your bread. Secretly you go to the little restaurants of your nationality—you wouldn't set foot in such places at home. You keep company with workers, waiters, bums. You talk politics. They don't understand you. Doesn't matter. They're your people. And when you die—they say you die speaking your own language."

He stopped talking.

"Who thinks of dying?" Moholy was embarrassed by Eisenstein's emotionalism and the heavy silence. "Death and language—nonsense. As an artist you have one adherence and that's your art. We liquidated countries fifteen years ago. Our nationality is the idea." He took a deep breath. "Nationalism is totally obsolete," concluded the man who, ten years later, would found the Council for a Democratic Hungary in Chicago.

For three months our little family group lived together. By January, 1934, one year after the collapse of the Weimar Republic, it had become clear that to remain in Germany was futile and dangerous.

As we stood beside the train that would take Moholy over the border, he smiled with infinite warmth, thinking back over the past weeks.

"I've never been so happy and at peace with myself."

A group of Jewish emigrants crowded together on the platform. They were tagged with white labels fastened to the

98

cuffs of their sleeves. Their luggage consisted of inadequate cardboard boxes. A string of black-uniformed SS men with rubber-stamp martiality on their faces stood on guard.

"They have both lost their identity," said Moholy, "the refugees and the rulers." He smiled at me. "I'll paint again as soon as we find a home." He took the latest of the baby pictures from his wallet. "There's my daughter and one day she'll ask what it was her father did to prove his identity."

This was one day after an episode which had illustrated the funereal irony of our world. Germany's withdrawal from the League of Nations had been preceded by a planned propaganda campaign stressing the "brotherly" unity between Germany, Italy, and Japan. Speeches and newspaper editorials were filled with eulogies on the eternal friendship between the Fascist nations, and with promises of the unlimited territorial and economic advantages which would result from this "axis." But to accept Mussolini meant to accept also his cultural program, which stood in striking contrast to the Hitler crusade against "Cultural Bolshevism." Not only had Mussolini supported the international style of architecture in his vast projects, creating new towns in the Ligurian swamps; he had also been a benevolent patron of "Futurism" in writing and painting, and had appointed Marinetti, the arch-Futurist, as his minister of cultural affairs.

With the same sleight of hand which later was to startle the world with a Russian alliance, the National Socialists decided to forget "cultural Bolshevism" for a week and to please Mussolini by inviting F. T. Marinetti and his circle to Berlin. In one of the many art galleries along the *Schöneberger Ufer*, empty now because their owners had either fled or were slowly dying in concentration camps, a large exhibition of Futurist paintings was put on show. Prampolini, Carra, Boccioni, Severini, Balla, were all represented by semi-abstract canvases and dynamic sculptures trying to "give the essence of movement without the thing that moves." In cubes and rectangles the material form of the object was dissolved, and its dynamism expressed in a wild symphony of interwoven lines and planes.

Marinetti's lecture was a last gathering of German artists and intellectuals just before the great diaspora. There wasn't

99

a uniform in sight. With his enormous cleverness, Marinetti had judged his audience at a glance. In brilliant French he stressed the international and progressive elements in Futurism.

> We declare that the glory of the world has been enriched by a new beauty: the beauty of speed. A racing car, its compressors roaring like fiery monsters, is more beautiful than the Victory of Samothrace.
>
> We are on the promontory of a new century. Why look behind? Past and tradition are dead. We sing the multivoiced surf of revolutions. . . .

he recited from his "Manifesto," which in twenty years had lost nothing of its youthful ecstasy. Neither the Axis nor Mussolini were mentioned. When he ended there was frantic applause. For a few minutes the abstract forms on the canvases had obscured the ideological alliance with Fascism.

The following night the German Press Association gave a banquet for the Italians, to which we had received a personal invitation from Marinetti. Moholy was unwilling to go. He had been shadowed by the SS; his refusal to submit his paintings to the censorship of the National Socialist Art Chamber to obtain a "working permit" had been followed by threats of arrest. His cleaning woman had stolen his mail and had delivered it to the *Blockwart* (political district warden), and some of his associates had disappeared mysteriously. He was done with Germany, and on his last night in Berlin he didn't feel like sitting down with the new rulers. But Kurt Schwitters, who was our house guest at the time, insisted on going, to honor the revolutionary in Marinetti, and he finally persuaded Moholy to join him.

Kurt was profoundly worried about the political tide. His rebellious days were over. At forty-six he wanted to be left unmolested, enjoying a secure income from his real estate and his typographical work, and puttering away on his gigantic MERZ plastic, a sculpture of compound forms which extended from a corner of his studio through two stories of his house, winding in and out of doors and windows, and curling around a chimney on the roof. There was nothing he dreaded more than emigration. He died a broken man in England in 1948.

100

The banquet offered a very different picture from the lecture the night before and confirmed all of Moholy's misgivings. Short of Hitler, all the Nazis were present: Goebbels and Göring, August Wilhelm of Hohenzollern, the president of the Berlin University, Gerhart Hauptmann, once the torchbearer of revolution but now a chipped plaster image of Goethe. Hess was there, and with him was fat Röhm, whose days were already numbered. These officials were sitting along a huge horseshoe table, while Nazi underlings and the artists whom Marinetti had insisted upon inviting sat at individual tables. Moholy, Schwitters, and I were sandwiched between the head of the National Socialist Organization for Folk Culture, and the leader of the "Strength Through Joy" movement. The disharmony between the guests was accentuated by the absence of speeches and an unlimited consumption of excellent German Rhine wine. Moholy was silent. His face was shuttered, and when our eyes met I saw that he was full of resentment. The more Schwitters drank, the more fondly he regarded his neighbor.

"I love you, you Cultural Folk and Joy," he said. "Honestly, I love you. You think I'm not worthy of sharing your chamber, your art chamber for strength and folk, ha? I'm an idiot too, and I can prove it."

Moholy put his hand firmly on Schwitters' arm and for a few minutes he was silent, drinking rapidly and searching the blank face of his neighbor with wild blue eyes.

"You think I'm a Dadaist, don't you," he suddenly started again. "That's where you're wrong, brother. I'm MERZ." He thumped his wrinkled dress shirt near his heart. "I'm Aryan— the great Aryan MERZ. I can think Aryan, paint Aryan, spit Aryan."

He held an unsteady fist before the man's nose. "With this Aryan fist I shall destroy the mistakes of my youth"—"If you want me to," he added in a whisper after a long sip.

There was no reaction at all from the "Strength Through Joy" man while the official from the Folk Culture Organization nodded droolingly, his round cheeks puffed up with wine and amazement. Schwitters took a sudden liking to him.

101

"Oh joyful babyface," he muttered, tears running down his cheeks. "You will not prohibit me from MERZing my MERZ art?"

The word "prohibit" had finally penetrated the foggy brain of the "Strength Through Joy" man.

"Prohibited is prohibited [*Verboten ist verboten*]," he said with great firmness and a heavy tongue. "And when the Führer says '*Ja*' he says '*Ja*' and when the Führer says '*Nein*' he says '*Nein.*' *Heil Hitler!*"

Schwitters looked wildly at Moholy, at me, at Marinetti, but before he could incite anyone to action, Marinetti had risen from his chair. He swayed considerably and his face was purple.

"My friends," he said in French. "After the many excellent speeches tonight"—the silent officials winced—"I feel the urge to thank the great, courageous, high-spirited people of Berlin. I shall recite my poem 'The Raid on Adrianople.' "

There was polite applause. Some nice poetry would break the embarrassing dullness of the dinner.

> *Adrianople est cerné de toutes parts SSSSrrrr zitzitzitzitzi*
> *PAAAAAAAAAAgh rrrrrrrrrrrrr*

roared Marinetti.

> *Ouah ouah ouah, départ des trains suicides, ouah ouah ouah.*

The audience gasped; a few hushed giggles were audible.

> *Tchip tchip tchip—Jééééééééééééééééééélez!*

He grabbed a wineglass and smashed it to the floor.

> *Tchip tchip tchip—des messages telégraphiques, couturières*
> *Americaines*
>
> *Piiiiiiiiiiiiiiing, ssssssssssrrrrrrrr, zitzitzit toum toum*
> *Patrouille tapie—*

Marinetti threw himself over the table.

> *Vanitéeeee, viande congeléeeeeeee—veilleuse de La Madone.*

expiring almost as a whisper from his lips.

Slowly he slid to the floor, his clenched fingers pulling the tablecloth downward, wine, food, plates, and silverware pouring into the laps of the notables.

Schwitters had jumped up at the first sound of the poem. Like a horse at a familiar sound the Dadaist in him responded to the signal. His face flushed, his mouth open, he followed each of Marinetti's moves with his own body. In the momentary silence that followed the climax his eyes met Moholy's.

"Oh, Anna Blume," he whispered, and suddenly breaking out into a roar that drowned the din of protesting voices and scraping chair legs, he thundered:

Oh, Anna Blume
Du bist von hinten wie von vorn
A-n-n-a.

5 From a number of possibilities Moholy had chosen work in Holland in preference to offers from England and America. He had not yet accepted the Hitler government as a finality. Each new outrage only strengthened his conviction that such a monstrous regime could not last. To renounce his old ties completely and to leave the Continent would have meant to admit total defeat. Holland was still close to Germany.

His new position as typographical advisor to a large Dutch printing firm paid well and promised a chance to explore color photography. Moholy divided his workday between layouts for textile magazines and book covers, and laboratory and darkroom work with a color expert. In February, 1934, he wrote to me:

> I'm learning my lesson like a good boy. I make tables of chemicals and exposures, and I work my way through a whole series of processes from a simple kodachrome shot to a very intricate multicolor print. As soon as I feel I have understood the technology of the thing, the real work will start. Up till now it's nothing else but photography made complicated.

And two weeks later he wrote:

> The only problem that matters for me in color photography is to go *beyond* nature. It starts to dawn on me that there is no such thing as natural color in photography because the chemical reactions and the mixture of artificial and natural light sources will always distort reality. What has to be tried is to find a photographic color process that permits controlled abstract color-combinations and their inexpensive correct reproduction.

When I visited him in April he was beginning to see that working with color specialists wouldn't teach him anything except skill. He dictated an article for an Austrian magazine:

> All these experts aim at the closest possible imitation of natural color, and they know they always fall short of their

104

goal. They're delighted if they can picture an apple looking red instead of brown and the surface of a lake blue instead of green. That's all right for scientific recording and reportage. But it has done great harm to photography as a creative process employing techniques unique to its concept. The language of gradation we've finally mastered in black and white is totally invalidated. We're back where realistic painters started in the Renaissance—the imitation of nature with inadequate means.

Our hotel room in Amsterdam changed into a laboratory. Strips of colored paper were tacked to the wall, and strewn over the bedspread were samples of colored gelatine, cellophane, glass, and plastics. I remember two nights when we slept on the floor because the arrangement on the bed couldn't be disturbed. With a battery of lights and borrowed cameras the same colors were photographed according to the Finlay color process, in Agfa color, Dufay color, and other systems I have forgotten. Then he went back to the laboratory of the printing firm, comparing the results. The color reproductions in his book *Vision in Motion* show some of the experiments.

One night Moholy remembered Goethe's *Farbenlehre* which he had read as a student, and in which Goethe tries to disprove Newton's color theory. Next day I scoured Amsterdam for a copy of Goethe's works, and for prisms of assorted sizes. Then, with different lights and different filters, we set out on a new round of experiments. The goal was to record the purely "abstract" color bands, produced through light refraction in the prisms. But the prints were uniformly flat, the finer gradations got lost, and the hues were never accurate.

His collaborators in the printing house didn't like Moholy's insistence on better color engraving and printing. They thought they had been doing fairly well so far, and they had no intention of revolutionizing the visual field.

"It's not that there's too little use of color," Moholy complained. "There's too much. It is daubed on the paper without discrimination. Every child knows that there are cold and warm color combinations; but even in the best reproductions everything has to scream with crude effects. In this mechanical color orgy,

105

the tense relationships between black-white and color are simply overlooked."

And in an article he wrote:

People's characters are judged by their handwriting. I'd know anyone by his relationship to color. In laymen as well as in artists it is the unfailing test for sensitivity and refinement.

He made a few color photograms but the results were unsatisfactory. Chemicals added to the developing solution colored the surface of the photogram, but control of hue and value was impossible and in time the picture faded. Moholy wrote to me in the summer of 1934:

I am convinced now that new aspects of color in photography have to come from kinetic experiments, from an interplay of color on film. There the third-dimensionality, which after all is the essential nature of light, can be combined with color. The superimpositions and the interplay have to come from optical instead of chemical combinations. If I had money and a laboratory—

But he had neither. The Dutch printers had become tired of his persistence. They withdrew their permission for the experimental use of their color laboratories and insisted instead on an unreasonable amount of typographical work. In a letter on June 23, he wrote:

I'm like a child who has to stay after school. You should see a day's work. Now I'm supposed to design lettering for Catholic tracts in addition to magazine pages and advertisings. Shall I leave—go back to Berlin where I'm a prisoner, or to Switzerland and join the bankrupt revolutionaries at Ascona? England? America?

The decision was made for him. In the summer of 1934 Moholy received two commissions which put his life back on its original course. The Stedelijk Museum in Amsterdam asked him to organize a one-man show of his work, and the Dutch Rayon Industry hired him to design an exhibition of their methods and materials for the Commercial Fair in Utrecht and the World's Fair in Brussels.

The invitation of the Amsterdam museum had an electrifying effect on Moholy. After the frustrating isolation in

Fig. 37. K IV, 1922. Oil on canvas.

Germany, the vicious attacks of press and government on abstract
art, and his self-imposed inaction as a painter, this offer was like
a rediscovery of forgotten standards. He made a trip to Berlin
where all his work was still stored, and for days and nights lined
up his paintings, collages, and water colors along the walls of
our apartment to make a selection. For the first time I saw the
creative sequence from 1916 to 1928, when he had stopped painting. I was still too uninitiated to comprehend the step-by-step
development from pigment to light and from two-dimensionality
to kinetics, which I came to understand ten years later. Perhaps
under the influence of the experiments in color photography in
which I had participated, I saw in Moholy's approach an additive
method, moving from the simple to the complex by amalgamating
additional visual elements into a new entity. One form-element
impressed itself upon me by its infinite variability. The segmented
circle appeared in the majority of canvases. In "K IV, 1922"
(Fig. 37) the forms were unintegrated, mere points of reference
to state the visual fact of the picture plane. By 1924, in the canvas
"Planes and Segments" (Fig. 38), the segmented circles were
already put into premeditated relationships. The rhomboid lines
with their depth function define not only the picture plane, but
a spatial equilibrium attained through construction. Two years
later, with "Z II, 1926" (Fig. 39), the segmented circle and the
depth-defining line were amalgamated with color transparency
and an inclusion of light as a new value. There is a first conscious

107

Fig. 38. Planes and Segments, 1924. Oil on canvas.

use of reflection from the reinstated textural pigment in the pictures painted after 1925.

The decisive factor in this first comprehensive show of Moholy's work in many years was his renewed contact with young people. It was one of the strangest features of the National Socialist regime that it had eliminated youth from daily life. They had either been drafted into the many Nazi organizations, imprisoned, or expelled. It was not until Moholy stood before a lecture audience in Amsterdam's Stedelijk Museum that he knew what had been missing from his life since he had stopped teaching at the Bauhaus. As he looked over his youthful listeners, who packed the room and stood along the walls, he put his prepared notes into his pocket and spoke directly from his heart. It was a gesture more indicative of his return to the Bauhaus idea than any rational explanation. He defined the position of nonrepresentational art in society:

> Isms, from Impressionism to Surrealism, are efforts to overcome the traditional forms of pictorial presentation. They are —all of them—fighting disciplines for a functional vision,

108

expressive of the primal human reaction to color, light, and form. Whether it is called "atmospheric impact" as in Impressionism or "reorientation in spatial infinity" as in Suprematism, it all is an attempt to liquidate traditional painting in which visual element and narrative are one. With the advent of photography the need for a separation between visual element and narrative has finally become clear. Photography is recording; painting is fundamental vision. Many different men have jumped into the arena. They all landed at the same spot: they faced the fact that optical creation can only be achieved

Fig. 39. Z II, 1926. Oil on canvas.

by optical and not by literary means. There will be no new isms. Nonobjective and representational are no longer hostile opposites. They are self-sufficient entities.

He spoke of the need to carry on the spirit of revolution that had moved the men of 1920.

We failed because we were not humble enough. We believed that all-or-nothing solutions would create a visual order expres-

109

sive of a new world. You can learn from us that it is the infinitely slow adaptation of the masses to new socio-visual standards that guarantees educational progress. Don't be impatient—don't be cocky. There's no task too small and no project too big to make it a manifesto of incorruptible design: a label, a photograph, or a million-guilder housing project. And there's no one too pompous or too humble to be made an ally—a big industrialist or the woman who washes your shirts. You take it for granted that it is your right to experiment with media and ideas unaccepted by the majority, and challenging to the prevailing esthetic and social views. You are proud to have convictions and to express them. Take a look across the border and you'll realize that free work is a priceless privilege and that it carries with it a tremendous obligation toward honesty and effort.

The warmth of Moholy's released enthusiasm carried the crowd. Many of them followed us all night. We drove to the "Y" and sat in old sailor taverns. At daybreak we stood in the *Oude Kirk*. The rising sun was streaming through the stained-glass windows, four hundred years old. Moholy pointed to the heavy lines of the lead filling, separating the panes and providing a structural contrast to the color harmonies.

"They knew," he said, "the old glass painters knew the balance of color, black, and light. They'd never have thought of one without the other. Look."

He took the lighted cigarette from the hand of a young man. As the silvery smoke mixed with a multicolored beam from a high window the evasive lines and ornaments of the smoke were concretized by the added color. He bent down and it looked as if he scooped the delicate color reflections from the stone floor.

"If only one could hold it—"

When we finally came back to our hotel there was still an unwearied group of students with us who wouldn't leave Moholy.

But after I had gone back to Berlin the exuberant joy in rediscovered creativeness changed to a more sober analysis. He wrote:

I have been back to the Stedelijk Museum time and again, and I know it now: my paintings are not yet ripe for mass

110

exhibition. They can only hold their own under the tenderest private care, under a patient observation which will reveal their actual values and the future potentialities still in ferment. There are hardly any people yet who want to see the tentative worth of this new language. They'll complain about monotony; they'll scorn the repetition of the same form and color problem in new combinations. Nowadays visual gratifications have to come fast—like the response of a jukebox, or the click of an amateur camera.

This is bitter because the real purpose of exhibiting my pictures is to make the spectator grow slowly as I grew in painting them. What a long way to go! Most people I watched in the exhibition looked like oxen.

And still, I shall exhibit wherever an opportunity is offered. I had inquiries from Basel and from Brno in Czechoslovakia. One day I'll be known as a painter instead of only as a photographer. This has to be prepared. The task now is to find a place to start painting again.

The exhibit for the Dutch Rayon Manufacturers was a large project involving thousands of guilders. In January, 1935, we went to Utrecht—both ill with a peculiar kind of swamp fever which is common among foreigners who go to live in Holland. The term "below sea level" had acquired a strange reality for us. The dense rain and heavy fogs fused with the endless marshes and canals into a submarine infinity.

The Rayon Exhibit would be done without compromise, Moholy had decided; the manufacturers would either let him do it his own way or he would not do it at all. They agreed to give him free rein but it meant that we had to do almost the whole job ourselves. The Utrecht workmen would listen to Moholy's instruction, take a look at the blueprints, and walk away. The only exception was a tiny Indonesian halfbreed called Teng. From thousands of samples Moholy had chosen some seven hundred fabrics. A fourth of these Teng and I cut with pinking scissors into free forms. With library paste we glued them on matting board mounted on a curved plywood wall which extended across the whole exhibition hall. This multicolored pattern was interrupted by glass panes. with black-and-white lettering set into the plywood wall, giving a view of the exhibition space on the

Fig. 40. Rayon Exhibition, Brussels, 1936.

other side. Two falls, twelve feet high, showed unicolored rayon in finest gradations, not in the customary spectral arrangement, but graded from black to white on a basic tone of blue. We cut oversized figures from double plywood frames, and hung rayon fabric between the panels, and we arranged a "harp" of vertical and horizontal chromium rods carrying large spools of rayon thread in carefully chosen colors (Fig. 40).

The exhibition was a success. The Dutch textile industry had never attracted such international attention and grateful manufacturers gave us a banquet in Amsterdam's largest hotel, to which we went with misgivings. Feverish and tired to death, we didn't feel in a party mood. But we needn't have worried. The frivolous habit of table conversation is not shared by the Dutch. From the hors d'oeuvres, consisting of kegs of oysters stationed on the floor beside the guests, to the dessert, depicting Moholy's rayon cascades in sherbet and spun sugar, our sole concern was food. Like a row of huge red beacons, the faces of the manufacturers floated above the table in almost total silence.

To reward ourselves for our labors, we decided to go to Paris. I had been there before with my wealthy first husband, living in the Ritz and "seeing the sights" in the prescribed way. This visit was different. It was the only time I really saw Paris.

I have forgotten where we lived; it certainly wasn't the Ritz. And I don't remember how long we stayed. All minor impressions have been erased by the men we visited—Brancusi, Tihanyi, Vantongerloo, Arp, Mondrian. They were Paris to me.

It was March and bitterly cold. There was no snow, but an icy rain seeped through clothes and shoes and into the studios, scantily heated by small iron stoves. After the bourgeois comfort of the Dutch houses, the frugality of the Left Bank was a humbling experience.

"I won't introduce you to Brancusi," said Moholy as we went down a flight of dark steps. "He wouldn't understand, and he isn't interested in people's names."

We entered a long, low room with bare stone walls and stone flooring. It seemed dark at first because the windows were small and high up near the ceiling. An old man turned from a stone hearth where he had poked a fire. He was covered with fine gray dust. It clung to the many wrinkles of his face and to his eyelashes, and it gave his smock a velvety texture. Only his white beard had a bright yellow fringe around the mouth. He smiled kindly but without curiosity or recognition, touching the small cap on his skull with two fingers. There was no inquiry from his side, and no explanation from ours. To visit an artist in his studio was a perfectly normal event. Silently, as a logical consequence of our appearance, he went from sculpture stand to sculpture stand, winding mechanisms that ranged from a simple string-pulley to an intricate combination of cogwheels. All the great pieces were there, many of them in different variations: "The Bird," "The Fish," "Leda," "The Penguins," and small models of "The Infinite Column." Marble, wood, stone, metal, plaster—every piece was mounted on a carved stand which now started to turn, set in motion by Brancusi. When everything moved,

113

he smiled. His vivid brown eyes looked at his work with benevolent pleasure.

"*Voilà*," he said with a sweep of his expressive sculptor's hand, and with a small extra bow to me, he repeated: "*Voilà, Madame.*"

I thought of a quotation from the catalogue of his New York exhibition in 1933: "Don't look for formulas—mystic or obscure. I give you pure joy. Behold my works as that which you see. The closer they're seen, the closer they are to God."

I told him of the deep sense of beauty his work had given me.

"How could it be different?" he said in a simple French that still had the accent of his Rumanian origin. "After all—there are your eyes. You can see. All seen reality is beautiful. It's man's thoughts that break the universe."

The end of his cigarette had set a spark to his beard. With a violent slap on his mouth he extinguished it, and I understood the reason for the yellow color-effect.

"You will excuse me. I have to work." He bowed and returned to the hearth. One by one the rotating platforms stopped. The beauty of the forms was again still when we left.

We stayed on in Paris till we could see Mondrian. He had been ill and Moholy decided to wait until he was up again. The wet cold had started to dampen my spirit. There hadn't been another experience comparable to the dedicated simplicity of Brancusi. We had visited Léger and Lipschitz, Arp, Delauney, Henri Laurens, and others. Some of the work we saw, and all of the men we met, were impressive through the passionate sincerity of their inner search. But in the approaching war agony of 1935 the general accent was on convulsion—a symbolic wrestling with turgid forms and highly subjective meaning, reeling between Surrealist fatuousness, and amorphous primitivism. The direct relation between social reality and creative vision had never been demonstrated more forcefully. It was this visual premonition of impending chaos that gave our visit to Mondrian's studio its significance.

He was glad to see Moholy. His white face flushed and he had to take off his glasses and wipe them. Cautioning us to step carefully around a white sheet spread on the floor, he motioned us into an alcove where kitchen utensils, paints, brushes, and canvases were stacked in impeccable order.

"I got a present yesterday," he said happily, "and you're just in time for the results."

He pointed to a pressure cooker standing on a small table. "I always wanted it so much—I wanted to have a pressure cooker to make my own *pot-au-feu*." Carefully he unhinged the lid. A delicious smell of meat and greens filled the chilly air.

"You must try it. It's the first *potâge* I have made in my gift." He ladled three portions into brown earthenware dishes. "I first got a small chicken," he said methodically. "I told the woman at the market that I wanted it not too plump—with meat, of course, but with only enough fat to make it agreeable. Then the celery. It had to be. . . ."

It was an intricate recipe, which I enjoyed but which bored Moholy. As soon as he had finished his portion he turned to the paintings—one tacked to the wall and one on an easel, half-finished. But Mondrian was not yet ready to talk art. Slowly he closed the pressure cooker again and stacked the dishes and spoons in a basin. Then he turned to Moholy:

"Look here. I've been thinking—" He knelt on the floor beside the white sheet we had avoided when we came in. There were several strips of black paper and a small piece of bright red.

"If this bar—" Mondrian pushed one black strip across the sheet, moving it fractions of an inch at a time.

"Stop!" Moholy watched intently. "Go back again." The black returned to its initial position.

"Now try upward."

"No—no—no, not upward," Mondrian protested. "To the left. If at all, it's only to the left." Moholy knelt beside him. As Mondrian moved his strip to the left Moholy pushed another one to the right, slowly, slowly, almost imperceptibly slow. For a while they said nothing.

"It's off balance," Mondrian finally exclaimed. "It's off balance. Don't you see?"

"Yes, I see." Moholy was crestfallen. "Now I know."

With swift moves he rearranged the black strips. Then he jumped on a chair, looking at the sheet on the floor. "Come up here," he called to Mondrian who was still kneeling. "From up here the tension is harmonized."

Mondrian looked for another chair. It was the one on which I was sitting. I relinquished it and now they both stood above my head, pointing—

"To the left—"

"Higher?"

"Higher—but to the right."

It was Moholy's task to execute the turns.

"*Non—non—non!*" Mondrian's quick-fire objections, so typical in the French language. "Too much, I say, much too much!"

"*Bien?*"

"Perhaps. See up here—"

"Not yet—one moment—there."

The room was chilly and my feet were ice-cold. I would have liked to leave. I was tired of standing. But I couldn't make my prosaic presence known. The two men on chairs were like seers, regulating the harmony of the universe with strips of black paper. The chaos of the finite world had been left far behind. They were living a "future life—more real, more pure; with needs more real, fulfilled more purely by the harmonious relations of plane, line, and color."[1] Optimistic, and serenely confident, they created a macrocosmic order of the absolute rectangle, endowed with magic powers more potent than the pentagram of old.

After his visit to Paris, Moholy knew he would not go back to Holland. He had sensed in her artists and intellectuals a hopeless defeatism, and even his Dutch friends from Bauhaus and CIAM days had become close-mouthed and sad.

There were other free lands left—Scandinavia, Switzerland, America—but in 1935 none seemed as promising to Moholy as England. The British tradition of free thought gave his first

[1] From a letter by Piet Mondrian to Moholy-Nagy, dated November 17, 1937.

London years the exuberance of a confirmed faith. Moholy loved Voltaire, who was the only one of the classical writers whom he had read systematically. Now he relived the *Lettres Philosophiques sur les Anglais* as a part of reality. Tolerance toward convictions as well as toward eccentricity; the love of understatement and self-irony; a plain seafaring sense of humor; the cool pride in being what one is—insular and English—and, above all, British amateurism, constituted a perfect psychological coincidence. After the years of enthusiastic apprenticeship, the heavy German professionalism had irritated Moholy. Once sure of his means, he wanted to work with pleasure for the benefit of his soul and as a concomitant to the all-embracing function of living. The German tendency to forego a full life for the accumulation of maximum information or maximum skill in one specialized field was alien to his nature. In all his lectures, he had attacked the German specialist who had given his country much of her greatness and all of her present disaster. England was the country of the amateur—it was his country. With delight he used to point out that almost all the leading English politicians had never had administrative training—Churchill, Chamberlain, Baldwin—that the Governor of the Bank of England was no banker and the president of the largest railroad company no businessman. He saw a greatness in this fact of which the English themselves were hardly conscious.

When he came back from his tragic visit to the Olympic Games in 1936, we were guests at the headmaster's house in Eton. A group of young men gathered around Moholy when they heard he had just come back from the Games. What did he think of the English team?

"Magnificent," Moholy said with enthusiasm. "Simply magnificent. They never won a medal."

The young men gave him startled looks. Was he making fun of them? "Did you say magnificent?" The poor showing in 1936 was a sore spot on English college pride.

"Of course! You lost, don't you see? You'll always lose."

"Pardon me, Sir!" A husky athlete moved a step closer with his teacup. "We have won the boat races in this and that time; we are the best cricket players in the world. Our polo—"

"Of course," Moholy shrugged off so much achievement. "But you do it for fun. The Germans, the Japanese, even the Americans, torture their teams half to death to make them competition-mad. Your boys went just as far as sport for leisure would take them."

"We do more sport in college than all you Germans together," someone said, totally missing Moholy's point. "Why should our team lose?"

"Because you're amateurs," Moholy said, paying the greatest compliment he knew to his hosts. But the effect was negative. No one talked to us again that day, and we were never asked back to the headmaster's house. We hadn't learned yet that the English delight in self-criticism is reserved for natives.

Moholy spent two years in England, from May, 1935, to June, 1937. He had been like "a young eager dog" when he joined the Bauhaus faculty in 1922. Twelve years later he was like Prometheus, dedicated to his fellow men who "saw, yet did not see; heard, yet did not hear; ignorant of how to profit from creation."

With a Titan's prodigality he poured his strength into three professions: design and display, film and photography, painting.

The German textile publication for which he had worked in Berlin had moved to London. It was in their office on The Strand that Moholy started his British career, shocking printers with his unorthodox ideas on type and layout and delighting the unspoiled English office help with candy and flowers which he never forgot to buy.

The publicity agency handling the account of "International Textiles" became interested in the new man and offered Moholy an unending stream of projects. He accepted them all. Together with Gyorgy Kepes, who after a long illness had joined him in London in 1935, he went on a sixteen-hour working routine, spending his days in the city and his evenings and nights in his studio in our home in Hampstead Garden suburb.

A fundamental difficulty arose from Moholy's prolific

118

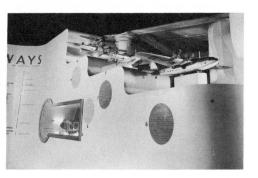

Fig. 41. Exhibition for Imperial Airways, London, 1935. In mobile railway car.

imagination. He was used to offering half a dozen solutions to one problem, and would think up six more if the first ones were rejected. But the English are realists. If art had to invade industry and commerce, it was the task of the artist to find the right solution. That's what he was being paid for—not to bother serious men with a lot of doodlings. There had been trouble with the "Trubenizing" people who wanted one good poster for their preshrunk shirts, not a sequence that explored every visual aspect of a nonwilting collar. When the Abdullah Cigarette Company asked for a new package, Moholy and Kepes turned out four, which disgusted the manufacturer considerably.

"I want to be served, not educated," he wrote to the agency.

But these were only the beginnings of work in England. By the end of 1935 Moholy had established contacts which appreciated his Continental prolificacy. Imperial Airways commissioned him to design a mobile exhibition which would tour the British Empire in a railroad car selling the idea of air travel. In addition he redesigned all their publicity material, from letterheads to posters (Figs. 41, 42). He was not yet done with the Airways when London Transport asked him for posters, and Alexander Simpson offered him and Kepes permanent positions as art advisors for his men's store on Piccadilly. This store in a functional building was the most Continental adventure on which an old English firm had ever dared to embark. It was intended to do away with the Saville Row tradition by which men's suits were tailored according to a prescribed ritual. The century-old

119

rule of no show windows or display cases for men's stores was to be liquidated, and high-quality clothes and accessories were to be sold in the Continental manner in large, light halls from stocks on display. The success of the venture depended on unimpeachable taste, which would quell any objections to cheapness or vulgarity by the quality of presentation. After the two-dimensional work on layouts and posters, and the purely structural organization for the Imperial Airways exhibit, Moholy was happy to work

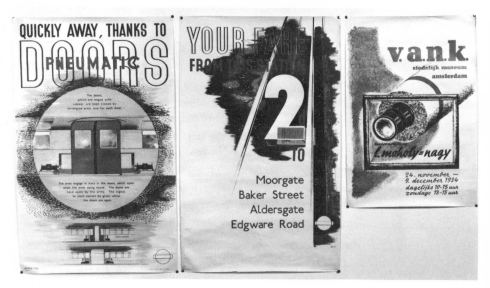

Fig. 42.   Three multicolored posters, 1934, 1935. Amsterdam and London.

again with actual materials. Here was his chance to translate his knowledge of light and color into reality, addressing not merely a select groups of gallery-goers, but everyone.

It seems that "grand openings" at all times and in all fields are harassed by the un-met deadline, by work unfinished, goods not delivered, accidents not foreseen. The opening of "Simpson's, Piccadilly" was no exception. I had grown used to the fact that Moholy was gone all day—swallowed by London, unreachable because he worked in many different places. His return at night was the only stable fact of our existence. But just before

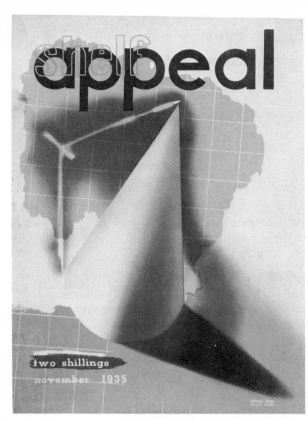

two shillings
november 1935

Fig. 43. Cover for
merchandising periodical
"Shelf Appeal," London 1935.

the Simpson opening he didn't come home at all. Telephone inquiries were useless; an army of workmen was moving through
the six stories of the building, I was told by the operator. No one
could be reached. I finally went to Piccadilly. It was early morning—a cold spring day with the characteristic London drizzle.
The big show windows at Simpson's were still shuttered, but
inside everything was ready—almost everything. On a stepladder
stood Moholy, shirt open, trousers crumpled, hanging fish netting
over a wall in the sports section. Below him clustered reporters,
looking up at his bare feet.

"Asymmetric advertising is like a mild electric shock
to the eye," I heard Moholy lecture as he dropped one side of
the fish netting to the floor. "The impact has to come from the
familiar object presented in an unfamiliar way."

As I listened I saw that his toes were bleeding.
Through a gray layer of plaster dust and floorwax I could see the
sores on his soles. I signaled him to come down.

121

"The familiar object in an unfamiliar presentation," Moholy grinningly repeated. "Just look at my wife's face over there, and you know what I mean."

We didn't find his shoes. He walked barefoot to a cab, and as we drove home, started a twenty-four-hour sleep.

The problem of display, of a visual unit seen from the street in the different light effects of day, dusk, and electricity interested Moholy immensely. He didn't care what merchandise he was asked to display. It was the visual effectiveness that mattered. On one of the rare occasions on which he permitted himself an evening of entertainment we had had dinner in a Soho restaurant and had seen a show. Our guests were a Swedish architect, his Russian girlfriend, and a young French painter. As we strolled through London Moholy decided to show them Simpson's. It was rather late and we planned only a quick look at the windows before going home. But when we got to the building Moholy noticed that the window dresser had not followed his instructions. In a display of leather goods neither the selection of colors nor the arrangement pleased him.

"You wait here, just a few minutes," he said with his biggest smile. "Stand right in front. I'll need your help."

He went in search of the night watchman, telling him that he had to get into the store to do some work. It took considerable time until the man had caught on to Moholy's highly personalized English.

"No," he said, insisting that he needed permission from the store manager to let Moholy enter the building. A series of telephone calls followed until finally Mr. Simpson, who was fondly aware of Moholy's zeal, gave his permission.

Standing outside in the dark we saw Moholy in his stocking feet appear in the window, his arms loaded with leather goods and pieces of transparent plastic. He beamed at us, signaling with his hands that we should direct his arrangements by gestures because the thick plate-glass windows were impenetrable to sound. For half an hour we talked in "body English." The young Russian showed her acrobatic skill by jumping high, crouching low, throwing her arms in wide circles. The young

122

Frenchman employed his national skill in gesticulation, and the Swede, unresigned to the impossibility of oral communication, shouted directions in booming German. A crowd assembled, growing steadily as time wore on and the four of us got more and more into the spirit of the thing. Suddenly two policemen appeared, tapping the Swedish architect energetically on his shoulder.

"What's this all about?" The Swede understood no English—least of all the Cockney drawl of a bobby; neither were the others capable of giving an intelligent explanation. They continued to act like dancing Dervishes while I tried to explain. The police got angry:

"You stop it and be fast about it. This is a public nuisance." I tried to inform Moholy of our dilemma but he was oblivious to the world outside. He only watched the acrobatic instructions, knocking angrily at the plate glass when our reactions were not fast enough. Finally I took one of the bobbies by his arm and, despite his angry resistance, pulled him so close to the window that even Moholy in his obsession had to recognize him. But he only smiled, happily acknowledging the interest of the authorities in the problems of display. It took another interview with the night watchman and the appearance of a London policeman in a Simpson store window to convince Moholy that his day's work was done.

All his commercial design of that period reflected his predominant interest in contour, the flow of curved and crossed lines stressing the perimeter and the profile rather than the solid form (Fig. 43). The Courtauld stand for the London Arts and Crafts Exhibition which he designed together with Marcel Breuer, the Isokon pamphlets, the book wrappers for Crowther and Gropius, demonstrate this trend (Fig. 44). Looking one night over typography and posters done during the Bauhaus years, Moholy said:

"I was much too heavy-handed. The solid rectangular beams, the filled dots and black cubes are a mistake. They stress detail and distract the eye from the unity of the visual impression. A printed communication should be a whole. Neither violent color-contrasts nor heavy typographical detail can achieve that. It's the line continuity that creates a visual entity."

123

Fig. 44. Dust jacket for J. G. Crowther, "An Outline of the Universe," 1937. Photomontage.

Fitted into this commercial art work were large projects in photography and film. In twenty-four months he produced three films: "Life of the Lobster," special effects for Alexander Korda's film on the H. G. Wells theme of "Things to Come," and "The New Architecture in the London Zoo." He made hundreds of Leica shots for three photographic volumes: *Eton Portrait* (Fig. 45), *An Oxford University Chest*, and *Street Markets of London* (Fig. 46) ;[2] and wrote the text for *Telehor*,[3] a four-language survey of his work. The Royal Photographic Society gave him a one-man show in their rooms on Russell Square, and he acted as member of the Advisory Council of the International Photographic Exhibition in New York in 1937.

This variety of expression was often criticized as an overextension of his abilities. But it was actually a coherent demonstration of Moholy's integration principle. His "amateurism," trying out all potentialities of a given medium, was based on the ultimate goal of total design. He defined the most heterogeneous tasks in similar basic terms. All through his life he was equally praised and blamed for his manysidedness, which was as natural to him as breathing. He shuffled his different jobs like a deck of cards, getting innumerable new combinations but finding them all part of the same game. The problem posed by a Simpson window display was basically no different from a setting for *Madame Butterfly*. Both had to convey a message; they had to appeal to perception and emotion in the onlooker, just as do painting and sculpture. The message was different, but the sense apparatus to absorb it remained the same. Design was indivisible. Most men waste their potentialities because departmentalization has made them fractional and inflexible. It was Moholy's peculiar gift to find, in various fields, the common denominator with which to make his particular contribution.

In the summer of 1935 we went to the Sussex coast to shoot the film "The Life of the Lobster." In working with the fishermen, listening to their native talk, watching their family and community life, Moholy created in himself a comprehensive

---

[2] Published by John Miles (London, 1936 and 1937).
[3] *Telehor, International Revue* (Brno, 1936).

pattern of English folkways. From an infinite variety of manifestations he abstracted, so to speak, some of the basic national characteristics. This knowledge helped him later to eliminate many obstacles in photographing the vendors who appeared in *"The Street Markets of London,"* to win the confidence of the Zoo keepers for "The New Architecture in the London Zoo," and it brought the crew in Korda's Twickenham studio around to back-breaking nightwork for "Things to Come." The producer of the Lobster film, John Mathias, was a wealthy young Englishman who in the best amateur tradition had switched from polo to movies. Living with him and his eccentric family in a Sussex manor, Moholy absorbed another pattern—that of British society. Things which irritated me—the feudal relationship between master and

Fig. 45. Fall afternoon, Eton playing fields. From: Eton Portrait, 1936.

servant, the clannishness of the men, the coldness of the women, and the drilled, unnatural politeness of the children—were for him object lessons to which he devoted himself with uncritical attention. He hadn't come to England to judge the English. He had come to demonstrate a new vision, and he was grateful for each clue handed him toward a right psychological approach. The intensity with which he could identify himself with his work compensated for the lack of time at his disposal. He was what he did, totally and imperturbably turning from task to task with

126

Fig. 46. Fireworks along the Cherwell. From: An Oxford University Chest, 1937.

equal concentration. But in addition he knew the secret of how to find helpers. With an almost hypnotic talent he could convince people that to work with him was the greatest chance of their lifetime. As the scope of his work grew steadily, and drove him to greater and greater intensity, he occasionally overstepped the psychological limits. Permanent collaborators became immune to hypnosis, muttering "exploitation" under their exhausted breaths. But with a shrewd insight into the mechanics of creative work Moholy was more interested in the helpmates and handymen who would execute the all-important detail. They were wooed with all the charm and generosity of a man who has ideas but no time. None of the janitors, secretaries, carpenters, mechanics, ever revolted. In the light of Moholy's demonstrative gratitude they gave their best.

The men who wrote the text for his photobooks— Bernard Fergusson for *Eton Portrait* and John Betjeman for *Oxford University Chest* dominated our life while the pictures were taken. Not that they themselves took the initiative. Their comments, the extent to which Moholy had decided to see England through their eyes, guaranteed the success of the books. Fergusson's boyish delight in Eton school life infected Moholy with enthusiasm for "Wall Games," "Fives," and "Blackberry Mess." And for the sake of *Oxford University Chest* he enjoyed Betjeman's whimsical mind which insisted that his house guests learn to sing Irish hymns and applaud the antics of a moth-eaten teddybear called Archibald. Betjeman in turn was delighted when at a Don's

127

Fig. 47.   Special effects for the H. G. Wells-Alexander Korda Film: "The Shape of Things to Come." London 1936.

Dinner at Balliol Moholy paid his respects to the host, an extremely dignified vestige of medieval college tradition, by saying:

"Sir, I thank you for your hostility."

Alexander Korda, who had a financial interest in the Lobster film, saw Moholy's "Light-play Black-White-Gray" in 1935, and commissioned him to do the special effects for the H. G. Wells film "The Shape of Things to Come." Moholy accepted the task mainly because it offered an almost unlimited chance for experimentation with new plastic materials, and he was fascinated by the idea of constructing scale models which through a skillful use of camera angle and lighting would create the illusion of superhuman dimensions. These models had to be tried out with quietness and leisure but in daytime his work got only hurried attention. Men and equipment were needed to shoot the actual play. Moholy decided to work at night, and for weeks his only rest were a few hours on a couch in a dressing room after his helpers had left at dawn.

The fantastic technology of the Utopian city of the future would, so Moholy dreamed, eliminate solid form. Houses were no longer obstacles to, but receptacles of, man's natural life force, light. There were no walls, but skeletons of steel, screened with glass and plastic sheets. The accent was on perforation and contour, an indication of a new reality rather than reality itself (Fig. 47). In its final version the film never lived up to the talent of its originators. The special effects were cut, and the character of the new metropolis, grown from the ashes of the old world, was indicated by the Wagnerian gowns of its inhabitants, and the chromium splendor of a Horn and Hardart Automat.

Often Moholy's day lasted twenty hours, divided between the film studio, commercial art work, advisory meetings for exhibitions and publications, and lectures in and out of London. When his second daughter, Claudia, was born in March, 1936, he had hardly time for a glance. As an infant she did not get the attention her older sister had aroused, but years later her father discovered in her an almost exact image of himself.

Late in 1935 Moholy brought home a large sheet of Rhodoid, a plastic of vitreous transparency. On it he painted his

129

Fig. 48. Oil painting on Rhodoid sheet, mounted two inches from white plywood background to produce mobile shadow play, 1936.

first "light modulator." It was the sketch for a canvas, painted the year before. After he had mounted the transparent sheet on a white plywood background, he compared the two-dimension effect of the canvas and the three-dimensional effect of the light modulator (Fig. 48). In the following months he made numerous pencil and crayon sketches, all marked "Third Dimension" (Fig. 48). He sketched in barber shops and subway trains, while he had luncheon or waited for an appointment. Every business letter had a sketch on its back, and his shirt cuffs and handkerchiefs were smeared with crayon, hastily wiped off his fingers before going into a conference or shooting a picture.

By the end of June, 1936, the first phase of his work in England had come to a close. "Life of the Lobster" and "Things to Come" were finished. Imperial Airways and London Transport had completed their projects and were not planning on new ones before the end of the year. The illustrations for *Eton Portrait* and *Oxford University Chest* were in the hands of the publishers, and

130

Simpson's had granted a two-months' leave of absence. We planned on a long vacation in Hungary, which I had never visited. Moholy looked tired, and his mood was tense and irritable. There was nothing more important than rest.

After all plans had been made, hotel reservations confirmed in Budapest and at Lake Balaton, and train tickets bought, a picture agency called Moholy for a conference. As he came back from the meeting, the exhaustion of the day before had left his face. It looked boyish with a new enthusiasm, and I knew our vacation was over.

"I'll do the Olympic Games in Berlin," he said. "I'll shoot a 16 mm. film and as many stills as I like. They want me to catch the spectator psychology, the physiognomic contrast between an international crowd and the rabid German nationalists."

I was unenthusiastic. "You need a vacation, not a new job. You're exhausted."

"Exhausted? Ridiculous. Female exaggerations! Don't you see what a chance this is? I've learned so much about filming people in action. Now I can apply it. I never really noticed German faces the way I've learned to see the English. And there'll be the continuum of the competitions, the constant motion of the games against the aggregate of the passive spectators. It's a unique opportunity. Of course I'll go."

He sailed for Germany in the middle of July. Two weeks later he suddenly turned up at Lake Balaton in Hungary,

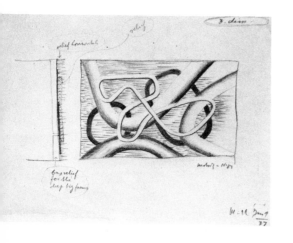

Fig. 49. Sketch for a three-dimensional construction, 1937.

131

long before I had expected him. As we floated at night on the water in one of the flat-bottomed boats, or climbed the wooded slopes to drink Badaconyi wine in the court of an old castle, he told me why he had dropped his assignment. The moral climate of a country under dictatorship had paralyzed him. Among his friends who had decided to remain in Germany in spite of their known opposition to the Hitler regime was a doctor. He was a pioneer of medical reform and had been a leader among the young rebels who had practiced a new biological faith, based upon vegetarianism, physical culture, and mental discipline. Moholy had looked forward to meeting him again—a silent hero who fought against overwhelming odds. But the revolutionary of old was a professor at the Nazi-dominated university now, and well equipped with verbiage to justify his position.

"We have to undermine the enemy from within," he had explained. "Good men working for a bad cause will eventually ennoble this cause. Believe me, I'll use every one of these new leaders for our own positive ends."

"I never felt so mute and so helpless," Moholy said. "I knew he was wrong, and that he was selling out. But who was I to tell him to accept either the physical suffering of a concentration camp or the moral anguish of emigration? Everyone I talked to in Berlin was suddenly two persons. They had all split into an ethical and a political self. I could not accept one and reject the other."

There had been another incident on the first day of the Olympic Games. As he entered the Stadium, Moholy had been greeted warmly by an officer in the hated SS uniform. He was a former Bauhaus student who admitted to being a political commissar.

"Don't worry about my convictions," he had whispered to Moholy. "I'm playing their game, getting myself into higher and higher positions. One day, at the right moment, I'll show my true face and take up where we left off in Dessau. But it takes cunning and patience. Nothing can be achieved with stubbornness."

I asked Moholy: "And what about your pictures? Did

132

you see them?" When I had moved our possessions from Berlin a year before, the van hadn't been big enough for the furniture and all the paintings. There had been no second truck available. Too many people were leaving Germany in a hurry. I had no choice other than leaving with a former housekeeper about thirty canvases and metal constructions. They were Moholy's earliest work, representing the transition from representational to abstract painting.

"There's nothing to look at anymore," he said slowly. "I went to see Frau Schwelker. Remember how she loved you, how she cried her eyes out when we told her we were leaving Germany? Well, she doesn't cry any longer. 'Those pictures,' she sneered at me, *'die ham'er lange schon kleenjemacht.'* ('We made kindling wood of them long ago.') When I protested that she had had no right to destroy my property, her grocer-husband threatened to call the police and have me arrested for *'Kulturbolschewismus.'* This all happened in the first two days I was in Berlin. On the third morning I called London and told them I wouldn't take a single shot of the Olympic Games. I'll never go back to Germany."

The loveliness of the Hungarian landscape and our visit to Budapest eased the Berlin nightmare. But it remained a smarting sore spot which was not to be touched. We rarely talked about Germany again.

The short span without work, without projects, and without haste, provided complete relaxation. It was the last real vacation Moholy was ever to have. After two weeks at Lake Balaton we went to Budapest to fulfill a dream of his young days. As a student in the penurious days after the First World War, he had envied the visiting Americans. For once he wanted to live like them, swim in the luxurious pool of mineral water in the Hotel St. Gellert, dance on the terrace, take rides in illuminated gondolas to the St. Marguerit Island in the Danube, and watch from the grandstand when the St. Stephen's Day Parade marched down the hills of Buda. We spoke only English, and Moholy beamed with happiness when the waiters took us for Americans. It was the only tragic note of this trip that time had destroyed the inner unity with his mother. "Édes Anyam," who had moved the boy to such tenderness and longing, had become an old woman, bitterly lonely, and stubbornly orthodox in her beliefs. Moholy had no patience to reawaken in her the charm and poesy he had once loved. While I wandered along the old streets and climbed the lovely hills, he spent dutiful hours with her, but our departure was in the end almost a flight.

The relationship to his older brother had never been close, because they hadn't spent their childhood together. Now that they met as men, they had a cool respect for each other's achievements, tinged with the slight ironic edge of the artist for the material worries of the businessman, and of the realist for the Utopian hopes of the professional dreamer.

His old friends and co-fighters were hard to find, but we managed to trace some of them in the city and in distant country retreats. They were the last representatives of the great days of the Hungarian Revolution. Their ranks had been decimated by exile, imprisonment, and death. The survivors were muted by the Horthy dictatorship, frustrated by the limitations of their unpopular language and the smallness of their audience. Moholy felt alien among them. Their common bonds were broken. They were all defeated men. But they still had the charm and the unique chivalry of the Magyars of old. It seemed as if there were no country on earth where a woman could be made more conscious of her femininity. All contact with men was courtship, fascinatingly balanced on the precarious line between deference and naughtiness.

When we went back to England neither the volume of Moholy's work nor the complexity of tasks had diminished. The commissions from Simpson and London Transport continued; the *Street Markets of London* were photographed; and the Museum of Modern Art, in collaboration with the Architectural Department of Harvard, commissioned a film on "The New Architecture in The London Zoo," a record of the extraordinary new buildings done by the Tecton architects. A new crop of commercial and typographical work had to be sown, tended, and harvested. But the emphasis had shifted. Perhaps it was in consequence of the Con-

134

tinental experience—of the German betrayal and the Hungarian petrification—that painting became the permanent center of Moholy's existence. It was a shift in accent—not in time. The multitude of tasks went on, but for the remaining ten years of his life the importance of anything he did was only relative to the supremacy of painting. It added immeasurably and finally fatally to the overstrain, but it gave him the maturity of final co-ordination he had lacked. From the autumn of 1936 onward Moholy never interrupted his painting again. He worked nights if the day didn't provide at least one free hour; he painted Sundays and holidays and during those brief summer interludes which other people can call vacation. For ten years he probed one problem, varied one theme: he thought, felt, saw, and painted three-dimensionality.

And he talked it. For the first time since the Bauhaus days he found men and women with whom to discuss his work. The unique English capacity for friendship, an objective unemotional association which warmed and stimulated without obligation seemed particularly strong among London artists and intellectuals. The young architects of the MARS[4] group supplied many new ideas. There was the Axis circle around Myfanwy Evans and John Piper whose courageous publications, *Circle* and *The Painter's Object*, maintained a level that had long been abandoned on the Continent. "Peter" Norton, vivacious owner of the London Gallery, organized Moholy's first English one-man show, which had a startling and gratifying response. A throng of hundreds jammed the opening and the large newspapers wrote detailed comments (Fig. 50). By and by a close circle developed—Herbert Read, Henry Moore, Jack Pritchard, Jim Crowther, Julian Huxley, Barbara Hepworth and Ben Nicholson. Ben's paintings and reliefs posed a visual problem related to Moholy's space modulation. Their three-dimensionality rested on the finest shadow effects, produced by advancing and receding planes. Barbara Hepworth had just broken away from Henry Moore's great example. Her sculptures sought a new organization of space displacement and multiple volume which Moholy had tried to solve in his early

[4] Modern Architectural Research, the English branch of *Congrès Internationaux d'Architecture Moderne*.

Fig. 50.   Exhibition of the work of Moholy-Nagy in the London Gallery, 1936.

Constructivist sculptures.[5] In their studio on Hampstead's old Mall one could sit and talk while the demonstration material was right at hand. The simple unpretentious dedication of Ben and Barbara to their work and their children as one inseparable unit was, I often felt, a creative experience comparable to Brancusi's pure craftsmanship and philosophy. Herbert Read had just published *Art and Industry,* the first attempt in the English language to establish standards of collaboration between designer and producer. There was much on which he and Moholy disagreed, conditioned mainly by a polarity of temperament and historical orientation. But Read's genuine convictions on the educational importance of art, his willingness to listen and to absorb, and his brilliant ability to find the precise formulation for the half-coherent stammerings of the unliterary mind, created a lasting friendship. There was Julian Huxley, whose vision and persistence had made the new architecture in the London Zoo a reality. Moholy loved his keen sense of humor, his independence from acclaim and reputation, which underbid even the usual British modicum, and his inexhaustible enthusiasm for new people with new ideas. And we all benefited from contact with Jack Pritchard, manufacturer of Marcel Breuer's plywood furniture and generous host to many a Continental refugee in his ever-open Lawn Road Flats. When we went to America it was the irreplaceable loss of this companionship that hurt most.

But as the importance of commercial work and of film and photo experiment faded before the urgency of painting, the teacher in Moholy grew more and more restless.

"Painting is not enough," he said as we watched a cricket game on Hampstead Heath. "Not even exhibitions are enough. The London Gallery show was fine. It was the first time I felt I had something distinctly original to offer. But it reaches so few and it reaches them in such a completed, rarefied form that the living problem gets obscured by the finish. There are very few people who can look at a picture and take its basic problem home to work on it. No money one makes in the industry and no satisfaction of shows and public recognition can equal teaching."

Yet England offered no chance. Its educational system

[5] See *The New Vision,* p. 44.

was untouched by the free-thinking tolerance of the London circle. By the spring of 1937 Moholy had become tired and melancholic. The Promethean drive had spent itself in an ocean of commercialism. The young men and women who should have been touched by its fire were out of his reach.

postal interlude

June 6, 1937

CABLEGRAM TO L. MOHOLY-NAGY, 7 FARM WALK, LONDON
Plan design school on Bauhaus lines to open in fall. Marshall
Field offers family mansion Prairie Avenue. Stables to be converted into workshops. Doctor Gropius suggests your name as
director. Are you interested?

ASSOCIATION OF ARTS AND INDUSTRIES, CHICAGO

CABLEGRAM TO L. MOHOLY-NAGY, PARIS   June 8, 1937
Forwarded Chicago cable today. Urge you to decline. German
example shows Fascist results when field marshals take over education. Stables and prairie sound just like it. Love.

SIBYL

CABLEGRAM TO L. MOHOLY-NAGY, LONDON   June 13, 1937
Marshall Field philanthropist and businessman, other sponsors
Avery, Gypsum, and Montgomery Ward; Kohler, Wisconsin;
Paepcke, Container Corporation. Their backing assured. Can you
come to Chicago for negotiations?

ASSOCIATION OF ARTS AND INDUSTRIES, CHICAGO

May 29, 1937

ASSOCIATION OF ARTS AND INDUSTRIES
700 NORTH MICHIGAN AVENUE, CHICAGO
Professor Moholy-Nagy
7 Farm Walk
London, England
DEAR PROFESSOR NAGY:

We are opening in the Fall a School of Industrial
Design, organized along the lines of the best Industrial Art Schools
in Europe, with workshop practice. We have the backing of a
large group of industrialists and have raised funds with which
to carry through our plans. Marshall Field II has given us his
family home to house the School and we are now about to remodel

139

the house for classrooms and the garage and stables for workshops. There are ample grounds to add other buildings which we intend to do in the course of a three-year program. These new buildings will be of modern design and eventually the house will be replaced by a modern structure.

We are starting without any hampering traditions and we think we have a real opportunity in this great manufacturing district of the Middle West to establish a school of the type so needed in the United States. In Sheldon Cheney's book recently published "Art and the Machine," on page 269 in the third paragraph he speaks of our Association and our experience. We have tried to establish our school in connection with the Museum School but the effort was a failure, as you may know it would be; so we separated ourselves and now plan to start the school along practical and real lines. We have always subscribed to the plan of the Bauhaus and it was of great interest to us when Mr. Gropius suggested that you might be available. With our background there is an opportunity to establish much the type of school you had at Dessau and I am wondering whether it would interest you to become the head of the school. We have a splendid man who would work with you; he has made a study of Industrial Art Schools abroad and has been one of the guiding spirits in our efforts. We have also an industrial designer trained in Hamburg who will be on the faculty.

Your telegram that this is of interest to you and to send more information is the reason for this letter. You will no doubt receive a definite offer from us shortly.

Yours very sincerely,

[signed] NORMA K. STAHLE
EXECUTIVE DIRECTOR

June 19, 1937

CABLEGRAM TO ASSOCIATION OF ARTS AND INDUSTRIES, CHICAGO
Send necessary confirmations to American Consulate in London. Passage booked SS Manhattan July first.

MOHOLY-NAGY

140

On Board SS Manhattan,   July 4, 1937
Darling Sibyl:

I might just as well sit up and write to you although it is well past midnight. Today was my first meeting with the American mentality. Until last night it was rough and I was seasick as usual. Now that we're well past Ireland, the sea is calm. To my surprise the dining room and the bar were decked out in red white and blue paper bunting this morning. There was a gala dinner at six o'clock. We all got whistles and noisemakers and horns, just as if we were small children. But the most extraordinary sight was bald men and heavy middle-aged women putting little paper hats on their skulls, singing and yelling into each other's faces. I've never heard such an uproar. This is America's highest national holiday—something like Bastille Day in France —but it seems to depend for success on a complete reversion to infantilism.

Do you know what they eat for breakfast? They have at eight in the morning a huge stack of pancakes, artfully decorated with numerous butter cones and a garland of small sausages. They pour sweet syrup over it, and when they're through they give the impression of being unable to get up. A Frenchman at my table couldn't stand the sight. He's now having his coffee and rolls on deck.

July 5, 1937

Today everyone is civilized again as if the wild merry-making of yesterday had never happened. There is a genuine friendliness about these people. Even their uninhibited curiosity seems to be without malice. But they shrink from no inquiry—no matter how personal. What a contrast to the English reticence. If this is a national characteristic, Americans will make wonderful students. They'll never be afraid to ask questions.

July 8, 1937

Barclay Hotel, New York
Dearest Sibyl:

This then is New York, and I've come all the way from a farm in Hungary to see it. How I remember the long winter evenings when Gusti Bacsi explained to me the pictures of Manhattan in *Over Land and Sea*. It seemed to me then that the skyscrapers of

141

New York were the destination of my life. Now they're just a station on a long way—but what a station, Sibyl, what a station!

I know America is a democracy, but this system has not yet been extended to the landing procedure. I waited nine hours while the first-class passengers and the American citizens were cleared. Then the officials went out for a two-hour dinner. Someone said: "If we don't get through today, we'll have to spend another night on board." I didn't like the idea. So I looked over the men with the rubber-stamps when they came back. They're Americans, I said to myself, they're neither English nor German. They must be human. There must be an affinity between them and the Austrian officials of my childhood. They too could accept a bribe with the innocent smile of a child, and come back for more. So I took a five-dollar bill and I went to the assistant purser.

"I'm a professor," I said as pompously as I could, "I'm expected by reporters."

And, Darling, it worked. I was the first passenger from the tourist class who came down the gangplank.

Sweeney [James Johnson S.] had waited faithfully. It was hot. We drove through streets that didn't look American at all. Two-story buildings, often clapboard, very often half-decayed. A slum worse than that around Victoria Station. But beautiful fire escapes. I made the car stop several times to look down narrow streets they call "alleys" to see the strange patterns made by fire escapes. This will make a fine film one day.

Then there's a big new building—called an apartment house—surrounded by small slum houses. A doorman in the uniform of a general and a very black man in the lift (elevator). Up, up, up! Another very black woman in a hall—but she smiles and takes my hat. Then Laura Sweeney—charming and full of friendliness. A room that looks like the best—very best Europe: white walls, matting, very little furniture—a Picasso, a Miro, and then—then, Sibyl, I step on a terrace so high I floated in the air. This was unbelievable. A river, called East River, with boats, steamers; a highway, an endless ribbon of cars, headlights make weaving patterns as they drift on, on. An endless ribbon of swiftly changing light. Sunset, the mere hint of a mountain against the sky, very far away—and then a bluish mist over the buildings.

142

That is what made it so fantastic—these buildings, the skyscrapers of New York. Obelisks, menhirs, megaliths—every shape, historic and prehistoric—straightly perpendicular, or terraced like a pyramid; in solid formations, or single—pointing.

There was no detail. Night came and even the sharp-edged contours melted. A million lights perforated the huge masses—switching, flickering—a light-modulation dissolving the solid form. Airplanes and stars—their lights of identical size—static and dynamic as contrast.

I got drunk—from seeing, although there was champagne served to celebrate my coming, together with an excellent meal: chicken, salad, on white Berlin china. Later we went to other places—many people, bars, a Hungarian restaurant. But I wanted to be up there again—on the terrace, see this incredible symphony of shape and light.

KNICKERBOCKER HOTEL, CHICAGO, ILLINOIS   July 16, 1937

DEAREST SIBYL:

If I didn't have to uphold my reputation as a valient male before you I'd say that my heart sometimes sinks below the gray pavement of this strange town. I've never felt so alone. It all *looks* familiar but when you investigate it, it is a different culture—it is no culture yet, just a million beginnings.

The skyscraper illusion of my first night in New York has vanished. Here I see it from below with all the detail thrown into focus. Why are they so afraid of the engineer who was their greatest genius? They quickly cover his construction with the façades of Trianon, Chartres, a mosque or a Doric colonnade. I have been quartered beside the only fair example, an enormous tower called "Palmolive"—not because it grows either, but because it was built by soap people.

It never gets dark and it never gets quiet in Chicago. I live one block off the largest avenue and all night automobiles honk their horns happily and police cars with screaming sirens seem to be incessantly on the way after some monstrous crime. Neon signs and shop windows remain lighted all night. It's a rich town—that much is sure.

There are wide streets near the lake, but also side streets with old dilapidated houses right around the corner. Gar-

143

bage in cans and even in cardboard boxes is put before the houses. In hot weather—and it is hot as Hades—it smells.

But what a lake, oh Darling, what a lake! Its color changes constantly, and it remains calm and moving at the same time. No limitation. An endless aspect to a very limited civilization.

July 27, 1937

CHICAGO

. . . The same friendliness that I felt on the boat is even more evident now. I have been invited to many houses—big industrialists who gave much money to the Association of Arts and Industries, professors who are interested in teaching if a school should be founded. They drink much, too much for my taste, but they eat well. And they bravely try out your first name, although you've never met them before. I never used my first name with men. It was reserved for the ladies of my existence. Now—how shall I help them out when they simply *have* to know my first name? I can't possibly have them call me Laci?

But that isn't the problem, Darling, the problem lies somewhere else. It lies, to be honest, in my own bewilderment. The men who invited me are the future trustees of a new Bauhaus if it should come about; they called me here—knowing what I stand for. They wouldn't have gone to all that trouble otherwise. But their homes, the style of their furniture, their architectural preferences, the pictures they hang on their walls, show not the slightest influence of any modern taste. What am I to believe? Shall I be an optimist and say: Everyone is a potential student; or shall I be a pessimist and say: Forgive them for they know not what they're doing?

The President of the Association, who is a particularly pleasant person, took me in his car through the northern suburbs of Chicago. There wasn't a decently designed building I saw, but he thought they were something to be proud of. K., a printer and book designer, has a mania for medieval eclecticism. He gave me two books he designed: imitations of Gothic prayer books. He must know about Bauhaus typography? Why would he join this whole venture? And P., who is the most charming of them all, has Madonnas all over his place, strange draperies, and imitation Louis Quinze furniture.

144

I am bewildered, Darling. Do they know what they're
doing?

8/8/1937

. . . Monday is the big day. I'll present to the Board
of the Association of Arts and Industries a full four-year program
and a draft for my own contract. You ask whether I want to remain
here? Yes, Darling, I want to remain in America. There's something incomplete about this city and its people that fascinates
me; it seems to urge one on to completion. Everything seems still
possible. The paralyzing finality of the European disaster is far
away. I love the air of newness, of expectation around me. Yes,
I want to stay.

August 13, 1937

CABLEGRAM TO LONDON
Signed five-year contract for Bauhaus. Opening October eighteenth.
Liquidate everything. Details follow.

LACI

August 16, 1937

CABLEGRAM FROM LONDON
Congratulations. Drop name Bauhaus. Identification with Ger-
many and past program unwise. Suggest American School of
Design. Love.

SIBYL

August 19, 1937

CABLEGRAM FROM CHICAGO
Your opinion re school name wrong and uncalled for. Official
name New Bauhaus. Inform London press.

LACI

145

6 In May, 1929, Margaret Anderson and Jane Heap had published in Chicago the last issue of their famous *Little Review*.[1] To summarize the ideas expressed for eight years in the foremost avant-garde magazine of America, they had sent a questionnaire to the artists and writers whose work had appeared in the review. It was one of those typical inquiries—naïve, indiscreet, and very clever. It attained its objective. The answers from such men as Sherwood Anderson, Jean Cocteau, Hemingway, Joyce, Lipschitz, Aldous Huxley, provided a comprehensive psychological picture of the postwar mentality. Moholy's replies to the ten questions were written at a time when he had just left the Bauhaus and had separated from his first wife. The depression was dawning, and he found himself faced with the necessity of making a new start in Berlin, which no longer considered the modern artist a pacemaker of social integration. What he answered to *The Little Review* was like a seismographic chart of his reaction to pressure. It was still valid eight years later when he faced the Chicago mentality from which the questions had originated.

> *Question 2:* Why wouldn't you change places with any human being?
>
> *Answer:* I'm satisfied with my fate. Chicken remains chicken. Moreover, I'm happy to be as I am. What could I do if I were better than I am? My failings give me impetus in the fight; they sharpen my effort.
>
> *Question 3:* What do you look forward to?
>
> *Answer:* That some time I'll be able to comprehend society, social relations, the relation of individuals to the mass, better than today. . . .
>
> *Question 5:* What has been the unhappiest moment of your life?

[1] *The Little Review*, Chicago, final number: Spring 1929.

Answer: I have never been, strictly speaking, deeply un-
happy.

Question 6: What do you like most about yourself? Dislike
most about yourself?

Answer: I like most about myself that I can be happy; the
least that I have a tendency to become a fanatic.

Question 8: What is your attitude toward art today?

Answer: I do not believe so much in art as in mankind.
Every man reveals himself. Much of it is art.

It was on the two last answers that Moholy built his
Chicago existence: a happy fanaticism and a supreme faith in man's
ability to reveal himself in art. On September 23, 1937, an unexpected crowd numbering eight hundred people jammed into the
ballroom of the Knickerbocker Hotel in Chicago to hear Moholy
outline his plans. For more than two hours he poured a stream of
analysis and suggestion over their unprepared heads, presented in
a language that shrank from nothing to be explicit, and omitted
definite articles to save time.[2]

> Well educated today means accumulate useful experience
> among historical and present ones. So far all right, but why,
> I ask you, has the specialist always to think down his channel?
>
> Age of conveyor belt, of disintegrated part, of screw driven
> into machine of which purpose and function he doesn't know.

He became entangled in sentence constructions from
which he could extricate himself only with a wide gesture and a
smile of infinite optimism.

> Books who should be friends one should get to, to find a
> rounded-up existence, not only as an excellent basis for spe-
> cialized education. . . .

But by ten-thirty that night he had put before the people
of Chicago a serious and substantial program. It defined the teacher
as the all-important bridge between specialist and student, the
pivot of social evolution. His much-quoted phrase, "everyone is
talented," acquired new meaning through a colorful demonstration of man's natural urge to exercise his senses.

> You speak: words, sounds, in joy, in horror. Are you a speaker?
> Oh no, you're just a human being. One day you notice that

[2] Moholy's original lecture notes, in English, have been left unedited.

sound is not only loud, it's beautiful. You try again and it makes you feel happy. Your ability to make sound beautiful liberates you—stomach, heart, up here [gesture to head]. You organize your ability to make sound, refine it, find pattern, watch effect. And you're a speaker, a writer, an actor. Good? —Good! And now color.—My little daughter wouldn't walk. Why should she? We carry her anyhow. But then she discovers red. Across a lawn are red toys she wants, and she walks because red forces her to take action. Now you who can already walk, you find that color means a life beyond food, drink, sleep. Pleasant, I know, I love to eat. But there's more. Everyone can buy it, without money, with openness of eyes, openness of feeling, readiness to learn. You understand? Everybody is talented. I told you so.

He attacked "beaux-arts" education.

It makes you feel low before you had a chance to fail. You aren't Michelangelo, not even Whistler. You can imitate them poorly and so can every other art student beside you. But if you extend the sensorial directness you had as a small child— remember the red toys—into creative work with materials and relationships, you feel for the first time that you are a supreme individual.

And he cleverly mixed compliment and plug:

Your American custom of night school is splendid. We in Europe don't know this. We spend our nights differently—we waste some; sometimes we have fun. But we don't learn. You use your time better. We shall give you a laboratory of form and movement, a place where all you've swallowed down inside of you during office hours and in factories gets liberated by experience and co-ordination. When you have been with us, your hobby will be your real work. Space-creation and color-creation can be taught like the alphabet.

"The illiterate of the future," he amplified his famous dictum, "would not only be the man ignorant of handling a camera, it also would be the man without a color and space concept."

To the industrialists and businessmen in the audience he presented a program of universal usefulness:

We don't want to add to the art-proletariat that already exists. We don't teach what is called "pure art," but we train what

149

you might call the art engineer. It is a remodeling of art-meaning we are undertaking. If our students become artists—this is their own job. We know that after they have learned to use materials, to understand space, to see color, they'll be better artists no matter how far removed they think they are from practical life. But to you—the industrialists—we offer our services for research. We shall work on your problems. In our workshops we shall provide research possibilities for synthetic fibers, fashion, dying, printing on textiles, wallpaper design, mural painting, the use of varnishes, lacquers, sprays, and color combinations in decorating; we shall explore for you typography, layout, commercial and portrait photography, microphotography, motion pictures in color and black-and-white, commercial art in posters and packages. We shall design stage display, window and shop display, exposition architecture, and all other architectural structures from a prefabricated bungalow to a factory; and we shall work with stone, glass, metal, wood, clay, and all plastics in the product design and the sculpture classes.

The curriculum he outlined was in accordance with his statement that "in the future we can never speak about a single thing without relating it to the whole." The students of the New Bauhaus would get instruction in biotechnique and biology, chemistry and physics, mathematics and geometry. Psychology, philosophy, and sociology, would supplement painting, sculpture, architecture, photography, weaving, and all branches of product design.

After he had signed his contract with the Association of Arts and Industries, Moholy joined some of his former colleagues from the German Bauhaus on Cape Cod. He wanted, he said, criticism and advice on his new program. When the outline had been read, it was apparent that its scope was much too big for the modest teaching staff available at a new school. Gropius voiced this unanimous criticism, analyzing point by point what Moholy planned to do, and separating the feasible from the infeasible. Moholy listened with intense interest, agreeing or objecting as the case might be. When Gropius had finished, he smiled with great relief:

"Thank you so much, Pius. All you said has made

150

Fig. 51. Moholy-Nagy at the opening of the New Bauhaus in Chicago, 1937. Photograph by Herbert Matter.

everything so much clearer to me. Thank God, the program is already in print."

When school opened in the remodeled Marshall Field mansion on October 18, 1937 (Figs. 51, 52), thirty-five students had sufficient confidence to expose themselves to this enormous vista. They came to understand that the program outlined for them was a vision, not yet a reality; that the actual school work was a step-by-step process toward the realization of a future goal. They became, and have remained, loyal supporters of an educational concept which, in the words of one of them, "veered my life at a 180-degree angle toward a future world that needs my personal contribution to come into being." Over the years a substantial number came back to the Institute of Design as teachers, and many others remained in close contact with Moholy while they organized similar programs at other schools, (Fig. 53).

The press reacted with unqualified enthusiasm. *Time,* the *New York Times,* all Chicago and Midwestern dailies, and art and architectural magazines here and in England, wrote hopeful reports, stressing the inadequacy of existing art instruction

151

Fig. 52. Sibyl Moholy-Nagy and children at the opening of the New Bauhaus in Chicago, 1937.

and urging support of the new approach. Many of the exercises done during the first year of The New Bauhaus are still standard illustration material today wherever the workshop method in art education is described. Hin Bredendieck, head of the workshops, extended the exercises of the Foundation Course, worked out by Moholy and Joseph Albers in the German Bauhaus, to new tools and materials.[3] In the supplementary instruction, Moholy made important adaptations to America and the education concept of a new era. The Foundation Course, which for the German Bauhaus freshman had been confined to a survey of visual means, was adjusted to college standards. In addition to workshop practice, which formed the core of the curriculum, such academic subjects as physics, biology, and philosophy were taught, supplemented in later semesters by sociology and mathematics. To teach these courses Moholy had won a unique group of men. They were faculty members of the University of Chicago, belonging to the "Unity of Science" movement. They joined The New Bauhaus

[3] See *The New Vision* and *Vision in Motion*.

152

because they saw a common denominator in its program and their own effort to define scientific terms according to actual function rather than to traditional usage. The ultimate end of their semantic approach was an equation of human thinking and acting, just as the Bauhaus aimed at an equation of function and design.

In the school's first catalogue, Charles Morris, Professor of Philosophy and teacher of Intellectual Integration at The New Bauhaus, wrote:

> Science, and philosophy oriented around science, have much to contribute to a realistically conceived art education in the contemporary world. . . . We need desperately a simplified and purified language in which to talk about art in the same simple and direct way in which we talk about scientific terms. For the purpose of intellectual understanding art must be talked about in the language of scientific philosophy and not in the language of art. . . . It is difficult to envisage the full possibilities of the systematic collaboration between artist and scientist to which the new [Bauhaus] program points.

Fig. 53. Seals of the Bauhaus, Weimar, 1922, and of the New Bauhaus, Chicago, 1937, designed by Oskar Schlemmer.

It was a fine Faculty roll but one name announced at the lecture in the Knickerbocker Hotel was missing. James Johnson Sweeney, who had agreed to teach History of Art and a sociocultural survey of related movements in literature and poetry, had withdrawn. This was a bitter blow to Moholy, who already had to cope with the inability of Herbert Bayer and Jean Helion to get entrance visas to the United States in time for the opening. As a young man Sweeney had worked in Chicago, dividing his time between a job in a mail-order house and the writing of art criticism for the *Daily News*. After one meeting with the Executive Committee of The New Bauhaus, he refused a contract. The issue between him and Moholy was not one of convictions: they re-

153

mained in agreement about all principles of education; the difference was between one who believes and one who knows. The question Moholy had posed himself a few months earlier—"Do they know what they're doing?"—had been answered for Sweeney by his previous contact with the Chicago business world. He knew their faces.

But the success of the first semester, the swiftly increasing number of students, the continuous interest of the press, made Moholy fanatically optimistic. The level of his school would soon be high enough to attract the best names in modern art. With the beginning of the second school year, Jean Helion would teach painting; Herbert Bayer, typography; and Xanti Schawinsky, display. Negotiations were under way with Hans Arp and Piet Mondrian, and Sweeney would—so Moholy hoped—soon be replaced by Siegfried Giedion, whose lifelong dream of an international institute for co-ordinated design research would be realized in Chicago as part of The New Bauhaus. The plans for such a cultural working center of integrated knowledge were formulated in great detail during the first year. Moholy approached several foundations and scientists whose response was favorable. A circular stated the objective:

> America has not yet built up an institution which strives for synthesis of all specialized knowledge. Since the Industrial Revolution we have been overrun with scientific discoveries and technical inventions without number; but we have lost access to their entirety because we have learned to concentrate on parts alone.
>
> There is an urgent necessity to create a collaboration between the different topics, to restore the basic unity of all human experience which could restore balance to our lives. The New Bauhaus, American School of Design, tries to achieve such unity. . . .
>
> When we design we must relate technical inventions and scientific discoveries to our psychological and physiological needs with a view to social implications which go far beyond mere innovation or increased financial returns. The structure, texture, durability and workability of materials must be systematized and their esthetic and technological meaning investigated. A hundred facts of life—work, recreation and

154

leisure, group response and personality growth—must be related to our designed environment. There is as yet no study which is contemporary in this deepest meaning of the term.

A group of collaborators in a cultural working center has to make the designers of man's physical environment conscious of the effect of their actions on the whole of mankind. Scientists who are responsible for plastic materials and new processes, artists who influence man's emotions through color, tone, and word, craftsmen who have explored the nature of man's basic materials: wood, stone, and metal, and finally designers who shape the tools of everyday living, must be brought together each year for a certain period to exchange findings and remind each other of the human denominator. American technology will thus lose its materialistic aspect and will become a servant instead of a menace.

And yet, in spite of all this visible success, there was —almost physical in its growing density—an air of dissatisfaction and tension in the school. Confidence between faculty and administration was riddled by rumors, and the symptoms of insecurity and dissent grew. The friction had started almost at the beginning of the school year. On October 30, 1937, twelve days after the opening, Moholy saw the need for a letter to the Executive Committee, stating

> . . . that it is impossible for me to run a school with good feeling when I have to be aware that unorientated members of the Board blame me for arrangements which were carefully planned and executed with the full knowledge of the president. It would be better and to the benefit of our work in the school if you would be in closer touch with each other and if you would inform each other more about decisions and agreements. . . . I think it would be desirable for the future to think about clear arrangements which allow me to be really responsible as director of the school, having knowledge and control of all actions which concern The New Bauhaus. . . . When all decisions in economic matters are with you, do not try to blame me now for things which I have never been in charge of.

The story which was prefaced by this letter is typical but unheeded, worth recounting for the benefit of future alliances between finance and education.

A minor cause of Moholy's irritation was the businessmen who

155

suddenly turned Maecenas. The big industrialists who formed the Board of Directors were glad to leave the functions of an executive committee to smaller people whose vanity was flattered by being sponsors to a cultural enterprise that had aroused international comment. They now offered an unending stream of criticism and naïve advice to students, faculty, and maintenance personnel, founded on no more than the necromancy of the checkbook. But the basic misapprehension lay in the fact that the integration principle which worked so potently in the curriculum had been totally overlooked in the organization of the school. Moholy knew nothing about the American system of money-raising and endowment, solidly founded on man's propensity toward benevolence and tax evasion. It was no secret that the $110,000 on hand when Moholy signed a five-year contract with the Association would necessitate annual contributions of $90,000. He wrote in a letter on August 18, 1937:

> Do you know how much that is? That is 360,000 German Marks or 18,000 English Pounds. They are absolutely sure that they can raise this sum with their left hand, so to speak. The executive secretary whose job the fund-raising has been for the last twelve years gets ten per cent of all she collects. To make this percentage attractive she certainly has to be sure of herself. Money rarely impresses me, but the ease with which it seems available here is remarkable.

These were the financial facts Moholy knew. When the enrollment for the second semester added twenty-five more students to the day school and twenty to the night classes it seemed beyond question that the goal of an annual addition of seventy new students could be reached. This was Moholy's responsibility. Anything else, he had been told repeatedly, was none of his business.

But the evidence of sedition grew louder from week to week. A meeting of four dissatisfied students had been attended by the Executive Secretary of the sponsoring Association of Arts and Industries, who told a puzzled inquirer:

"We might have to close down for one semester to get rid of Moholy's contract."

Long after everyone else knew about it, Moholy, with

156

his protective lack of interest in hearsay and grapevine, became slowly aware of a planned campaign to undermine his prestige. True to his character, he fought off this knowledge as best he could. When one bewildered teacher reported that a member of the Executive Committee had accused Moholy of spending $134,-000 over the school budget, and darkly hinted at a financial collapse as a consequence, Moholy said:

"This Executive Committee acts like bad children who invent tall lies to show off with what looks like inside information. How could I spend even a dollar over the school budget when I've never signed a check? If there were any financial difficulties, the Board would inform me first."

But in the spring of 1938 it could no longer be concealed that the Association needed funds which had to come from other sources than the futile money-raising efforts of the Executive Secretary. Moholy's reaction was characteristic. He forgot his disappointment in not having been taken into the confidence of the Board, and he decided to raise the money himself, without the benefit of a ten per cent commission. With the blessing and the gratitude of the Board, and "with the knowledge but without the approval" of the Executive Committee (as the court action later stated), he planned a car trip through the Middle West and the East. His mission was to interest big industry in the Bauhaus idea. Moholy had almost no recommendations. All he could rely on for success were his personality—alertness, enthusiasm, Hungarian accent, and personal magnetism—and the sincerity with which he could plead the cause of American youth once he stood face to face with the man he was after. "The man he was after" is a cliché used advisedly because there are no other words to describe his man-hunt. From a Dun and Bradstreet directory he had selected nine companies in Michigan, Ohio, Pennsylvania, New York, and New Jersey. Of some he knew the name of the president, of many he didn't. But he saw them all, and, with the exception of one milling company in Michigan, he was never turned down completely.

The summer of 1938 showed all the symptoms of an approaching depression. The stock market was low; unemployment was rising, and—more symptomatic than the actual facts—

most businessmen fell into a psychological paralysis as they stared at the revived specter of 1930. It was an unpropitious moment to ask for donations, tax-exempt or otherwise. If Moholy wanted help it had to come from a collaboration offer rather than from a request for cash. As we went from State to State we mapped the strategy for the next interview. There was for instance Eastman Kodak in Rochester, New York. For once we had decided to shun the hated cabin camps, which fitted our carefully planned budget, but whose closeness to highway traffic undermined all rest. Extravagantly we planned to spend the night before the Kodak offensive at a resort on Lake Erie, in an old mansion on a peninsula far removed from highways and traffic. But, when we had settled down, a caravan of omnibuses arrived, carrying all the Woolworth employees of Rochester who had chosen this spot to celebrate their summer outing. It wasn't the Fourth of July but the symptoms were similar, aggravated by an intoxicated couple who had locked themselves in the only available bathroom on our floor, unwilling to be disturbed until the door had been broken down. When we stopped next morning opposite the main gate of the Eastman Kodak plant we hadn't slept an hour, and the day promised a good ninety-degree temperature. As Moholy vanished inside the factory grounds, he carried with him a small selection of photographic work done by him and the best of the students, several carbon copies of his article "Paths of the Unleashed Color Camera," and a smile of infinite confidence in the farsightedness of American industry. I was to wait in the car until he'd either concede that his mission had failed, or send out word in which hotel to meet him.

At seven in the evening, with the last of the workers leaving the plant, Moholy reappeared, exhausted but happy. He was amazed and considerably annoyed by the fact that I had found my nine-hour vigil without food or drink distracting. As we drove out of town, because he had decided to have a swim before eating supper, he told me the steps which had taken him, hour after hour, from the secretary of the public relations assistant to the office of President Lovejoy. At five in the afternoon, Mr. Lovejoy had called in the Vice-President in Charge of Production and together they had planned the visit of an expert to Chicago to investigate the possibilities for a large-scale program of collaborative research. In the meantime a substantial grant of photographic materials would be given.

"How did you do it?" I asked again, as I had asked uncounted times before.

"By not being discouraged," Moholy said, with obvious reference to my own spirits, still depressed from waiting, "and by not forgetting that my work is bigger than my vanity." After a long pause he added:

"And by making people feel important when I ask their help for an idea."

"All right, I understand that this works on the executive level. But there are so many little people one has to by-pass to get to places where ideas count."

"I don't by-pass them, I infect them. On a high level, ideas are cheap. But in the monotonous existence of a secretary or a foreman, they have glamour. The little people of America have a tremendous respect for ideas, especially when they don't fully understand them. You should have seen the face of the receptionist when I gave her a photogram as I left; she blushed as if it were a rose."

When we returned to Chicago in August, Moholy had seen men like Kettering and Knudsen, Schwab and Stettinius, and he had started a friendship with Frederick Keppel, director of the Carnegie Foundation, which lasted until they died within a few months of each other.

The trip had not yielded any cash contributions, for which in fact Moholy had not asked. But substantial grants of working materials for the photographic, the metal, and the plastics workshops had been promised. Two companies intended to refer packaging and lettering problems to the school, and the Carnegie Foundation sent an investigator shortly after our return from the East.

In his mail Moholy found a form letter, signed by the President of the Association of Arts and Industries, advising all faculty members of The New Bauhaus to look for other positions since the school would not reopen in fall. Moholy's first reaction was not despair at seeing his work wiped out but fury at the short-sightedness of the directors who had made this final decision without hearing his report on the new contacts he had opened up. In addition to the humiliating fact that he knew no more about the school policy than the janitor, he now appeared as an impostor who had solicited support for an institution already bankrupt. There wasn't a Board member available for comment or discussion. Not even the Executive Committee could be reached. Well-instructed secretaries informed Moholy that none of the directors would be back in town before Labor Day. The young faculty members of The New Bauhaus had no savings to fall back upon, and no chance to secure other positions so late in the summer. Since no salaries had been paid for two months, many of them were in acute embarrassment and we decided to share our resources. Much to the disgust of the uniformed elevator men, our apartment in Astor Street became a community enterprise for the common use of cooking gas, telephone facilities, canned food, and cigarettes.

When finally the Executive Committee consented to a meeting, Moholy asked for an immediate appeal to the big-name industrialists who had figured so conspicuously in the Association's first cables, and who adorned the front page of the Bauhaus catalogue. But haltingly at first, and brutally in the end, the Executive Committee made it clear that these men had given their names in lieu of financial contributions; that a famous name could be bought with a promise of no further solicitations. A list of sponsoring names for a nonprofit organization, Moholy finally understood, is purely ornamental.

The teachers felt that more was at stake than their pay checks. In a last attempt to save the Bauhaus idea they issued a "Declaration of Loyalty of the Members of The New Bauhaus for L. Moholy-Nagy":

We whose privilege it was to teach in The New Bauhaus during the first year of its existence wish to express our sense of the loss which education and the Chicago cultural community has sustained in the failure of The New Bauhaus to reopen this fall. The first year has convincingly shown the promise of the school under the leadership of L. Moholy-Nagy and we felt

160

that the future development of the school was secure. It came as a great surprise to hear late in summer that there was even a question as to whether the school was to reopen.

The very lateness of the decision worked great hardships upon students, upon the existing faculty, and upon those who had given up positions to become new members of the faculty. Whatever the circumstances, the fact remains that the Association of Arts and Industries has failed in its side of the venture, whether the failure lay in starting the school at all upon an inadequate financial and organizational basis or in being unable to continue the school at the moment when a promising future seemed assured.

In its failure the Association of Arts and Industries has placed difficulties in the way of realizing a significant educational venture whose program is congenial to the best educational leadership and the deepest educational needs of this country. It is to be hoped that this administrative failure will not be interpreted as a failure of The New Bauhaus itself, and that L. Moholy-Nagy and the Bauhaus idea, fitted as this idea is to play an important part in the liberation of American creativity in the arts, will receive from some other quarters the support necessary to insure its success.

> *Signed:* ALEXANDER ARCHIPENKO
> HIN BREDENDIECK
> DAVID DUSHKIN
> CARL ECKART
> RALPH GERARD
> GEORGE KEPES
> CHARLES W. MORRIS
> ANDI SCHILTZ
> H. H. SMITH

This declaration had no practical results, but it meant everything to Moholy's spirit. With the confidence of his co-workers assured, he set out on a battle which would be hard to match for tenacity and conviction. Within a month after the closing notice had been issued by the Association, he had secured for himself a position as art advisor for the mail-order house of Spiegel in Chicago. His salary of $10,000 he offered to the Association for the continuation of The New Bauhaus. He also submitted a plan for the solicitation of contributions from the many friends and acquaintances he had made during his first year. Their help, Moholy felt, could be secured if he were given a chance to follow the same tactics which had been so successful on his solicitation trip in the summer.

The industrialists forming the Board wanted to accept Moholy's plan to save the school. They acknowledged gratefully Moholy's irreproachable motives, and his success as a teacher. On August 30, 1938, the President of the Association wrote a letter to Walter Gropius in which he stated that economic conditions and not ideological failure had caused the closing of the school.

> . . . In October, 1937, we entered a very bad general business depression. We were forced to sell securities to operate the school, at 50% to 60% of their former value, and have been unable to secure additional funds from new sources or from sources that have subscribed liberally to the Association in the past.

> . . . I personally feel that if the school could be kept going on almost any basis for another year, our troubles would be over.

> . . . None of us relishes the idea of having our names connected with a school that is forced to close after one year of rather brilliant success due to the work of Moholy and his staff.

But the Executive Committee refused to give Moholy a free hand in saving the school, arguing that a revision of the Association's by-laws was undesirable. A consistent effort of the Board members would have been necessary to overcome this resistance and to prevent a futile and ludicrous attempt to save the Committee's reputation by forcing a lawsuit. But no one was willing to invest time in a problem outside the scope of benevolent sponsorship. While Alden Jewell, art critic of the *New York Times*, printed the revealing letter of the Association's President in the Sunday issue of January 1, 1939, followed by a reply from Moholy, the Association filed an answer to his claim for salary spiced with such a profusion of dark hints at immorality, fund embezzlement, plagiarism, and gossip, that the *Chicago Times* stated in a brief account: "The meat was rotten, says the bankrupt customer."

162

The final verdict was fully in favor of Moholy, award-
ing him in place of money a mortgage on the school building,
and distributing among the teachers whatever equipment hadn't
been removed by other creditors.

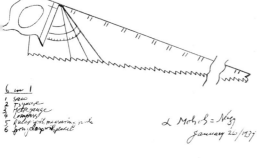

Fig. 54. A "six-in-one-saw"
designed by Moholy-Nagy
for the mail-order house
Spiegel, Inc., Chicago, 1939.
First sketch.

But The New Bauhaus was gone. Eighty students who
had applied for enrollment for the second year had to be told
that their hopes for a new art education were idle. While Moholy
designed hardware (Fig. 54) and revised the typography of a
mail-order catalogue, he pondered the lesson. His moral obligation toward the young people who had joined him during the first
year became almost an obsession. The Bauhaus idea had to go on,
and only a new school could prove that it had not failed. But even
if it had been available, sponsorship by industry under the usual
terms would never again tempt him; and the $3,000 left in his
bank account seemed a ridiculous capital after a $100,000 had
been lost within a year. The year 1938 ended on a note of defeat.

7   In his reply to the questionnaire of *The Little Review* Moholy had written: "My failings give me impetus in the fight; they sharpen my efforts." Four months after the closing of The New Bauhaus he had analyzed his failure to the extent that he could draw constructive conclusions.

OMAHA, NEB., Jan. 5, 1939

DEAR SIBYL:

I have five hours to wait for my next train. It is incredibly cold and dreary outside. I have been wandering through the streets of this most typical of all so-called typical American cities, reminiscing about the last time I was here, a little more than a year ago. At that time S. tried to interest the Chamber of Commerce in making our school part of their university. How superfluous it seemed then to consider such an offer after one had realized The New Bauhaus.

I'm not expecting a success from my talk with L. mainly because something in me doesn't want to leave Chicago. I have never been able to stand unfinished canvases, half-written books. You know yourself how you've kidded me about my eternal return to that certain canvasboard and the Silverit plate, no matter where you hide them. Chicago is not only an unfinished canvas. It is a smeared-over sketch which I have to clean up and set straight. Do you understand that?

It's not only that I want to clear my name. Of course I do. Any man would after what has been spread around about me. I want to get my hands back at the problems of art education before I've forgotten what I learned during the last year.

When I started in Chicago, I took the whole finished complex of Bauhaus philosophy and derived from it applications and details of instruction. What I have to do in the future is to think, not in terms of a fixed program, but in terms of students, in the *human* proportions of this country and this period. I'd let them investigate each visual problem as it presents itself— display, for instance, and the effect of light and color on trans-

164

parent materials, or positive-negative relationships in film and photogram. From these experiments, done with their own hands, they would come to conclusions about the general validity of our approach, its formative power. There should be more induction.

That is why I'm so doubtful about a job with any university. One day I'll *have* to accept one to keep us going because I know I cannot work for the industry without the compensation of teaching. But within a fixed curriculum, the result to which the student has to come is already determined. It's like cutting a wedge from a melon. It'll always fit exactly in the old place.

I'm going to catch an hour's sleep on a waiting-room bench before going on. I'm dog-tired, darling, but my head is very clear. Not much use for all this insight just now. The only consolation is that I can share it with you.

Love,
LACI

This trip to negotiate a university appointment brought no result because Moholy's terms seemed unacceptable to the head of the Art Department. But he was unconcerned about the outcome. Like a student who has discharged a distasteful duty, he felt infinitely relieved that he had proved to himself that he had no chance with academic institutions. The conflict between the conventional obligation to look for economic security and his pent-up drive toward a realization of his pedagogical convictions had been resolved. His drawn face became open and smiling again and he painted with increased vigor after his day's work in the mail-order house was done. One morning late in January he called to me from the bathroom. He kept a memo pad beside the mirror because he claimed that his best ideas came while he was shaving. The memo pad was covered with figures and names.

"We'll start our own school, if you're with me," he said pausing to watch my reaction. "We have $2,500 in the bank with which to start. My job at Spiegel's is good for another eight or nine months, and after that we'll be established. If we're careful, we should be able to make it."

I smiled. The detour was over. Moholy was on his way again.

Twenty-four hours after the new school had been

founded in our bathroom, five members of the previous New Bauhaus faculty met in our apartment. Gyorgy Kepes, George Fred Keck, Robert Jay Wolff, Andi Schiltz, and Charles W. Morris agreed to teach in the new school. They also agreed to teach without pay for at least one semester. It was a unique and risky arrangement because it meant that each man had to maintain a full-time outside position while experimenting with a new curriculum. Carl Eckart and Ralph Gerard, both full-time professors at the University of Chicago, joined this group of educational volunteers who kept faith without exception, missing not a day or a lecture in two full semesters. Moholy's total collaboration principle had met its supreme test.

When the question of a name for the school came up at the first meeting, Moholy made a vigorous speech for dropping, at least for the moment, the name *Bauhaus*.

"It is too often identified with Germany," he reasoned, "and it could be misconstrued as the slavish repetition of a program which we have adapted to a new age and a new mentality."

As I grinned happily, remembering our exchange of telegrams about the name *New Bauhaus*, Moholy inserted an aside in his exposition:

"If there's anything I can't stand, it's the typically female attitude of I-told-you-so."

It was decided that the name of the new venture would be "School of Design."

At the end of January, 1939, five hundred letters were mailed to former students and a list of names compiled from educational directories and club membership lists.

SCHOOL OF DESIGN
1210 ASTOR STREET, CHICAGO, ILLINOIS
TELEPHONE SUPerior 3413
The undersigned intend to open a *School of Design* and will start at the end of February, 1939, if sufficient demand is manifested to justify the effort.

We feel that the response of the American youth to the Bauhaus program has been such that it is worth while to form a new nucleus for an independent reliable educational center, where art, science, and technology will be united into a creative pattern.

166

To keep our independence it seems to be advisable to start modestly and to rely more than ever on the conscientious collaboration of each student.

The program remains the same as in The New Bauhaus in the last year. Tuition fee: 150 Dollars for a semester in the day school, 60 Dollars in the night class. Registration fee: 5 Dollars for both. Workshop fees: 20 Dollars.

We send this announcement to you as one who may be interested in our work—either in attending the school or in recommending it to others. The sooner we receive some idea of the volume of registration we may expect, the more efficiently planned our program can be.

Sincerely yours
L. MOHOLY-NAGY
Director
School of Design in Chicago

Two weeks after the mailing we had received sixty-two inquiries.

"But who'll back your school?" friends asked who heard about the new project. "You can't expect any students if you haven't a board of directors whose names give prestige to a school."

It was an inquiry ill fitting Moholy's mood.

"I won't have a board," he said. "I'll disprove the myth that a list of names from the social register or the financial page is the prerequisite for educational success. I'll ask a few men to give their moral support because they understand what I'm trying to do and want me to succeed because they share my convictions."

These men were: the philosopher John Dewey; Walter Gropius, the founder of the German Bauhaus and chairman of the Department of Architecture at Harvard; Dean Joseph Hudnut, of the Graduate School of Design at Harvard; Julian Huxley, Moholy's collaborator on the London Zoo film and Director of the London Zoölogical Society; W. W. Norton, New York publisher, who had brought out the first American edition of Moholy's *The New Vision*; William Bacharach, Chairman of the Committee on Education of the Chicago Association of Commerce; and Alfred

H. Barr, Jr., of the New York Museum of Modern Art, who, in sponsoring the Bauhaus Exhibition in 1938[1] had answered inquiries as to why he considered the Bauhaus so important, with nine reasons:

1. Because it courageously accepted the machine as an instrument worthy of the artist.
2. Because it faced the problem of good design for mass production.
3. Because it brought together on its faculty more artists of distinguished talent than has any other art school of our time.
4. Because it bridged the gap between the artist and the industrial system.
5. Because it broke down the hierarchy which had divided the "fine" from the "applied" arts.
6. Because it differentiated between what can be taught (technique) and what cannot (creative invention).
7. Because its building at Dessau was architecturally the most important structure of the 1920's.
8. Because after much trial and error it developed a new and modern kind of beauty.
9. And, finally, because its influence has spread throughout the world, and is especially strong today in England and the United States.

With sponsors and faculty secure, everything depended on finding a suitable building in which to house the School of Design. January of 1939 brought blizzards which heaped layer after layer of frozen snow and ice on Chicago's unswept streets. In our little Ford we scoured the Loop and the Near North Side of Chicago for empty space. It became routine to park with misgivings in a snowdrift before an empty building and for Moholy, Kepes, and Wolff to have to push the car away from the curb and often well down the street when the inspection was over. Finally a row of dark and dirty windows caught Wolff's attention, and, early in February, Moholy rented the second floor of 247 East Ontario Street on Chicago's Near North Side. It took an enthusiasm beyond the reach of discouragement or despair to see in this empty loft a future school of functional design. A commissary which had occupied the space years before had gone into bankruptcy and left

[1] Bauhaus 1919-1928, The Museum of Modern Art, 1938.

168

without cleaning up. The cockroaches had developed into a new species. They measured easily two inches in length and an inch in breadth and they were touchingly tame. The window panes were broken, and, as we stood in what might one day become an office, the snow drifted in onto the stone floor. The building was in receivership and the rent cheap, but the redecorating was our own responsibility. With buckets, scrubbing brushes, and bottles of disinfectant, we started to clean up. Two former students of the New Bauhaus joined the mopping faculty, and with their help window panes were replaced, walls whitewashed, and doors and shelves installed. There wasn't much more equipment to start with than the benches and lecture chairs Kepes had received in lieu of his salary from the Association of Arts and Industries. Wolff contributed an old desk with which to start an office, and every chair, table, and shelf that wasn't absolutely essential vanished from our apartment in Astor Street. Two huge iceboxes, which once had served the commissary, became darkrooms, protected by endless lengths of black satin which I sewed together, and stocked with Moholy's personal photographic equipment. The baking ovens, connected with a gallery that gave the empty halls an unusual architectural articulation, were earmarked as storage space for plywood, metal, and plastics—but for the time being they were empty.

It was almost ten o'clock on the night before the first registration day when the weary faculty and its assistants trudged down Ontario Street. On the other side of Michigan Avenue was an inviting sign: KUNGSHOLM, Swedish Smörgasbord. Without giving it another thought we walked in and heaped our plates with salads and cold meats.

Boldly Moholy ordered some wine, to drink to his crew. The next day, he mused, would decide the wisdom of our challenge. If, say, at least twelve students enrolled, our faith would be justified and the backbreaking labor of this last month would be a bow to American youth. If not. . . .

When the bill came we couldn't pay. Under the glare of the assembled waiters we pooled every penny in our possession, feeling foolishly and delightfully amused by our dilemma. It took Moholy's wristwatch as a pawn to release us. There was something almost symbolic in Moholy's emphatic assurance that he would bring the money the next day. As we parted we reassured each other that this had been our last day of trouble. Tomorrow would be a day of paying old debts.

One week later, on Washington's Birthday, eighteen day students assembled in the main drafting room to start their first semester with the School of Design; they were followed during the week by twenty-eight night students. In the small strongbox which I had kept since my high school days, and which now represented the school's safe, was $2,300. In an opening address, Moholy told the students:

> This is not a school but a laboratory in which not the fact but the process leading to the fact is considered important. We depend on everyone of you to give all you have to further this process. If you really give your best, the results will be extraordinary. I have found the best in every man to be pretty good. You as total human beings are the measure of our educational approach—not you as future furniture designers, draftsmen, photographers or instructors. Your brains as well as your hands, your emotions and your health, all this is part of the process. Don't think that you can neglect one to perfect the other. It would destroy the totality of your performance. You depend on each other to shape and mold what lies dormant in you. If you succeed in organizing among each other a working community, your combined strength will surpass in its results any technical school with the finest equipment. I believe in the creative supremacy of the human mind.

The curriculum differed from The New Bauhaus plan in more than the number of staff members and square feet of occupied space.[2] The ramifications of the first American program had been dropped. The emphasis was on fundamentals, not on complexity. The shopwork under Andi Schiltz and Eugene Bielawsky followed basically the original Bauhaus line, confining itself to the materials of man's immediate daily environment: paper, wood, metal, their tensile strength, pliability, structure, and surface treatment. The light and color workshop under the direction of Gyorgy Kepes had a clearer visual and intellectual structure than before. He related technique and the social impact of visual presentation

[2] For detailed descriptions of the work done at the School of Design see L. Moholy-Nagy, *Vision in Motion* (Chicago, 1947).

to each other. A tonal score leading from white-gray-black gradations to chromatic scales, color mixtures, and color textures,
awakened the student to a comprehension of visual organization.

The unique effectiveness of the school's program rested
on the fact that by necessity and choice one man encompassed all
that could be taught in one field. The atomizing specialization of
college training was avoided. Kepes, for instance, would develop
in his students a comprehension of all visual aspects from finger-
paints and kodachrome shots to camouflaging a city or designing
a sophisticated fashion display.

Robert Jay Wolff had as his field the problem of
volume in all forms and materials. His "volume family" became
a basic principle of sculptural analysis. Under his guidance

> . . . volume was transformed by a new contrapuntal rhythm,
> by the architecture of space and motion, by the total influence
> of environment. . . . We propel the motion of change. How
> does the object look, now, now, and now again? We don't
> care. *We ask how is it changing?*[3]

The Architecture Class under the chairmanship of
George Fred Keck moved from a space modulator in simple
three-dimensional relationships to "an orthographic projection"
of plan, elevation, section and perspective. Physical, psychological,
and socio-economic factors were co-ordinated in a step-by-step
development from the "primitive" dwelling of rural inhabitants
to the complex requirements of a city settlement.

Marli Ehrmann's Weaving Workshop translated the
color and tactile experiences of the Foundation Course. It produced textiles that answered practical and esthetic needs and
would lend themselves to mass production in new synthetic fibers.

Moholy's special delight was the Children's Class
which met on Saturday mornings under the guidance of Gordon
Webber. Boys and girls, ranging in age from four to twelve,
visited the Aquarium, the fruit markets, the Zoo (Fig. 55), or
looked at the light pattern of the city at night. Then they recreated
what they had seen in form and color. The "Locks of the Chicago
River," a "Deep-Sea Dream," a "Clock Ballet," inspired by a
dismantled alarm clock, were created in one winter. Saturday

[3] R. J. Wolff, *Curriculum for a Sculpture Class* (1941).

171

Fig. 55. Announcement for the Saturday Children's Class at the School of Design, Chicago, 1939, done by the children themselves.

morning should have been Moholy's time for rest; but around ten o'clock he'd take his Leica or his 16 mm. film camera and appear among the youngsters. Those particularly active in their work would be asked to his office to see his latest painting and get some Rosemarie chocolate. He jotted down well-formulated reactions to abstract art, delighted by such definitions as: "Oh, it's speed, it's airplane speed."—"This picture isn't empty, it's painted air." —"That's easy to see: it's a picture of tumbling."—or his daughter's stern rebuff of an adult who had called the color print of a landscape a picture: "This is no picture, this is a story. A picture is what my Daddy does."

Due to the architectural peculiarities of the school building, lectures had to be scheduled so that they wouldn't interfere with workshop instruction. While the students finished their color or form problems, they couldn't help listening to a discussion on Economics with Maynard Krueger, or on Sociology with Lloyd W. Warner. It was integration by necessity, drawing each student into the whole orbit of the school.

172

Occasionally all instruction had to stop—drowned out by the beat of a hundred tapping feet on the ceiling. The practice room of the Chez Paree Night Club was on the floor above, supplying variations of music from hot jazz to a Viennese waltz. Excess suds from the night club's kitchen seeped down the drain pipes and formed pools and rivulets on our worn stone floor. But the most obvious nuisance was an all-pervading odor of grease and frying meat which annoyed the satisfied and tortured the hungry.

For four months I was secretary, bookkeeper, registrar, and auxiliary janitor. Conscientiously I entered money received on the left side of a little black book, and money spent on the right, feeling very efficient when at week's end the cash tallied with my summation of credit and debit. But when at the beginning of the first summer session office help could be hired, my efforts were deemed totally inadequate. A bookkeeper, working a few hours each night for a fee which he invariably donated to the school, tore his hair when I couldn't remember whether a certain sum had come under capital investment, discounts, general expenditure, or any of a dozen other headings. The pedantic mysticism of bookkeeping, I decided, would be forever beyond my comprehension.

The $2000 we had invested in basic equipment, rent, and a minimum of publicity, was gone. The next step was to induce the businessmen of Chicago to donate machinery, materials, and services. We had no time to wait for "connections" to function, and for telephone calls of recommendation to pass from one manufacturer to another. Moholy selected from the classified telephone book firms who manufactured woodworking machinery, small tools, plywood, and engravings. Then he set out to visit firm after firm. He still hadn't learned to drive, and I became very much at home in my car, writing with gloved hands a novel about Germany's political history while I waited. At the end of 1939 Moholy had solicited basic equipment for the workshops, and printing services for a richly illustrated catalogue.

The lesson learned from this experiment was simple and timely. The donation and endowment policy of higher education excluded the businessman of medium means from participation. A firm with a carefully balanced minimum budget seemed

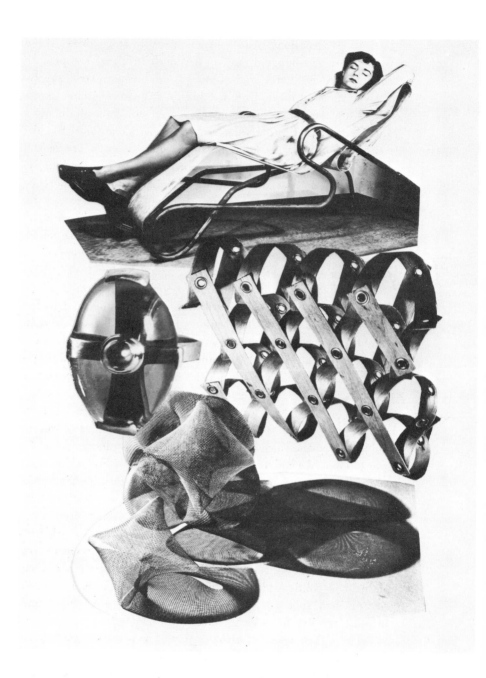

Fig. 56. Registered inventions made by students of the School of Design, Chicago, 1939/43: elastic plywood chair; self-magnifying pearl and Plexiglas ring; wood inner-spring mattress; cushioning for soldier's helmet.

rarely capable of contributing cash to a benevolent cause without having to go through a tedious process of reallotment. Gifts in kind were more easily granted for such plausible activities as research, experimentation, and promotion. The inherent American interest in technology and construction, and the common pride in educational institutions, could be utilized for material contributions on a large scale. When Moholy died, the Institute boasted workshops which were suited to almost any form of design research, and none of the equipment had been bought.

The results produced during the first two years of the School of Design justified not only Moholy's exhausting efforts but also the contributions made by a dozen small and medium-sized firms. Margaret De Patta, now a leading jewelry designer, utilized Kepes' instruction in the behavior of light to develop a new method of setting stones and pearls into a magnifying matrix, providing brilliant visual effects. Wire-bending exercises were applied by a student co-operative to the production of elastic wire-mesh cushions which, joined together, served as shock absorbers. Orin Raphael gave the mobile and paper-cut structures their logical application in a new longchair, and Charles Niedringhaus and Jack Waldheim developed a new line of plywood furniture. Within two years the students of the School of Design filed seventeen applications for patents, and an uncounted number of small inventions were incorporated into the daily workshop production (Fig. 56).

These were the external results of group co-operation. The more significant success showed in human relations. Richard Filipowski, who graduated in 1944, recounted in a letter how Moholy handled the frictions and complaints which cropped up among a group of high-strung individuals:

> Anyone could go into his office and air his grievances, no matter how late the hour or how tired the director. Everyone coming back from these conferences smiled, his spirits heightened and his energies renewed. "Well, what did he say?" we would inquire. "What's his opinion on the case?"

> And the complainer would suddenly realize that he hadn't had a chance to speak about his troubles. Moholy had asked him about his health, his family, his living conditions; he had

175

shown his latest picture or photogram. He often asked the visitor's advice on a sentence or an expression in a manuscript or he read a paragraph from his book in progress. Gradually he'd start to discuss the school aims, and the student—although he received no answer to his query—went away with the conviction that Moholy had known his complaint beforehand and had chosen this roundabout way to supply an answer.

At the bottom of the infinite faith we had in Moholy was the fact that he never criticized the work of a student in terms of good or bad. Even the poorest work had a fragment of merit which—Moholy emphasized—could be developed with imagination and industry. Nothing was all bad; each idea contained a spark of quality.

This could have been termed simply as a teaching technique. But it really was much more. It was an expression of Moholy's deep-rooted optimism, based on his faith in the validity of the human mind, and on his inexhaustible joy of constant discovery.

The School of Design won many prizes in national competitions for textiles, posters, and ideas for display. Decorations for Chicago's Architects' Ball in 1941 were furnished as a group project, a woman's apparel store was designed, and a special light display for a hotel bar was invented. Each winter brought a Fancy Ball and a Santa Claus Party, given by the students in the school, where Moholy judged costumes and presents ranging from a personification of Léger's "Abandoned Farm," complete with broken wheel, barbed wire, and sweet potato, to a "Constructivist Moth Bag," looking like a mobilized Mondrian painting.

The School of Design experiment refuted the belief that endowment and expensive equipment determine educational success. After the hierarchical character of the German Bauhaus, and the deceptive opulence of industrial sponsorship in the American New Bauhaus, Moholy proved to himself and his staff that education is solely the responsibility of the teacher, and that no material aid can take the place of the sustained power of personal inspiration.

Wealthy Chicagoans who had been so enthusiastic about Moholy's coming felt little inclination to accept the court verdict against the Association of Arts and Industries. Cause and

176

victim were readily identified, and our social contacts broke off. The exception was Walter Paepcke, President of the Container Corporation of America, who had been one of the trustees of the Association. In the spring of 1939 he offered Moholy a vacant farm and two acres of land on a purely nominal lease if the School of Design wanted to conduct a summer school in the country. When Moholy told me about the offer I was delighted.

"I want a place where the children can get away from the dangers and restrictions of the city," I said, looking down into the filthy back alleys of Chicago's Gold Coast. "If only they can be in the country for a few months each year."

"This is a plan for a school, not for a nursery," Moholy said reproachfully. "If we accept the house we'll do it because it gives us a chance to carry cooperation and integration to a point that can never be reached within a city group."

But it was obvious that neither he nor any of the teachers could add the organization of a summer school to their schedule. They were greatly overburdened with teaching and the necessity of supplementing their minimum salaries by outside commissions.

"You're the only one who could do it," Moholy said. "If you want a country place for the children, you'll have to work for it."

"I accept," I said, feeling as sure of my ability to shoulder this new obligation as when I had pledged myself to the support of our first child.

The "Rumney Place," five miles out of Somonauk, Illinois, and two hours drive from Chicago, was badly run down. The last tenant had abandoned it five years earlier, and nothing had been done to prevent the rapid disintegration that befalls unoccupied buildings in the country. The main part of the house was over a hundred years old (Fig. 57); the ancient beams in the basement sagged precariously, and the window frames broke like brittle cake when one tried to lift them. There was no plumbing, no electricity, no water—but there were beautiful old trees in the yard, acres of meadowland and open timber on each side, and a deep ringing calmness in the air. Blissfully unaware of

177

Fig. 57. Main Building of the School of Design Summer Camp near Somonauk, Illinois.

labor conditions in the country, I decided that the restoration of the farm would be done with "typical American speed." But in spite of my exasperation, all negotiations for repair work had to be couched in an abundance of conversation, starting with the weather and leading slowly toward the core of the matter. It would have been highly improper to conduct business in any other way. There still wasn't any wiring, and water was pumped from a temperamental gasoline pump when the first students arrived. But we could offer some comfort, thanks to Frederick Spiegel, Moholy's employer in the mail-order business, who had contributed furniture and appliances at a generous discount. James Prestini, instructor in Woodcraft, an untiring friend of the school throughout its existence, installed his superb collection of tools along the walls of the workshop barn, and Gyorgy Kepes and Robert Jay Wolff had planned a curriculum for visual design and sculpture that utilized all elements of the outdoors.

Our newly established Art Camp, far off in an unknown

178

corner of the country, advertising a collaborative program that differed from anything offered by other summer schools, at first attracted predominantly such students as were either afraid of competing with the average crowd or incapable of adjusting socially to their environment. Of the thirteen men and women who enrolled for the first season, all but four were, in one way or another off the beaten psychological track. There was a doe-eyed divorcee with an insatiable hunger for male attention; a young Texan who confessed that his sole reason for attending the school was his mother's exasperation at his ravenous appetite; and an Amish schoolteacher who had brought all her vociferous prejudices and repressions. They quarreled among each other and complained to me, venting their tensions less in creative work than in fights that often reached the hand-to-hand stage. I had not yet learned to evaluate dissatisfaction and bickering as symptoms of emotional instability rather than well-founded criticism, and in my efforts to meet all demands I exhausted my emotional and mental resources.

Each Friday when Moholy arrived at the farm the black sheep turned an innocent white, listening attentively to his lantern-slide lectures, following his corrections of their work, and joining in a mannerly fashion social gatherings at the Old Mill, a lovely tavern of prohibition-day notoriety in the meadows of the Fox River Valley. He paid no attention to my reports of the troubled situation during the week. The first summer session of the School of Design in Chicago posed new problems with substitute teachers and vacation schedules, and his commercial work absorbed the rest of his energies. With a belligerent indifference he refused to become interested in any problems not related to his own work. Once he had delegated power, he rejected all further responsibility. To recognize this unsympathetic attitude as self-defense had been one of the hardest tasks of my life. It demanded a self-restraint which doesn't come easily to a young woman in love.

At the end of the summer session I was deeply discouraged with the results. For once my optimism in shouldering responsibilities had been excessive. The labor put into this project seemed wasted, and I was infinitely relieved when the experiment

179

was not repeated the following summer. Alfred Neumeyer, head of the Art Department at Mill's College in Oakland, invited Moholy and the faculty to conduct a summer school there along Bauhaus lines. Late in June, 1940, Moholy and I set out for California. It was a perfect trip, full of long silences, the common enjoyment of visual discovery, and intellectual stimulus. We stopped on the desolate salt flats of Utah to hear the radio report of the fall of France, which we both loved as a spiritual homeland. We followed some deer off the Grand Canyon Road at three in the morning; and when our differential broke down at the top of a Nevada mountain, we succumbed to gambling while waiting for repairs. I became an expert at stopping dead-short at sixty miles per hour when I heard the familiar cry, indicating that Moholy had spotted a "photogenic" vista, and I melted patiently in 108 degrees heat while he recorded every angle of the Boulder Dam, and every interrelationship of nature and technology.

By the time we arrived at Mills College, Moholy had lost most of his English vocabulary. During the trip he had insisted on speaking only German, which he loved. But even though he had lost his facility of speech, he had regained the spirit of high adventure which had been his most distinguished characteristic as a young instructor. He consented to a schedule of thirty teaching and lecturing hours a week. Together with five of his best teachers he put a group of eighty-three students through an intensified Bauhaus curriculum, including every workshop and every major exercise. Late at night or on the few free Sundays, we would drive into San Francisco. We loved this unusual town, its clean contemporary structure, the golden color of the wild oats on the hillsides, and the red bark in the forests. In his painting "Mills #2, 1940" (Fig. 58), Moholy has translated the color-light interplay of the Bay region into a composition of glowing transparency. For the first time since we had left Europe, the atmosphere of a city seemed filled with an enjoyment of nonmaterial values—art, music, theatre—not as demonstrations of wealth and privilege, but as group projects of young people and of the community. The museums, co-operative units, studios, and schools offered a hospitality of the spirit that had been unknown to us in America.

"One day I'll come back," Moholy said as we drove

180

Fig. 58. Mills #2, 1940. Plexiglass Space-Modulator.

over the Bay Bridge for the last time. "One day I'll have $10,000 in the bank and I'll spend two years in San Francisco."

We arrived back in Chicago without a penny. To give the students at Mills the full Bauhaus curriculum, Moholy had split his own salary with his staff. We had to borrow money to pay the rent and buy a month's supplies. But the School of Design had established its reputation, and a dozen students who had attended the summer session at Mills enrolled for the fall term to finish the work they had started during the summer.

The discouraging experiences of the first summer term on the Somonauk school farm never repeated themselves. A very different group came in the summer of 1941 and the following years. The workshop collaboration became one of the most fruitful and creative branches of the school work. By an unwritten agreement, students of graduate ability worked in the country, while the younger crowd preferred the city and the greater technical facilities of the Chicago workshops. Sometimes four or five heads of college art departments lived on the farm, combining intensive work with the quiet recreations of country life. Once it was organized, the summer session became Moholy's greatest enjoyment. The abundant nature around us presented an unending variety of form and function. There were the smooth, many-formed pebbles in the creek and the gravel pit, the cattle bones that were dug up in the fields, and the texture of living bark. Mushrooms, fungi, wasps' nests, fragments of shell from bird's eggs, piled up on shelves and tables and rotted quietly in the hot summer air. They were magnificent photographic material. A cabbage leaf, eaten into intricate designs by a caterpillar, was as fascinating as a tangle of rusted wire on a slab of limestone. The wooden floors in the old house had worn hollow, the hard substance of the wood showing like the veins on an old hand. Moholy was fascinated by this process of wood attrition, and, with pencil, crayon, and colored chalk, he did rubbings on paper and canvas to study the texture and the rhythm of line and color (Fig. 59). After his return to the city each Monday night, the small working community was noticeably hushed. For the following four days they devoted themselves with silent industry to an exemplification of

181

what they had learned over the week end, presenting the results proudly and anxiously on Friday night. When the war created a food problem and the lack of help forced the discontinuation of the farm summer sessions in 1944, we felt we had lost one of the most joyfully rewarding aspects of our work.

Fig. 59.   Colored wood rubbing of old floor boards in Somonauk farmhouse, 1942. Black and Orange.

The School of Design had completed six regular terms when Moholy faced another threat to his work. During the fall term of 1941 more than half of the teachers and students had to leave for the Armed Forces, and after Pearl Harbor the exodus became almost universal. Plywood, photographic materials, metal, and paper rose in price and soon became unobtainable. Highly paid factory jobs lured away maintenance personnel and office help. Moholy had little time to map a new strategy to save his

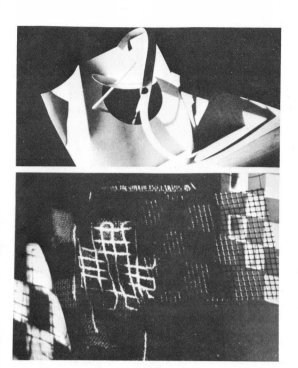

Fig. 60. School of Design, Chicago, 1943. Camouflage workshop exercise. Instructor: Gyorgy Kepes.

school. He had to think fast. Eight weeks after Pearl Harbor, when the spring semester of 1942 opened, he had found three connecting links between the program of the School of Design and the war effort. The analysis of visual elements, and the psychology of light and color perception, could be applied to camouflage techniques. The creative co-ordination of hand and eye, shaping new forms and exploring new uses for known materials, could serve disabled veterans in occupational therapy; and, thirdly, the knowledge of wood and its infinite adaptability could lead to a replacement of metal parts by wood forms. There were many instances of quick conversion in American industry. What distinguished Moholy's program was its organic incorporation into the school curriculum, providing students, not with a curtailed or compromised version, but with extended vistas and applications.

On December 19, 1941, Moholy was appointed to the Mayor's personal staff in charge of camouflage activities in the Chicago area. During blizzards and rainstorms, in fog and in brilliant sunlight, he had to take flights to absorb air views of

183

the city under diverse weather conditions. While he fought air sickness, which he never overcame completely, he pondered how to conceal the vastness of Lake Michigan with a simulated shore line and floating islands. In January, 1942, the School of Design became a certified school for camouflage personnel. As head of the Camouflage Workshop, Gyorgy Kepes produced a wide range of new techniques and concepts. When they were displayed for the first time in 1943, they aroused wide attention (Fig. 60).

The Occupational Therapy Course entailed unending visits to hospitals, rounds of lectures and conferences, and strategic battles with the wardens of charity. Moholy's interest in the therapeutical aspects of crafts and design had always been part of his teaching. In his books *Malerei-Photographie-Film* and *The New Vision*, he had pointed out the psychological blocks to a fearless realization of man's creative urge. Dr. Franz Alexander, whose friendship with Moholy dated back to the days when both had been students of Alexander's famous father at the University of Budapest, offered advice and help. As head of the Chicago Institute for Psychoanalysis he had made psychosomatic interrelationships his life-study. He had often sent to Moholy patients who required creative work as part of their treatment, and he now consented to give a series of introductory lectures to the students of Occupational Therapy at the School of Design. During the first war year, Moholy built up a program that aimed at

> . . . an understanding of the handicapped as having the same potential source of creative energies as is inherent in every human being. His best qualities have to be considered and brought into the open in order that he may not only try to restore the standard of his previous state but attempt to rise beyond it to a higher efficiency and a higher productive level.[4]

Moholy's goal was

> . . . a planned vocational rehabilitation following hospitalization. The person handicapped as a result of an accident, having been imbued with the idea that he may rise above his former capability, will orient himself toward such an accomplishment.

[4] "Better Than Before," by L. Moholy-Nagy, *The Technology Review*, Volume XLVI, Number 1, November 1943 (Massachusetts Institute of Technology); also available as a reprint.

Naturally, in practice, one should not hope for superhuman results. But we cannot accomplish anything by teaching a single craft. The patient has to be stimulated by a well-rounded program in order that he may be activated to a full evaluation of his own situation. He can then attempt to strive for the new goal which is to realize the maximum extent of his capacities in the industrial world.[4]

Dr. Konrad Sommer, head of the Illinois Neuropsychiatric Institute, and Franz Alexander supported Moholy's ideas. They sent students, nurses, and social workers to attend classes at the School of Design and they arranged for Moholy's appearance before several medical conventions. For two years a selected group worked on extended applications of the principles laid down in "Better Than Before" for the training of occupational therapists. But the appointed guardian angels of the crippled and the handicapped didn't like Moholy's ideas. They resented his efforts to take rehabilitation out of the grasp of charity and incorporate it in the Social Security Act; they ridiculed his demand for a training program that was to include psychology, art and technology to produce better therapists; and they fought back with patriotic clichés when Moholy proposed that the disabled soldier, the injured worker, and the mentally deficient should come under the same rehabilitation program, securing in this way an equal standard of professional assistance. Wounded veterans had to keep on listening to benevolent ladies who considered basket-weaving or lamp-shade decorating adequate work for a mature man, and the bane of the injured war worker remained the social worker of whom George Edward Bartin had written in 1919:

> It is unreasonable to suppose that an anemic, neurasthenic woman, bored to death with her own life and incapable of firm decisions or strenuous endeavor, should be able to instil into the mind of a sick man the very qualities which she herself lacks.

But like all seeds scattered on the earth, Moholy's concrete suggestions germinated in many different places where the nurses and young doctors who attended his courses now worked. They also helped, together with the Camouflage Workshop, to see the

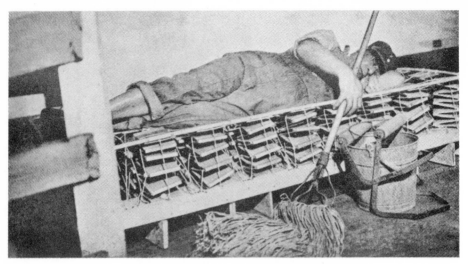

Fig. 61. Wood-Spring Mattress developed at the School of Design for Seng and Co., Chicago, 1943.

School of Design through a severe crisis caused by dwindling manpower and increased expenses.

The third project, "Wood-Springs," developed organically from woodcuts, made by hand and machine, which gave to a rigid board a rubber-like elasticity. Once cutting, laminating, and gluing had been carefully explored, it was a logical step to find a practical application for this unexploited quality of man's oldest material. In *Vision in Motion* Moholy reported on the twenty-four different types of wood-spring developed in the school workshop. Finally Jack Waldheim, in collaboration with a Hungarian carpenter, Kalman Toman, who had the unobtrusive genius of the craftsman of old, arrived at a spring which could be easily produced and which provided the comfortable elasticity of a metal box-spring. Frank J. Seng, a Chicago manufacturer, found it worth his while to supply a set of special machinery and a working capital of $10,000 to produce the first nonmetal all-wood bedspring (Fig. 61). When in July, 1943, the *Saturday Evening Post's* Robert Yoder wrote a report about Moholy and his school,[5] he photographed the janitor, Gus, taking a noon nap on the comfortable contraption.

Prices rose and the income from tuition fees dwindled. Personnel came and left in quick succession, and the students who remained were worried more about their draft status than about

[5] "Are you a Contemporary?"

their work. It was then that Moholy remembered Frederick Keppel, President of the Carnegie Corporation of New York, who had listened so sympathetically to the report on the American New Bauhaus. In a long letter Moholy explained the new aspects of the curriculum, adding a portfolio of clippings and illustrations. But the result was negative. The war, Mr. Keppel replied, had put before the Foundation tasks of greater urgency. Art education would have to wait for peace and the re-establishment of normal conditions. Two days after the depressing news, Moholy inquired about our bank balance. This was surprising because we had come to an agreement that he was not to be bothered with our personal money. The school budget, he had insisted, was all the financial worry he could take. Our income tax, checks, and bills were to be my burden. When I told him that we owned about $1,000 he was delighted.

"Splendid! I'll go to New York Sunday night. Please get a Pullman ticket."

"But why go now? You're so desperately needed at the school?"

"This is more important. After all, money has to come first."

"Money? Do you have any prospects?"

"Sure. The Carnegie Corporation."

"But they have just refused. They said quite clearly that they have to support the war effort."

"That's just it." Moholy grinned. "I'll take them up on their own statement. I'll argue our place in the war effort to a point where they can't deny their support without looking downright unpatriotic."

Three months later the School of Design received a grant of $5,000 from the Carnegie Corporation which was followed in one year's time by an equal amount; and in June, 1942, the Rockefeller Foundation's amicable and progressive directors, John Marshall and David Stevens, succumbed to a similar campaign of attrition and granted $7,500 for photographic and motion-picture equipment.

At the end of the spring semester, 1942, the first class of seven students graduated with bachelor's degrees. They had

studied eight semesters at The New Bauhaus and the School of
Design. In his commencement address Moholy could proudly
state that

> . . . the past four years have proved the workability of the
> Bauhaus Idea in American vocational training. It was the spirit
> of collaboration between students and teachers that made us.
> Everyone working here, from the office force to the visiting
> professors of the University of Chicago, realized the adversities,
> but they also realized that at all times our goal was greater
> than our obstacles.
>
> Since the outbreak of the war, students and faculty have been
> confronted with queries as to whether our work is not a luxury
> in times of strife. We have been urged to "teach something
> real" instead of insisting on experimental work with pencil,
> brush, camera, tool, and loom. It is in answer to this question
> that I want to define our moral obligations toward society.
>
> It *is* a great privilege to be allowed the exercise of one's skill
> and ambition in times of war when millions die and additional
> millions barely survive. But it is a privilege granted to you by
> society, an investment made for the future benefit of man.
> You are the men and women on whose sincerity and effort
> depends the future progress of education. It doesn't matter
> whether you make wood-springs or chairs, design a house or
> a poster, work with veterans or children. It is all education,
> adding to the crude struggle for physical survival, the qualities
> that distinguish man from beast.
>
> Democracy is based upon an exchange of equivalents. It is the
> obligation of those who were permitted to develop their finest
> capabilities to exchange one day their creative skill for the
> productive and harmonious existence of a new generation.

8 When the day was done, Moholy went home to paint. During a normal week he had taught Advanced Product Design, Motion Picture, a seminar on Modern Art; and a night class in Painting. There were an unscheduled number of hours which had been spent on administrative detail, solicitation of contributions, student counseling, and the commercial design work which provided our financial support. During the war years there were long meetings with the local Office of Civilian Defense, hearings on draft deferments, and weekly sessions with the American Federation of Democratic Hungarians.

This group was a curious assembly of doctors, lawyers, shopkeepers, artisans, and workmen, who had no more in common than their Hungarian nationality and their devotion to Moholy. Driven by the same nostalgic loyalty which had seemed so ridiculous to him in his friend Eisenstein ten years earlier, Moholy tried "to form a permanent organization to work for the defeat of Hitler and the liberation of Hungarians from despotic rule, and to assist in the undercover democratic movement in Hungary." It was the ultimate aim of this group to establish Count Michael Karolyi, Hungarian land-reformer and exile, as Prime Minister of a democratic Hungarian government. Moholy spoke before steel-mill workers in Gary and coal miners in Pennsylvania; he sat through endless amateur shows which are the peculiar obsession of all foreign language groups; he went to Washington to enlist the support of Eleanor Roosevelt for the cause; and he spent hours on the telephone, trying to pacify the fiercely individualistic tempers of his followers.

Around ten o'clock at night he came home, ate a substantial dinner, and started to paint. He usually worked until one o'clock, and he painted each Sunday. If he had to travel, or if visitors and invitations cut down his schedule, he worked until

189

two or three in the morning. On train and airplane trips, and on the rare days when he didn't go to the school, he dictated the manuscript of *Vision in Motion*.

He never painted in his office, but each morning he picked up the half-finished work from the night before and took it to school. This became our badge, the special attribute that distinguished us from thousands of other couples driving toward the city at 8:30 in the morning. On the back seat of our car rested an abstract painting, and beside it sat a workman's lunch pail. Moholy was a lover of fine food, and the average restaurant meal was unacceptable to him. He preferred a box lunch of cold meat, salad, and fruit.

In a burst of optimism I had once put a narrow couch into his office, hoping that he would lie down and rest between day and night work. He never did but the gray cloth of the cover offered an ideal background for a canvas, a water color, or a piece of sculpture.

"I work subconsciously during the day," Moholy said once when I objected to a particularly heavy piece of plastic which we had lugged back and forth for weeks. "When I look up from my desk, my eyes catch form and color. I never think about it consciously during the day. But by nighttime the next step has clarified itself. It's like a meal, left to simmer slowly on a corner of the stove."

There were few cabs during the war years, and when I was not free to pick him up at night, Moholy relied on a lift or the bus to come home. But there were occasions when no car was available, and the crowded buses wouldn't take on a passenger with a painting half his own size. Then Moholy walked four miles, protecting his canvas with his coat.

He rarely used an easel; it was an emergency device to which he resorted only if the canvas or the plastic sheet were too big to fit on the dining-room table, on my desk, or in his favorite spot—the floor space between couch and bookshelves in the living room. On Sundays he took his work into the nursery, painting while the children played and talked, listening to their fairy tales and radio programs. He liked the original Oz books with their fantastic color imagination, and he never tired of

190

Mortimer Snerd on Edgar Bergen's show. He had great sympathy for the unsophisticated yokel lost among the wisecracking city dwellers. From his rural childhood he had retained a deep suspicion of verbal smartness, and he delighted in straight earthly fun. "Shaggy-Dog Stories"—of talking animals and dumb humans —were his favorites, and after his death I found that several pages of his notebook were filled with key-word reminders, such as: "Performer, dog, parrot, piano, ventriloquist." Now and then Hattula and Claudia were permitted to stipple the corner of a canvas or scratch a line on a plastic surface. Every picture made by his daughters was carefully dated and collected, and he composed a radiant collage around one of Hattula's childish figures. When he wrote *Vision in Motion* he included work of both of his children,[1] and their visual progress was a steady point of reference in his lectures.

Plexiglass for sculptures and space modulators was heated in the kitchen oven. When he was ready for the execution of a new piece while the Sunday roast was in the making, the dinner was postponed and we all participated in the creation. Moholy had tried to mold the hot plastic while wearing gloves, but it impaired his sensitivity, and the fabric left flaws on the polished surface. So he bent it with his bare hands, jumping wildly up and down while he burned his fingers. The children took his agonized leaps for antics, and watched delightedly. After each twist had been realized, the hot piece had to be held in shape until it hardened sufficiently to be submerged in warm water in the bath tub where it cooled off slowly and became solid again. Many hands were needed to keep the plastic form from collapsing, and the children became experts in applying a strictly prescribed pressure.

Moholy's distaste for working in solitude never changed. As on that night in 1932 when he had conquered the paralysis of political defeatism and had again started to paint, I remained the lion in the cell of St. Hieronymus. When he fell ill in 1946 and had to agree to a vacation in the country, he complained bitterly that the smallness of the rooms and the poor light conditions in our old farmhouse near Somonauk would make

[1] Pp. 118, 324.

painting impossible. I decided to fix a barn loft as a studio. The big openings through which the grain had been loaded were screened. Easel, working table, stools, were brought from the city, and the rough floor boards were covered with linoleum in case he wanted to paint on the floor. But he never used it. He did not even look at it. Unexpectedly, he settled down on the kitchen porch of the Somonauk farmhouse. There he was close to the smell of food, the clatter of pots and pans, the back door at which appeared neighbors, peddlers, and strangers who had lost their way, and to the clicking of my typewriter. He didn't speak while he painted, and he never participated in the conversations. It was the sustaining atmosphere of togetherness that he needed.

When Moholy had joined the Bauhaus in 1923, he had already realized two distinctly different directions in his painting. His Expressionistic period—unconscious during his war years, and conscious in Budapest and Vienna—had come to an end shortly after he arrived in Berlin. When he dropped the realistic model, he also dropped analytical color and form representation inspired by Cubism. It had accomplished its task of "shaking his visual lethargy," and it had taught him to observe the structural reality of matter. Cubism and Expressionism had been the grindstones on which to sharpen his senses. Beyond that they offered him no development toward unexplored goals.

The second period, characterized by Suprematist and Neoplasticist influences, had lasted approximately three years, until 1924. The Suprematist attempt to render objectified emotion through "the suprematism of the plane (with the additional element of the Suprematist straight), and the suprematism of space (with the additional element of the Suprematist square)"[2] had emphasized a mental and visual discipline that transcended purely personal expression. Through Malevich, Moholy had grasped economy of means and universality of meaning. He economized on line and plane, and started to think in terms of an objectified suprapersonal appeal.

[2] Kasimir Malevich, *Die gegenstandslose Welt* (*The Nonobjective World*) (*Bauhaus Bücher*, No. 11, Munich, 1927).

Fig. 62. "A II," oil on canvas, 1923. Showing strong Suprematist influence.

Neoplasticism, through the work of Piet Mondrian, added tension and harmony to Moholy's comprehension. Mondrian had written:

> It is important to discern two sorts of equilibrium. First, a static balance, and second, a dynamic equilibrium. The first maintains the individual unity of particular forms; the second is the unification of forms, or of elements of forms, through continuous opposition.[3]

Mondrian's attempt to establish a new "absolute reality" through the rectangle and the three primary colors, confirmed and clarified Moholy's intuitive knowledge of the laws of tension and balance. Through Mondrian he understood structure as an intrinsic law to be revealed in form relationships, and not an intellectual concept to be imposed from without.

1923 was a year of adjustment to the Bauhaus and its specific tasks, but by 1924 Moholy had clarified the fundamentals from which to compose his own visual language. It could neither

[3] Piet Mondrian, *Plastic Art and Pure Plastic Art* (Wittenborn and Co., New York, 1947).

193

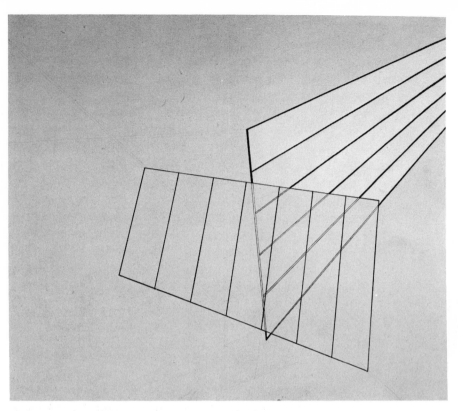

Fig. 63. "B 100," oil on canvas, 1928.

be the illusive reality of traditional painting, nor the illustrative rendering of simultaneity and motion as with the Cubists and Futurists. His vision would transcend Suprematism and Neoplasticism because it surpassed structural harmony and spatial tension with a rhythmic interplay of light, color, and form, unafraid of emotional connotations. And it envisioned beyond the dynamic third, a kinetic fourth dimension. For twenty years, between 1923 and 1943, Moholy was like a gem-cutter, adding with infinite patience facet after facet to his intuitive vision. At the end of his life, in one moment of total fulfillment, the six faces of his magic stone were all visible. Its transparent planes, worked to perfection by a lifetime of craftsmanship, referred to one center—light—perceived from six different angles.

The first facet had been the sharp surgical cut toward fundamental simplicity, the *tabula rasa* cleared of the remnants of literary symbolism in art. The canvas "A II, 1923" (Fig. 62),

194

is a factual statement of form in space. It confirms the visual reality of line and color as self-expressive and nonsymbolic. The Suprematist cross, and the rectangular harmonies of Neoplasticism are evident, but a first attempt at superimposition is already visible to indicate the next facet—space penetration through transparency.

"B 100" is the accomplished effort toward this space penetration which had started to occupy Moholy in 1923. Three-dimensionality here is no longer identical with the illusion of a perspective view into nature. Depth-creating lines, and the finest gradations of superimposed gray and white pigment, are the perspective elements to render space. The slightest change in the position of the two grills would annul the third dimension. The emotional experience of flight into depth, and the harmonious equilibrium of pure form, have merged in "B 100" (Fig. 63).

To realize the first two facets of his vision, Moholy had relied more on line than on color, and more on transparency than on pigment. With "Large Aluminum Picture, 1926" (Fig. 64) begins a third phase, color, that allowed for infinite variations. The formal and the spatial were supplemented by the dynamic. "A II, 1923" and "B 100" held the eye of the spectator in a central position. Once he had grasped the point of equilibrium where the two crosses overlap just below the center in "A II," or his sight had traveled along the receding screen to the farthest vanishing point in "B 100," there would be a static rest. But the floating structure of the "Large Aluminum Picture" was dynamic. The converging lines from top to bottom of the plane, and the three winged spheres rolling to the left and pointing to the right, are nonstatic. Their dynamism persists in spite of the fixing gaze.

The visual wealth contained within these three facets —the self-sufficiency of form, the depth indication of transparency, and the dynamic color construction—occupied Moholy for many years. The variations were unending and he played with them joyously and creatively throughout his life (Fig. 65).

The philosophical basis of this art was an esthetic collectivism, born and nourished from the revolutions that had formed his character. The protest against the caste spirit of the Imperial world and the deceptive sentimentality of the old iconography had been sublimated into

195

Fig. 64.   The Great Aluminum Picture, 1926. Oil on matte aluminum plate.

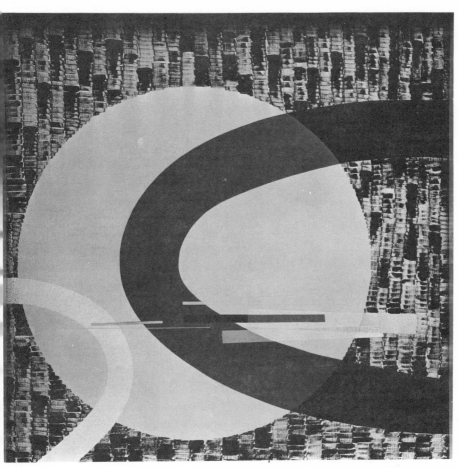

Fig. 65.　"Ch XIV," oil on canvas, 1939.

. . . a fanatic will to build constructively and to create jubilantly. The Constructivism that is our new dimension has no other purpose than *to participate in life*. It is essentially one with the spirit of evolution that created science, civilizations, and the systems that govern social life. Like them, constructive art is processual, forever open in all directions. It is a builder of man's ability to perceive, to react emotionally, and to reason logically.[4]

But the means of expression had not yet transcended those of the Renaissance painter; only their application had been varied. Line, gradation, perspective, and pigment had become nonsymbolic, yet

[4] Excerpt from "The Spiritual and Social Aspects of Constructivist Art," manuscript of a lecture given before the Bauhaus students, November, 1923.

Fig. 66. "LAL II," oil on Silverit plate mounted on light-gray plywood, 1936.

they still represented the maximum extension of man's ability to render pictorial illusion. The activation of light, as the fourth facet in Moholy's hexagon, would be the first attempt to draw the surrounding atmosphere actively into the picture plane. The aluminum picture and "LAL II, 1936" (Fig. 66) show pigment modulated by light on a polished surface that absorbed and reflected all gradations from darkness to a silvery luster. Oil paint was applied in thick layers. After it had dried, Moholy sandpapered it down to complete smoothness. Then he applied another layer, and repeated the process until a light-bridge led from the texture-less brilliance of the metal surface to the vivid modulations of the rough pigment.

But there was no shadow. The minute recesses and concavities of the painted texture were too delicate to give the roundness of the living world which Moholy had considered so essential in his film work. His own dictum for the film-maker, that "there's no life without shadow," became the impetus toward the fifth facet. In rendering shadow he was glorifying light.

His early celluloid and gallalith pictures before 1925 had been attempts to render *lighted* pigment, to give to the known

198

Fig. 67. Plexiglas space modulator with cutouts mounted two inches from white plywood background, 1936.

color values a new radiance expressing the joy of perceiving an infinite variety of hues. But the media were unsatisfactory. Celluloid cracked and yellowed, gallalith warped easily, and the commercial dyes were too crude to blend with the carefully mixed oil paints. Although they were discontinued these experiments

> . . . had inevitable repercussions on my thinking concerning light problems. To produce true primary relationships (my former idea of an "objective" painting) was not the only reason for my use of smooth flat surfaces. It was also the nearest to the transition from color into light, something like an objective texture invention for a delicate and evasive medium. By producing real radiant light effects through transparent dyes on plastic, and through other means, one has no need for translating light into color by painting with pigment. Light-painting had arrived.[5]

[5] "Abstract of an Artist."

199

Fig. 68.   Free-standing moulded color and light modulator, 1945. Plexiglas sheet
oil paint on black reflecting Formica base.

The first of the light modulators, done in London, had been no more than a translation of form into a medium that would include the shadow of that form. The sketches that followed probed two potential variations of this inclusive light pattern: perforation, and warping of the surface. In five years Moholy realized these two notions of light modulation within the picture plane. "Modulator 50, 1936" (Fig. 67) shows a perforated center. The brilliant white of the sprayed wood background contrasts with the filmlike transparency of the plastic sheet, creating a center of vision along the black diagonal line that ranges from jet black to a smooth, unpigmented white.

The "warped surface" found its most accomplished realization in "Handshaped Plastic, 1942."[6] Here the molded plastic sheet had been shaded by three different colors. Light either reflects from the curved surface or is filtered through the transparent material to create a dramatic variety of shadows on the white background. There are plexiglass modulators of many sizes and concepts, from the gay "Papmac, 1941," which utilizes a natural flow in the plastic material, to the imposing "Space Modulator with Highlights, 1942"[7] and "Color and Light Modulator, 1945" (Fig. 68). In each modulator the plastic sheet was held in place either by chromium clamps, extending two inches from the background, or by two rails screwed into the wood. Rhodoid was more flexible than plexiglass and needed a more rigid support, but plexiglass was smoother, so that the painted areas were always in danger of peeling. After the years had dried out the pigment, it became obvious that a method had to be found by which to hold oil paint on a plastic surface. Moholy started to roughen it with a network of fine hairlines, incised with a sharp engraver's needle. These scratch patterns called for infinite patience. They tired his eyes, which often looked red and swollen after he had completed a picture. Later he discovered that it would increase the adhesive effect if the lines were of different depth and applied in a crisscross pattern. The verticals were engraved with a heavy needle, and the horizontals with a very fine one. Then color was rubbed into the network before the final coat

[6] *Vision in Motion*, Fig. 213.
[7] *Ibid.*, p. 66.

was applied. If the plexiglass was to be perforated, or if a future sculpture had to be cut out from a sheet of plastic, only the finest jigsaw blade would do. Even so, many sheets cracked or splintered until Moholy decided to leave the protective paper coating on the sheet. He drew his sketch on this brown packing paper, and he and his old friend Kalman would meet in school after class hours to do the cutting. Then the paper coating was removed.

But in spite of seemingly countless variations, around 1944 the light modulator came to an end as part of Moholy's development from form to motion and from pigment to light. Because even the light modulator remained a *static* painting, no matter how dynamic its composition. The spectator was still compelled to view it passively like any other work of art born from the Greek tradition. With the instinct of the teacher, Moholy knew that to recreate the art experience of the painter demands of the spectator a high level of emotional and intellectual sensitivity given to few. The re-creative *action* became his goal, the establishment of an immediate relationship between spectator and object.

The first step in this direction was of Gordian directness. When he left London for Chicago in 1937 he had completed two plastic "leaves" made of clear celluloid. Each measured ten by fifteen inches. One of these leaves carried on the front side delicate black hairlines and an oblong perforation, and strongly textured blue and white forms on the reverse side. The other leaf had a pattern of four straight horizontals. On a smooth wide background "screen" of sprayed plywood floated a sphere in brilliant orange-red.

"Have the two leaves spiral-bound down the middle of the white background," Moholy told me when he left for America. "The leaves have to move like the pages of a book. Is that clear?"

I thought it was, but I was in the minority. For days I canvassed the London binderies, carrying board and leaves like pieces of armor.

"Where's the text?" the foreman would ask after a disapproving glance at the designs. "These are covers, but what's to go between them?"

202

"Nothing. Just put them together with spiral binding and fasten it to the middle of the board."

"What for?"

I was fooled into honesty. "To create new light effects, superimpositions." I held the leaves against the light. "See?"

"No, I don't. Tell you what——" A binder in Chelsea was at least willing to give the matter some thought. "Let's call up your boss, and if he confirms the order I'll do it."

"He's—he's in America."

"In America? Why would he want us to do such an odd job if he's in America?"

Guiltily I took my burden home.

The spiral binding was done in Chicago. Assembled, the white and red background painting and the transparent, perforated leaves created a kinetic painting that depended on the action of the spectator. By turning the leaves and varying the air space between the different picture layers, he could create a variety of light and color combinations of his own choice (Figs. 69, 70).

There are several designs for further "leaf paintings" among Moholy's sketches, but he never executed them. As school work, commercial and civic jobs, writing, and lecture tours pressed harder and harder, he became obsessed with the passing of time. His experiments aimed at the solution of one problem. When it had been solved, he prepared for the next step. And this next step, the last facet in his total vision, was the kinetic sculpture—sculpture modulated by the kinetics of light and the kinetics of motion. The wood, nickel, and glass sculptures Moholy had made during his years at the German Bauhaus had grown organically from his work in the Metal Workshop. There was no esthetic difference between a fine lamp and a fine piece of sculpture; they were both conceived as carriers of light. Twenty years later Moholy's plexiglass and chromium sculptures grew organically from the light modulators. They were destabilizations of designed form.

"I have come upon a strange rhythmical simultaneity," he said in a lecture dealing with the potentialities of plastics as

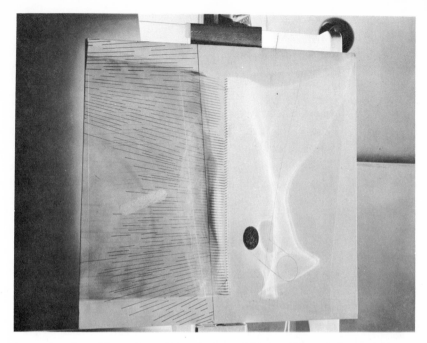

Fig. 69. Spiral-bound mobile picture, 1936. Oil painting and engraved lines on celluloid sheets bound to painted background, position I.

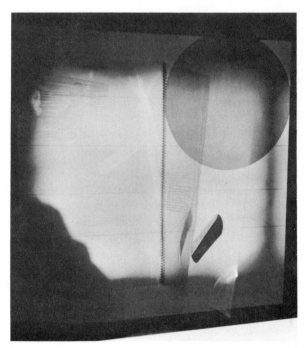

Fig. 70. Same as Fig. 69, position II.

sculptural material. "This urge of mine to supersede pigment with light has its counterpoint in a drive to dissolve solid volume into defined space. When I think of sculpture, I cannot think of static mass. Emotionally, sculpture and movement are interdependent. It seems illogical to invite the spectator to adjust himself to kinetic painting and then to immobilize him before a carved stone or a piece of sculptured plastic."

In 1943 he had completed his first plexiglass and chromium-rod sculpture. Two heavy planes of perforated plexiglass were held together by chromium rods; as the suspended form turned, it created a virtual volume of reflected light or it merely vibrated as the air around it moved (Figs. 71, 72). It was up to the spectator to animate the sculpture according to his own intensity. His re-creative pleasure could express itself in a gentle twist or a powerful whirl. The sculpture of 1943 has two companion pieces, dating from 1945 and 1946. They were the closest Moholy came to a kinetic solution. Like Cézanne, he knew that he was "only the primitive on the way he had chosen," but he also knew that his light mobiles bear in themselves the potentialities of a new kaleidoscopic sculpture.

What is a painter's relationship to his public? How much of a showman must he be to establish contact between his imagination and those he wants to influence? For Moholy this problem was perhaps less important than for many other painters and sculptors because the integration of his art and his design, his writing, lecturing, and teaching, provided contacts and gratifications missed by the "studio artist." He loved acclaim and success as much as any man, and he was well aware of the advantages bought with money: independence, and the good things he loved—expensive working materials and publications, good clothes, hospitality, and good food. But he rarely promoted his art. He had an unconquerable suspicion of art dealers, dating back to the crude and dishonest treatment he had received as a young painter from two of Berlin's foremost gallery owners.

Moholy entered his paintings in competitions only if he was invited, and he never sought contact with museum

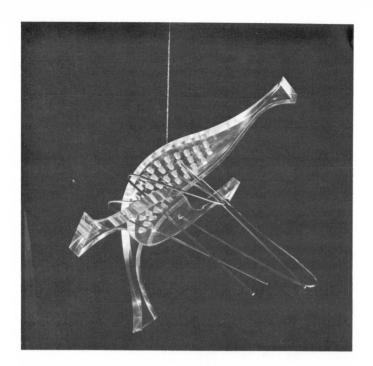

Fig. 71. Plexiglas and chromium-rod mobile suspended from steel wire against black cloth background, 1943.

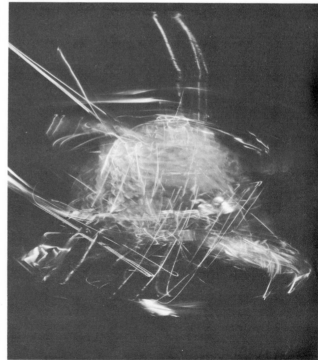

Fig. 72. The mobile of Fig. 71 in motion, creating a virtual volume.

directors. The one-man shows that came his way in America were offered to him without request. They were, at first, a fine, well-promoted exhibition in Katharine Kuh's modern gallery in Chicago in 1939, a survey of his own work and that of his faculty in the gallery of Mills College in Oakland in 1940, and a comprehensive show, covering his whole production, which the Contemporary Arts Society sponsored in the Art Museum in Cincinnati in 1946. He sold paintings regularly during the last eight years of his life, but the buyers needed no prodding. They were mainly industrialists for whom he worked as a designer, or colleagues with whom he shared his educational convictions. He was a regular exhibitor with the American Abstract Artists, but his main opportunity to show his work was the Museum of Non-Objective Painting in New York.

In 1944 the art dealer Karl Nierendorf, who had been the co-editor of the catalogue of the first big Bauhaus Exhibition in 1923, came to Chicago with an offer to handle Moholy's art work. After thinking it over for a week, Moholy turned down the offer, and, in a letter, explained his reasons.

October 11, 1944

Mr. Karl Nierendorf
53 East 57th Street
New York City
DEAR KARL:

I enjoyed our dinner last Sunday very much, and I was quite moved by your response to the work I have done lately. God knows, this recognition is necessary, and since it is such a rare occurrence it is doubly enjoyed.

I have pondered a good deal about your kind offer to become my New York representative, and to handle my work exclusively; and Sibyl and I have been both very much aware of the great advantages such a connection could bring in our present situation.

And yet, I feel that the condition attached to your offer is one I cannot meet. I do not want to sever all my connections with the Museum of Non-Objective Painting, and I do not want to tell them that I won't participate in any further exhibitions of theirs.

207

I am very well aware of the discrimination against me resulting from this connection, and I know that possibly in the long run their purchases of my work won't amount to what I might make if I had my work handled by you. But there is a consideration involved which goes far beyond money.

I had a hard time finding recognition; and it meant more than I can ever say when Guggenheim and Rebay[8] bought my first painting in 1929. I was proud then, and I knew that I had built a bridge across the Atlantic Ocean. When I came to this country, I saw their collection, which—unfortunately—is packed away in the Plaza Hotel. And I came to the conclusion that this is the most essential, the most far-reaching, collection of modern art. No other collection here or in Europe can approach the complexity and at the same time the fundamental singleness of conviction in the Guggenheim selection. I know there are many, many paintings neither you nor I would ever buy or even look at. But that proves nothing. It cannot devaluate the brilliance of the other pieces.

A few years from now the negative attributes of the Foundation will be forgotten but the collection will remain. There is nothing that could dim my pride and my gratitude for being part of it.

I am sure that you'll understand this attitude, and that it'll be possible for us to arrive at some agreement by which you will handle some of my work without insisting that I sever my connections with the Guggenheim Foundation.

Sibyl joins me in warmest greetings. Cordially yours,
MOHOLY

There was no reply from the Nierendorf Gallery, and Moholy never had a representative among art dealers.

If light was the *leitmotif* of Moholy's art, industrial design was the orchestration, providing opportunities for infinite variations. Ideas which had been born and developed in the realm of nonapplied art were tested and broadened to prove the indivisibility of vision. The three large projects, executed in the last four years of his life, denounce more convincingly than lectures and books the artificiality of the barrier between "fine" and "commercial" art. In Moholy the designer and the painter were

[8] The owner and the curator of the Museum of Non-Objective Painting.

one, and the elements of his vision were subject to the same laws of development and carriers of the same message.

In 1943 the Baltimore & Ohio Railroad commissioned him to design a passenger car which would provide postwar standards and compete successfully with the luxuries planned by the passenger airlines. Traveling on day coaches and in Pullmans, Moholy developed his suggestions, which had one unifying factor: space organization. Through transparent, floating, adjustable partitions, through different seat levels, curved walls, and tubular light fixtures, the confining narrowness of the train corridor was broken. The disappearance of solid wall units, and the use of light materials and perforation effects gave a feeling of breadth and spaciousness. The accent was on variety, a psychological antidote for the monotony and boredom of long train trips. Like many a postwar dream, the great rejuvenation drive of the American railroads bogged down and died, and Moholy's train was never built. But its design opened an exciting vista into the future where the elements of speed and time will be adequately expressed through a truly streamlined design.

Exhibition architecture had been one of Moholy's favorite tasks since the days of the Bauhaus Exhibition in 1923. In Europe the opportunities to add new elements to his experience had been frequent. But he had been in America eight years before he got his first chance to design an exhibition. The United States Gypsum Company asked him to create a display at a builders' fair in Chicago. There was a minimum of space available and a maximum of material to be shown. Together with Ralph Rapson, who then was head of the Architectural Department of the Institute of Design, Moholy concentrated on two elements: light-shadow effects, and superimposition. By perforating the narrow exhibition stall with porthole-like openings, he drew the eyes of the spectator away from the narrow front wall; and by using depth where breadth was not available he created many space units reaching far behind the actual exhibition space. Contrasting light effects distinguished the different "stages" from each other. Units close to the spectator were darker than those farther away, and the sober lettering on the gray front wall attracted attention by long shadows (Fig. 73).

209

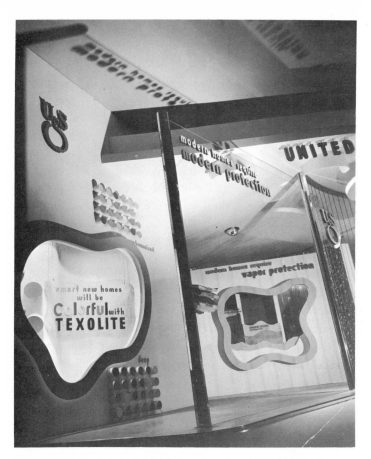

Fig. 73. Exhibition Stand for United States Gypsum Company, Chicago, 1945. (In collaboration with Ralph Rapson.)

"There's no task too small, and no project too big, to make it a manifesto of incorruptible design," Moholy had told the young Dutchmen who had crowded into his exhibition in Amsterdam in 1934. In 1944 he got a chance to demonstrate this point. The Parker Pen Company appointed him as art adviser. It was a working relationship well suited to Moholy's disposition. Once a month he spent two days with the company in Janesville, listening to questions and problems ranging from the printing of an ink-bottle label to projects for a new factory building. His spontaneous fondness for people made him a patient and concentrated listener, and his lifelong experience as a teacher had taught him to formulate advice simply and slowly. The company

210

had adapted the therapeutic technique of self-analysis to the technical field. Everyone was invited to discuss his work problems with Moholy, and it became evident that an hour of formulation was worth many weeks of solitary effort. When Moholy returned to Chicago he had absorbed the practical atmosphere in which his designs were to be realized. Together with his gifted collaborator, Nolan Rhoades, he worked on pens, clips, inkstands,

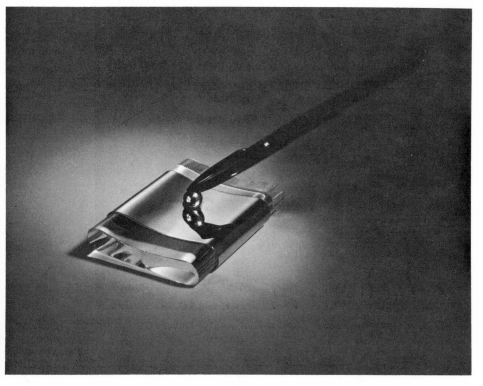

Fig. 74.   Desk set with magnetized ball holder in polished chromium for Parker Pen Company, 1946.

packaging, posters, stationery, and showrooms. These designs were as much part of his work as an artist as had been the B. & O. coach or the Gypsum exhibit. Through many years of experimentation Moholy had developed a "sense" for plastics. He knew their properties, possibilities, and limitations. And from the days of

211

the Bauhaus Metal Workshop he had retained a working knowledge of metals and alloys. He now combined transparent and solid materials, and light and heavy ones, to go into pens and accessories. Harmonious lines and the imaginative use of fine materials were the sole indicators of high quality. The ostentatiously rich ornamentation had been dropped. It was a first attempt to create a functional luxury trade (Fig. 74).

With the beginning of 1945 Moholy's personal life had reached a level that was deeply satisfying to him. His work as a painter and sculptor had progressed toward new solutions. *Vision in Motion* had been achieved—a "synonym for simultaneity and space-time; a means to comprehend the new dimension . . . the projective dynamics of man's visionary faculties."[9] The six facets of his art were all cut and polished. His design work provided a direct and stimulating contact with the practical tasks of contemporary society. He felt himself part, not particle, of his times. *The New Vision* was selling well in its third edition, and the publication of *Vision in Motion* was planned for the spring of 1946. His income was satisfactory and promised a secure future for his children. At the age of fifty, he felt a harmonious balance between performance and recognition. In a curious state of dual existence, Moholy, the painter, the writer, the designer, the man of many achievements and influences, was consciously and gratefully happy, while Moholy, the teacher, faced defeat.

[9] *Vision in Motion.*

9 After six years of existence the School of Design reached a crossroads. In spite of a minimum budget and the impediments of war, it had proved itself as a unique design center. The projects carried out in the different workshops were shown throughout the country, and graduates were working in many schools and industries. It was Moholy's singlehanded publicity campaign that had put his school on the map. He wrote from a lecture trip into the Northwest:

> Since we can't afford to advertise, I have to be the advertisement. If Idaho can grow the best potatoes, there's no reason why it shouldn't grow good future designers. But the strain of this new gospel mission is considerable. It's not the lectures, believe me. It's the social exploitation of the lecturer, the cocktails and teas, and dinners and luncheons. I sometimes feel like a ball of knitting wool, thrown from the lap of one matron into that of another.

No college nor club was too small, and no trip too inconvenient. He went wherever an opportunity offered to talk about his program. Equipped with kodachromes and photographs, he gave lectures on the social, the practical, and the esthetic implications of the Bauhaus approach. If he didn't get paid, he chalked it up as one more contribution to the school; and if he got an honorarium it went into more slides and more prints.

In the spring of 1944, the accumulated evidence of the workability of this new design-education intensified the interest of a group of Chicago businessmen. They proposed to form a Board of Directors under the chairmanship of Walter Paepcke. In return, Moholy would submit to the customary control of a board over the school's finances, publicity, and the appointment of administrative personnel. To stress the progress from a small educational laboratory to an institution on a par with colleges

213

and universities, the name "School of Design" was to be changed to "Institute of Design." Moholy would be relieved of administrative detail to devote all his energies to teaching and planning, and a competent trio of manager, executive secretary, and accountant would direct noneducational matters. It was a decision of great consequence for his lifework.

Moholy's reaction was strangely divided. He no longer had the optimistic belief that each businessman is a potential student, a belief which had made him sign a contract with the Association of Arts and Industries six years earlier. He knew that his educational plan had to succeed in spite of public opinion, not because of it. But he had acquired respect for the willingness with which men of capital and civic influence served orchestras, theaters, universities, and philanthropic organizations. It pleased him that in the midst of a war and a feverish boom his idea carried enough weight to merit attention and support. It was part of Moholy's philosophy of total involvement that he accepted businessmen as readily as artists. They were functioning elements in the totality of contemporary life. But, though he understood their place in society, he questioned many of their motivations.

> The success theory of the profit economy pays a high premium to the anti-artist. Artists are considered effeminates who do not have the stamina to participate in economic competition. This is very tragic, since art is the only field where convention does not completely impair sentiment, and where the omnipotence of thought and independence of emotion are kept relatively intact. No society can exist without expressing its ideas, and no culture and no ethics will survive without participation of the artist who cannot be bribed. . . . The silly myth that the genius has to suffer in order to give his best is the sly excuse of a society which does not care for its productive members, except if immediate technological or economic applications with promising profits are in sight.[1]

The inner conflict resulting from this critical insight, and his need for outside support to carry through his program, was expressed in two letters, dated April 23 and 26, 1944:

[1] Catalogue for the retrospective exhibition sponsored by the Contemporary Arts Society at the Art Museum in Cincinnati, February, 1946 (private printing).

DEAR SIBYL:

I slipped out of Washington as quickly as I could and I am now on the train to New York. I spent two days with H.D., the key man of government research who, in peace time, is president of a technological college in New Jersey. This experience has intensified my dual reaction to the developments in Chicago.[2]

This man in Washington is so typical of the "enlightened" businessman, but oh so far from the humbleness of real insight. Progress, in his terms, means increased efficiency, and success is an upward trend in figures. He has never learned to think in human proportions. His reaction to my detailed suggestions as to the use of the infrared oven, the wood-spring, the rehabilitation textbook, and the mass-housing research, was a barrage of impatient questions: "How much time will it take? How much will it cost? How large is your endowment? How many square feet of laboratory space?" He didn't contemplate for a moment the actual worth of our ideas, or inquire about the qualifications of the men involved in this research. The smallness of our school made him squirm, and he angrily hit a stack of files and said that he could have the help of institutions ranging in endowment anywhere from four to forty million. In the end he dropped all pretense of politeness and told me that the government wasn't interested in lending its prestige to a peanut affair.

It was this peculiar expression that linked this interview with the school situation in Chicago. How often have I been told by the Board that I have to make up my mind whether I want to head my own peanut affair or an institution that counts. What a strange insecurity that measures the importance of an idea in square feet of occupied floor space, and the number of personnel. . . .

Léger and I reminisced today over a bottle of Rosé about that nightmarish dinner in the Arts Club [on the occasion of the Container Corporation Poster Exhibit]. Léger imitated the speaker who was a poll-taker for advertising agencies and who reported so proudly how the designs of Moore, Helion, Kepes, Bayer, Léger rank by plus and minus points against the output of the commercial studios. We felt both ashamed in a strange sort of way that none of us had protested, save under our breaths. I guess art directors buy artists to advertise advertising, and to camouflage the mediocre quality of the

[2] In March, 1944, the new Board of Directors had been organized.

215

anonymous designs. The provocative statement of modern art is constantly annulled by checkbook and cocktail party. Am I on the same way?

Darling, darling, let's hold on to what was built during the last years. . . ."

But the choice was between existence or liquidation. The school needed a moratorium in which to survive the war emergency without losing identity. Moholy hoped that the prestige and the contributions of the Board would sustain the school according to its original concept.

In contrast to the Association of Arts and Industries, some of the new Board members lived up to the obligation assumed. Both their financial help and the time given for money-raising campaigns were considerable. Without their support, the Bauhaus idea would have foundered a second time in this country. But the transition from "peanut affair" to "institute" was slow, much too slow for businessmen who think in terms of figures and who know nothing about the slow growth of ideas.

"The genuine businessman is actually quite a romantic," Moholy once said wistfully after a conference. "He's the dreamer and I'm the realist. He still thinks in terms of Horatio Alger stories and the fast and fabulous successes that'll make the financial page. I try to tell him that genuine success is measured in intellectual influence that can be achieved, not in a lifetime, but in the lifetime of generations."

The whole dilemma of endowed education centered around the simple fact that a school is not a business, that it operates according to different psychological and economic laws. Each board meeting was a gentlemanly battle between economic and pedagogic motivations. Seen in the perspective of a whole country resting its higher education on the hostile union between educator and trustee, the expenditure in effort and nervous tension seemed absurd. The business managers of the reorganized Institute of Design, who were hired by the Board from commercial employment agencies, were an uninterrupted sequence of failures because their "noneducational" approach was a fallacy. If they were to succeed, they would have to become obsessed with the supreme importance of the school's program. The methods they

216

had employed successfully in selling whiskey or drug products didn't work with art education. Their pathetic attempts to establish a "normal business routine" in a design laboratory run by imaginative and individualistic personalities were doomed to failure. Moholy's highly successful publicity campaign bogged down and petered out the moment a publicity agent took over. Whereas Moholy had tried to sell the prospective donor a stake in a future world, the professional money-raiser tried to sell an income tax deduction. In a naïve transference of prestige standards, business executives accused him of an incurable "janitor mentality" because the preservation of tools and materials, the cleanness of the premises and accommodations for the students were for him intrinsic elements of the school program.

Moholy was increasingly aware of the abysmal difference in basic principle between him and his Board. For more than a year he steered his school on a precarious course between what he called a board mentality and his own integrity.

"There's a symbolic meaning in those chocolate-covered filberts Moholy brings to every board meeting," Crombie Taylor, the young Executive Secretary of the Institute, once told me. "They're typical of his attitude. He has a hundred different ways of coating a tough problem, and they're all sweet and tasty. But once the coating is removed, there's nothing but solid hard nut. I've never seen him give in at the kernel of a problem."

When in the spring of 1945 the enrollment was still below one hundred and no immediately saleable products had been turned out by the workshops, much of the initial interest of the Board members faded. Established academic art schools started to profit visibly from the rising stream of returning war veterans. Why didn't the Institute of Design? Where were the famous European names who had been linked with the original Bauhaus and who were now in this country? Why didn't they join the faculty of the Institute, attracting students by their prestige? And where were the short-term courses that would give men who had lost years in the Service a chance to acquire skills quickly?

These demands were met by Moholy with a deadly determination.

"Our curriculum doesn't fit into the competitive mood

217

of an approaching postwar boom, because we refuse to promise a two-semester training for a breadwinning job. And we won't give a thought to fashionable trends in design unless they're sound and functional. Visual fundamentals are a slow-acting ferment. They have to be absorbed and applied in a hundred different ways before they produce an integrated vision and mature results. I shall keep on considering the process of education more important than the finished result."[3]

And to the taunting inquiries as to why his former associates from the German Bauhaus did not join his school, Moholy replied with a statement that later was supplemented in a letter, dated May 11, 1945.

I'll tell you why recognized artists and designers dislike teaching: they find too little compensation for the great effort involved. If they are to resign themselves to the small income paid to teachers, they should at least have the freedom of their convictions. They can work for the industry and be paid decently. In an endowed school they still work for the industry which controls the board. The only difference is that there's less pay and more interference.

But there's another problem involved, less general and more deadly to us. Creative people don't seem to thrive in the Chicago atmosphere. Scores of them have come with high hopes over the last fifty years, and all of them have left again. . . . The enthusiastic support given to new projects, new ideas, dies too quickly. There's no stamina, because there are no convictions.

When the dissatisfaction of the directors with the slow progress of the Institute of Design finally climaxed in a blunt request that the school be discontinued, Moholy remained calm.

"I won't close the Institute," he replied to the Chairman of the Board, "because I know that my program is good. It will serve American youth when they have recovered from the hasty postwar adjustments. They'll be a minority, I know, but they'll be those who value creative integration above quick skills and a fast-earning job. The Institute is the only place where a young man can train his brains, his hands, and his emotional

[3] From a lecture given on May 20, 1945, in Milwaukee. Wisconsin.

218

sensibilities without intimidation of his ethics. When he leaves the school his contribution will be proportionate to the time spent. If you drop the chairmanship, I shall still go on. I have done it before, and I shall again plow every penny from my industrial designing that I can spare back into the school. There are too many young men waiting to come back once they are released from the Army."

And they came back. Within one year the daytime enrollment jumped from 92 to 366 students, and the income from tuition fees totaled $40,000. It was the justification for which Moholy had hoped, and it convinced the Board of Directors. They remained faithful to the Institute of Design.

But the battle had only begun. The school building on Ontario Street was sold, and a half-forgotten clause that the premises would have to be vacated within sixty days became effective. Amidst the sudden scramble for housing following V-E Day, the Institute had to find new quarters. There was no choice but to sign an unfavorable lease for a second floor on North State Street. While classes grew by the week and new administrative personnel had to be broken in, bricklayers and carpenters transformed a former night club into a school. The unsuitability of the building and the pressure of time raised expenses to high figures. The only way to cover the conversion costs was to accept more and more students. The leisurely pleasure of working with a select group of graduates during the summer was a thing of the past. Under the GI training program a full semester had to be wedged between spring and fall. Teachers were still scarce in 1945. Moholy taught twenty-two hours a week all during the summer, using evenings and nights for his money-earning design work and for painting. On Sundays he came out to the farmhouse in Somonauk and wrote on his manuscript for *Vision in Motion*.

Since 1943 he had assembled material for a book that would record the fermentation and transfiguration of the Bauhaus idea in a new era and a different civilization. The time for coordination and formulation was always lacking, but he had managed to put down a rough draft during the winter of 1944. In the spring of 1945 the Rockefeller Foundation granted him $5,000, "to study the place of arts in liberal education." It was a generous

219

gesture of the Foundation's Humanities Division to offer a grant that carried with it no other obligation than the completion of *Vision in Motion*. When Moholy received the news he was delighted.

"I'll hire an assistant director for the Institute," he said. "He'll take over half of my obligations, and I'll have two or three days a week to finish the book."

But the assistant director somehow did not take to the job and seemed unable to grasp the specific problems of the school. He soon stopped trying, and Moholy had to attend to administration detail as before. Weekends remained the only writing time.

Verbal formulation didn't come to him easily, and some of the chapters were rewritten more than a dozen times.

"I'll never write another book," Moholy vowed. "It's an unbearable temptation, to sit next to brushes, paint, and canvas, and have to keep a pencil in one's hand. How I thrive on *seeing*, and how this whole delight withers when I have to translate it into words. This book is the greatest sacrifice I have ever made for my students. It is a kind of visual testament, something they can go by when I'm dead."

It was one of the frequent references to death that appeared in Moholy's conversation toward the end of that hot and frantic summer. They startled me because he had seemed so determined to ignore the threat of the advancing years. His childhood among old women on his grandmother's farm had made him intolerant of age. He shunned the company of old people.

"Age is fiction," he told me on his fiftieth birthday in July, 1945. "I shall remain as I have always been."

But in the late autumn a growing melancholy started to influence his motions and his speech. It didn't show in public. He put on his cheerful smile like a mask as soon as he left his home. But at night he would sit in his chair without working, staring vacantly into space, or speaking in short, labored sentences. His appetite lagged, and the Sunday morning romps in the park with the children became to him exhausting walks. When the fall semester enrollment listed eight hundred day and night students, he did not smile.

220

"If only we didn't have to accept them," he said. "They don't know it, but they strangle each other's minds. How can one co-ordinate such a throng?" And with a wistful reference to past decisions he added, "It's no longer a peanut affair, but a multitude of peanuts."

He refused to see a doctor, in spite of nervous skin disorders and frequent dizzy spells.

"A doctor who's worth his money will laugh at me," he insisted. "When I tell him what I've worked during the last eight years he'll either tell me to go and get a good rest or examine my head. I'm just tired—incredibly tired."

In November of that year he collapsed. As he lay on the couch, struggling for breath, with severe pain in his left side and black spots before his eyes, we were certain he had had a heart attack. A day later we knew that he had leukemia.

In a family where no one had ever been sick, the seriousness of the diagnosis didn't sink in at first.

"I feel like one of those rare babies who get a Christmas tree in July," Moholy joked as we waited for the doctor's car, which would take him to the hospital. "If I didn't feel so rotten I'd send my picture to the newspaper."

The idea of being nursed by a pretty young woman roused him to a vigorous protest.

"I'd rather die than undress with one of those flippant young ladies around," he insisted, and it was decided that he'd go to a hospital run by a Catholic order and staffed exclusively by men.

The first diagnosis showed such an increase in white blood cells and such a deterioration of the spleen that his imminent death was hinted. But the Brothers had never seen a dying man of such vitality. While blood and glucose drained into his arm, and one doctor after another examined him, he sketched versions of his bed with one hand. The many parts of this contraption—screws, bolts, boards, and bars—delighted him. During the third night of his absence from home the telephone rang.

"The professor wants crayons and sketching paper," a bewildered Brother told me. "And he wants them right away."

221

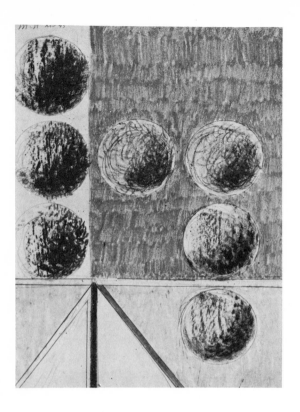

Fig. 75. Hospital Bed, November 1945. Sketch in pencil and crayon.

"It's past eleven o'clock," I said. "Tell him I'll bring it first thing tomorrow morning."

But I hadn't counted with Moholy. The next ring was directly from his bed.

"I won't have another transfusion for forty-eight hours. If you don't bring what I want, I'll send one of these friars to scour the town for crayons."

He did a series of abstractions of a hospital bed that night, the visual hold of a painter on a world he didn't want to leave (Fig. 75).

As soon as the transfusions were over he decided to select the illustrations for *Vision in Motion*. For two weeks I carried a collection of sixteen portfolios into the hospital which he had filled with clippings and photographs and sketches. At first I held each piece before his eyes. Later when he could sit up I arranged a sequence on his bedspread. Suddenly he remembered another illustration, originally meant for a different chapter or a different book. Then would start a frantic search which often extended to school files or the many drawers at home in which he

222

had collected teaching material. There was no letup until the piece was found, discussed, and discarded or accepted. Injections, blood counts, medications were secondary to this activity. Moholy endured them as bothersome interruptions of his work.

After three weeks in the hospital he came home. His blood count had hardly improved, he had great difficulty in walking and breathing, and his appetite remained poor. But his spirit had reached a high pitch of determination. He had faced death, and every ounce of his energy, every thought, and the entire emotional power of his heart, were concentrated on living. He received ten successive X-ray treatments which were an agonizing experience. His system revolted against the effects of the radiation. He became sick after each treatment, and his body trembled for hours. But his blood count improved rapidly. The white cells reduced to normal, his spleen contracted, and four weeks after the last treatment his health picture was normal. By Christmas he was safe, and in an overflowing emotion of infinite gratitude he painted a large canvas, "Leu I, 1945."[4] He wrote in a note, attached to the gray canvas, "Ch XIV, 1939," for which I had asked as a present:

> This is a wonderful Christmas. It is the most wonderful Christmas I have ever had. Thank you for loving me, nursing me, being a mother, a friend, a wonderful cook. Now I know what life really is. I hold it all in my hands—space, color, light. I have never been so clear with my eyes, my thoughts, my feeling. I am so grateful.

At the beginning of January, 1946, he went back to the Institute.

His illness had had a curious effect on the faculty and the Board of Directors. Men who had done their work in a spirit of necessity suddenly did miracles. The office force, the janitors, and all the teachers doubled their efforts. In spite of the half-finished building and a curriculum that was poorly fitted for mass education, the students did what Moholy had always urged them to do: they gave their best. When he came back after an absence of eight weeks, the remodeling had been completed. The student work was on a level of creativeness and accomplishment reminiscent of the best results achieved under Moholy's direct supervision.

[4] *The New Vision and Abstract of an Artist,* p. 85.

The most advanced group had completed an experimental film, "Do Not Disturb," which utilized all the color and light effects Moholy had planned; and the Foundation Course, which was faced with the most severe problem of overcrowding, had been ingeniously organized by Nathan Lerner to work in shifts of cooperative units. In infinite gratitude and optimism, Moholy arranged a "housewarming party" to open the new school premises to the public.

It was a great success. Instead of an expected two hundred people, more than eight hundred came to see the workshops. They were ushered by students and faculty and entertained by the Board members and their wives. As we drove home that night, Moholy said:

"This leukemia business was a great stroke of luck for me. Without it the school would have bogged down. The Board would have lost interest in the face of all the difficulties, thinking that we were just an unsuccessful box factory. Did you notice how all the ill humor is gone? The incompleteness of the workshops and the overcrowding has suddenly turned from an excuse to an incentive. When I got sick they realized that they were part of an idea that might not survive if I died. That shook them out of their doldrums. If we can keep this spirit alive, I'll have no regrets. I shall always remember this sickness as a great ally."

Moholy was sincere. He believed in his recovery. But a subconscious realization of death remained in his mind. It drove him to an intensification of effort that can be compared only to a man running down a steep slope, unable to check the acceleration until he crashes.

In the spring of 1946 the Cincinnati Contemporary Arts Society offered him an exhibition. It was the first one-man show in six years, and he accepted enthusiastically. For a month he added to his teaching, writing, and designing schedule the task of selecting, assembling, cataloguing, and framing his work. He edited a catalogue and supervised the making of blocks and the printing. When he asked me to inspect his selection of pieces to be exhibited, we did not agree with each other.

"This is such a unique opportunity," I tried to argue.

224

"The public is so unfamiliar with Constructivism. Why not choose some pleasing pieces, the brilliant light-effects of the space modulators, the radiant colors of your latest canvases, and the mobile sculptures in plexiglass and chrome? These early paintings and drawings are for connoisseurs. They can only be appreciated by people who already know and love abstract art. Why show so little of your latest work and so many of your earliest experiments?"

"Because they were experiments," Moholy explained. "There is nothing more important to me just now than seeing my whole development in retrospect. I want to get a continuous picture of how the relationship of pigment and light, and of line and space, developed. I used to reflect so little on what I did. I want to find out how precisely my instincts worked."

"But people won't understand it; they won't buy this type of painting."

"Too bad for them." It was rare that Moholy scoffed at the public. "All the time while I stared at the walls of my hospital room, I covered these walls with my past work. I tried to remember the sequence, the order of development. It became an obsession. I craved to see how I had used my life. Now I can find out. Do you think I'd pass up such an opportunity?"

The show was not a popular success and nothing was sold. The rows of drawings, pencil sketches, and collages, lovingly matted and framed, and the large number of darkened canvases, showed a fascinating variation of basic elements, a gradual additive vision, moving organically from the simple to the complex. It might have been a feast for an art scholar. For the people of Cincinnati it remained enigmatic. But Moholy was happy. On the train ride back from his opening lecture, he filled many pages with sketches, using numbers to indicate color. It was then that the large work done during the summer of 1946 was prepared.

Toward the end of spring, all of Moholy's students and collaborators were convinced that he was cured. When the lease on North State Street was suddenly canceled and the Institute of Design was faced with another move and the loss of $10,000 in remodeling expenses, everyone had full confidence that Moholy was the man to save the school in this new peril. We took up where we had left off a year before, and canvassed Chicago's

225

North Side in search of a building. It was a strenuous and depressing job. The postwar expansion had pushed commercial rents beyond control, and fire, police, and safety restrictions narrowed the choice considerably. When the deadline for leaving North State Street was less than two months away, a contract was signed with the Historical Society to purchase their old building on Dearborn Street for a reasonable sum. The Board rose to the occasion and donated $20,000 as a down payment. The future of the Institute of Design was once more assured.

But the effort showed in Moholy's health. Unnoticed by anyone else, and vigorously denied by his doctors, the earlier symptoms of his illness returned. The radiant optimism that had carried him through the winter faded. He became highly irritable and reproachful at home, and there were new undertones of hopelessness in his complaints. His blood count was still close to normal, and the specialist was sarcastic about my anxiety. My diagnosis was more psychological than physiological; to rate the mere fact that Moholy suddenly agreed to a prolonged stay in the country as an alarming symptom must have seemed ridiculous to anyone who didn't know Moholy as I did. In June we moved into our farmhouse near Somonauk.

But in spite of his admitted need for rest he didn't know how to live during a vacation. It was too late for him to learn the conventional meaning of the term. The work for the Parker Pen Company continued, and we drove frequently to Janesville where he had long conferences with directors and employes. I was worried about the strain involved, but Moholy enjoyed it. He could not live without teaching, and the young designers replaced his students. On week ends there were many visitors, teachers, former students, friends from the East and West Coast who stayed over night, and the finishing touches were put on the manuscript of *Vision in Motion* whose completion had been delayed by his illness.

Twice a month he went to Chicago to see the doctor, to supervise the remodeling of the new school building on Dearborn Street, and to meet with a group of young architects and town-planners. Harry Weese, who was the moving spirit of this group, has described Moholy's influence upon them.

226

In March, 1946, Moholy had Charles Wiley and me at the Tavern Club for luncheon. He asked us whether we had a sort of Professional Five Year Plan. He prefaced this question with a cogent statement on the necessity for principle and direction in architecture, showing a warm optimistic interest in the possibility that our plans might have progressive implications. Out of this meeting grew the City Planning Group. It became Moholy's instrument in doing something about the projects submitted to the Better Chicago Contest, sponsored by the *Herald American.*

He was dissatisfied with the insincere handling of the efforts of many good men in this contest, and the way significant ideas had been treated by reactionary judges. He had withdrawn his own name from the jury because he felt that the winning solution could not compare to another one of high imagination which involved an outer Lakeshore Drive on a continuous dike, forming large bathing lagoons and removing traffic from residential areas. He also thought highly of Ralph Rapson's suggestion of artificial islands for new housing.

Moholy liked the character of a giant centralized city in contrast to a romanticized garden city. But he found many suggestions to humanize it. The idea of a centralized industrial area toward the west in a strip plan found favor with him because it secured the lake border for housing.

The central goal of our group under Moholy's guidance was to take an architect's and planner's stand on such problems as the unhealthy emphasis on single-family dwellings and forced individual ownership, the lack of building control necessary to prevent future slums, the migration away from established communities to the suburbs, and many others.

Moholy took these meetings seriously.

"If I let them down, how are they ever to make sacrifices for the community," he asked me once when I objected to a trip into town on an oppressively hot day; and to his friend Giedion, who had canceled a promised series of lectures during the summer session of the Institute, he wrote:

Of course I understand your difficulties; but my first thought was that all of us have great difficulties and yet we have to do what is expected.

227

Fig. 76.   Moholy-Nagy explaining a problem at photo seminar, 1946, listening to student questions and giving his answer.   Photographs by Arthur Siegel.

After six weeks of this sort of vacation he went to town for another conference. He looked appallingly ill when I took him to the station, but he rebuked me sharply for my concern.

"I've done what you wanted; I have moved out here. This is more than anyone else at the school can afford. Don't destroy my good will toward this arrangement by overanxiousness. This is a hot day, and I don't like heat."

A few hours later the doctor called me. Moholy's blood count had deteriorated catastrophically. The X-ray treatments had to be repeated immediately.

When I arrived in town, Moholy was busy in his office dictating letters, making telephone calls, looking at building blueprints, and selecting plastics for pens and inkstands. On our way to the clinic where the X-ray treatments were given, he showed me the program for a series of lectures on photography he planned to give the following week during a special seminar for photographers at the Institute.

"But you had told me you'd cancel these lectures," I protested. "You told me in the country that you'd ask Siegel and Newhall to take your place."

"That was weeks ago when I didn't feel so good,"

228

Moholy shrugged. "Now that I'm going to have more X ray I'll get well fast. It would be a waste of time to be in the city anyhow and not use the time for teaching."

For a nightmarish week Moholy went early in the morning for his X-ray treatments, which upset his system as much as the first time. Between ten and five he lay in a dark room covered with ice packs, recovering from the shock. At six o'clock he started his lecture followed by a seminar or a discussion; and it was usually past ten o'clock before we got home. I sat in the first row, ready to take him home if he should collapse, but he always made it alone except for the three flights of stairs to our apartment. They became the crowning ordeal of the day. The special photographic session was a brilliant success, and early in August we returned to the country (Fig. 76).

But Moholy was a changed man. The very fact of a relapse, after he had been so sure of a complete cure, had produced a mental shock much deeper than his first realization of death. We never talked about his health, and the word leukemia, which we had bandied around so lightheartedly in the beginning, became taboo. The shadow had grown too big. Moholy could no longer look up and face it. His stunned soul expressed itself in a wordless affection and a frantic immersion in artistic creation. It was as if he sought a deeper order below the surface of his destroyed equilibrium. The inexpressible could only be revealed in new plastic forms. It was with the impact of illness and the anticipation of defeat that Moholy's work admitted for the first time an emotional symbolism.

The dropping of the first atomic bomb on Japan had made a profound impression on him. Although he usually stayed aloof from political events, he felt a personal concern. For months he lived through an intense inner struggle, weighing the official claim of a shortening of the war against the implications of an amoral precedent. In spite of the scope of his work and his failing health, he read through the complete Smythe Report, anxious to grasp the potentialities of nuclear fission for constructive uses. While in the hospital in November, he cut circles from packing paper, shading the surface with crayon. Then he would tear a circle into small pieces, arranging the scraps on a large cardboard disk. His first canvas after he was up again was the large "Nuclear Bubble." Immediately following it, he put this nuclear monster into a structural relationship to man's existence.

Fig. 77. Nuclear painting,
1946. Oil on canvas.

"Nuclear II, 1946" is essentially a commentary on the first version. The fearful void of the bubble is emphasized by iridescent color variations around its rim, extinguishing with their deadly brilliance man's rational, orderly pattern of streets and city blocks (Fig. 77).

Of the two dozen water colors which Moholy did during the six weeks he remained in the country, some were symbolic. There were several interpretations of Béla Bartók's "Diary of a Fly." Others showed an abstracted pattern of roads and footpaths between fields and swamps, and a charming ephemeral reminiscence of fish in the clear water of the pool. But beyond these interpretations of a world he loved, it was as if he relived his whole development as a painter. There were line-form organizations similar to his early collages, and the severe arch and segment compositions of his first independent canvases. Line again became important in itself, swinging, crossing, merging, as it had in the dark war landscapes of his first sketches. With infinite patience he created a rich pattern of finest hairlines, ranging from light gray to deep black, centering around white cores. (Fig. 78). He felt sick from the strain on his eyes after the two large ink drawings were completed, but he wouldn't rest. After line his obsession now was color—a stronger, gayer, purer color than he had ever dared before. There were wide radiant areas in unmixed primaries, or delicate superimpositions like those he had done during the Bauhaus years. Yellow and black appeared in many combinations, and there was a predominance of purple, graded from a delicate rose color to a dense violet. Some psychiatrists claim that an increased use of purple in the work of an artist indicates a subconscious death anticipation. Moholy knew nothing of this theory, but purple and a contrapuntal variation of greens are predominant among the rich production of August, 1946 (Fig. 79).

At the beginning of September, this intense period of painting came suddenly to an end. Without an explanation Moholy put his casein colors in their cardboard boxes which he labeled carefully. He cleaned the dozens of brushes he had used and dried them in the sun. The water colors were put into large portfolios, and the sketches into file folders. The next morning when the

231

Fig. 78. Snake forms in ink,
1946. On board.

kitchen porch showed no longer any trace of the quantity of work
produced there, Moholy went to the workshop and started to work
with wire. With pliers and metal shears he formed a wire construction which he accentuated with bright yellow paint and a solid
form of plastic. After four days the "Wire Outdoor Sculpture"
was ready to be mounted. There were some high oak poles on the
back lawn which had once served as laundry poles; time and
weather had aged the wood to a deep bronze. On top of one of them
Moholy mounted his wire form. The effort to lift the construction
and hold it in place while I drove the iron clamps into the wood
was too much for him. He became violently sick and had to lie
down on the grass. But as the dizziness passed, he climbed the
stepladder again. The sun was setting with a red glow when he
stepped down, and he smiled with infinite happiness as he watched
the golden reflections on the plexiglass form.[5]

"I've added this to my place," he said. "It'll remain

[5] *The New Vision and Abstract of an Artist*, p. 87.

232

Fig. 79. Purple Water Color, 1946.

here, just like my trees," and he looked affectionately over half a dozen Chinese elms he had planted eight years ago and which had thrived magnificently under his care.

For days he was too weak to work. He lay on the ground, unwilling to use a long chair when he could feel the earth under his back. He watched the changing cloud formations in daytime and the stars at night. All his assertiveness was gone. He needed love as a tired child does. He remembered things far back in his life—songs the shepherd had sung on the plains of the river Drava, stories the old coachman had told, and poetry he had written forty years ago. He wanted to hear German folk songs which I had sung when our children were small, and he asked me to recite Heinrich Heine's

> Denk ich an Deutschland in der Nacht
> so bin ich um den Schlaf gebracht—

and

> Ich hatte einst ein schönes Vaterland. . . .

He spoke of Germany with infinite sadness and affection. His bitterness was gone. He only remembered what Germany had given him. He read Voltaire's *Candide* again, and we spoke of religion and the freedom of the spirit.

"If atheism means the supreme self-reliance of man, I certainly am an atheist. My instinct as a social being has been quite sufficient to make me morally conscious and responsible. But if religion means devotion to the spiritual in man, I do believe."

And spinning the thought over many days, he concluded one night:

"I do believe that man can make himself independent of his biological limitations. His spiritual force can surpass the mere process of changing food into energy. I have discovered lately that I am stronger than my body."

Later I read Carr's Bakunin biography to him. "The child, the barbarian, the scholar" delighted Moholy. He re-experienced his own bitter insights after the unsuccessful Hungarian Revolution in Bakunin's words:

233

A revolution must be social, not political. I believe that we can reach this goal by the development and organization of the non-political, social, and therefore anti-political power of the masses in town and country.[6]

And to his friend Carola Giedion-Welcker, Moholy wrote:

I love him because he was a man without compromise. His faith in the self-determining dignity of the individual was so outrageous that he had to live it every minute of his life to prove it to himself. In a totally dark world he had only himself to burn up as a guiding flare.

On the fifteenth of September, 1946, we had to return to Chicago.

"Let me take down the wire sculpture and store it in the house," I said as we stood for the last time in the yard. "The winds are ferocious out here, and the rain and snow will ruin it."

Moholy shook his head. "It is meant to be an outdoor sculpture. The impact of the weather will add to its form. I want to see next spring what has become of it."

Our eyes met, and I realized that he knew his fate. He returned into the house. It was the only time that he broke down and cried.

The Institute of Design moved to Dearborn Street amidst falling plaster, splintering beams, and obstructive scaffolding. With frozen smiles and labored cheerfulness Moholy, with his staff, faced hundreds of freshman students and those Board members who had suddenly discovered within themselves untold architectural abilities. They took over the plans for the remodeling of the building, insisting on a prestige policy in locating executive offices and reception desks that would have done full justice to a manufacturing concern. For a school to have to fight for abundant workshop and classroom space was an uncalled-for complication. The cost of this remodeling scheme was so staggering that anyone who applied had to be accepted as a student. With an enrollment of one thousand day and night students, the Institute finally looked like a "normal" school. But Moholy knew that

[6] E. H. Carr, *Michael Bakunin* (London, 1937).

234

he'd lose his lifetime fight if he could not tame this throng with a mature and creative faculty. He went to New York to look for the best men in the design field, but on October 4, 1946, he wrote:

> The postwar boom is even more noticeable here than in Chicago. Anyone who can do as much as hold a pencil tries to cut himself some bacon. Z. who couldn't buy a pint of whiskey a year ago now gets two hundred a week making clay models for motor cars, and even P. designs radio casings. Teaching? They just laughed at me.

The teachers who carried the curriculum into the fall term of 1946 were former students who had graduated before or during the war years. They were devoted and serious, but Moholy was worried about their lack of experience and maturity.

"We should have a faculty seminar each month," he said as we returned from a faculty meeting. "To mull over all that comes to our minds, as we've been used to doing, is fine. But it isn't enough any longer. If we could get together for a day or two every other month or so, they'd learn to be more than just teachers."

And in a burst of optimism he added:

"Mark it down on the calendar: December 26 and 27. That's when I'll give the first faculty workshop."

But deep within himself he knew that it wasn't lack of faculty training but sheer numerical load that crushed the spirit of the Institute.

"There's a strange contradiction in number," he said once as we stood on the second-floor landing, looking down at the milling crowd in the lobby. "Young people work better in crowds. They hate solitude, or conspicuous single effort. Yet they crave attention, and they fret if you don't know their first name. I wanted a big school eventually, and I dreamed of our own campus. But it should have been an organic growth as in a family where each arrival has his gestation period. I knew it would take a lifetime or perhaps more. If only they had been patient with our insignificance—just for another five or ten years—"

It was only in his night class for painters, and in a seminar with the oldest students, that he felt at home. With a

235

desperate determination he clung to these groups as the justification of all his efforts.

The preparations for the publishing of *Vision in Motion* had been infinitely slow. Now the first galley proofs had come, but Moholy felt that the introduction needed a new emphasis. In two nights of intense concentration he wrote:

> One of the functions of the artist in society is to put layer upon layer, stone upon stone, in the organization of emotions; to record feelings with his particular means, to give structure and refinement as well as direction to the inner life of his contemporaries.
>
> It is the artist's duty today to penetrate yet unseen ranges of the biological functions, to search the new dimensions of the industrial society, and to translate the new findings into emotional orientation. The artist unconsciously disentangles the most essential strands of existence from the contorting and chaotic complexities of actuality and weaves them into an emotional fabric of compelling validity, characteristic of himself as well as of his epoch.
>
> This ability of selection is an outstanding gift based upon intuitive power and insight, upon judgment and knowledge. *and upon inner responsibility to fundamental biological and social laws which provoke a reinterpretation in every civilization.*

"I couldn't have written this a few years back," he said, when he felt the formulation was satisfactory. "I saw in emotion only a precious individual barrier against the group. Now I know differently. Perhaps because I was a teacher so long I came to see emotion as the great adhesive, the ray that goes out to warm, and the response that comes back and confirms."

And to the first chapter of *Vision in Motion* he added:

> By concentrating insight, passion and stamina we may recover the neglected fundamentals. Our generation must accept the challenge to reinvestigate the elements of healthy living so that they can be used as yardsticks to clarify conditions around us. By integrating this newly gained knowledge with the existing social dynamics we could direct our steps toward a harmony of individual and social needs.

Now all the writing was done. The water colors and drawings from the summer were put away like an intimate diary. In our living room stood two heavy plexiglass sheets, a full inch thick and flawless and reflective like clear water.

On October 29—it was my birthday—Moholy came home late from a Board meeting. We had waited with dinner because of the special date. The children had put candles on the table, a garland of tiny fall asters surrounded my plate, and we had intricate doilies made of colored tissue paper under our glasses. Moholy had never remembered any of our birthdays. But in 1946 it was different. He had bought a lovely fox jacket which he now put around my shoulders. It was the first actual birthday present he gave me, and it shook me to the core. It indicated a concern and tenderness that was frightening. I fought my tears all through dinner, and when I finally dared to look at Moholy I knew that he understood. That night he marked the plexiglass with an engraver's tool. Swooping down on it almost like a bird, he outlined a large area with a deeply incised line which then was subdivided by two central cuts. Within a few minutes the form of "Double Loop" (Fig. 80) had been determined.

For half an hour he rested on the couch. He seemed asleep and I tried to cover him with a robe. But he waved me away and got up. This time he engraved two identical forms on the plexiglass sheet, two oblong "fish forms" which had appeared in his first kinetic sculpture of 1943. No correction was possible; the mark of the needle was final. Slowly Moholy aimed his tool, hesitated, contemplated, made a new attempt, until the actual incision was made. Exhausted, he finally got up from the floor, and with a tired relaxed smile he went to bed. At one o'clock he got up and returned to the living room. Next morning I saw that he had outlined a third form. I hoped he would sleep, now that the creative tension had been released, but he was up at seven, talking to his Hungarian carpenter.

Kalman Toman was a wonderful fellow. He came from Hungarian peasant stock, a short stout man who in his late sixties retained a radiantly youthful complexion and an indefatigable capability for work. Moholy loved him and felt happy and relaxed in his company. It was Kalman who had made the farmhouse the

237

Fig. 80. Double loop, 1946.
Molded Plexiglas sheet on
black Formica base.

place we loved. For years he had spent his week ends in the country, building porches and workshops, furniture and roads. Each fall he and Moholy got together for the old European ritual of making "*caposta*," shredding cabbage into wooden barrels for future sauerkraut. I could not enter into their conversation, but 1 loved to hear their roaring laughter when they told each other the primitive jokes of peasants and soldiers, or whistled to each other the tunes of their young days. Kalman made Moholy's picture frames and the backgrounds for the light modulators; he fashioned bases for sculptures, and he was the only person to whom Moholy would entrust the delicate business of cutting out the sculptures from the plexiglass sheets. Moholy, who had long since decided on the final cuts, would bend every effort to make his friend feel his appreciation.

"Do you think this cut is right?" he would ask anxiously. "Please, friend, I urge you, don't cut if you think it isn't in the proper place."

Kalman, whose artistic preference ran toward highly decorative intarsia panels which he did for his home, felt in turn the obligation to show how much he appreciated his friend's appreciation.

"Considering everything involved," he'd say very slowly, squinting his eyes and cocking his head sideways. "I think you have done right, Moholy—ur."

And the bandsaw or the drill cut into the material, carefully guided by Kalman's skilled hands.

That morning in 1946, Kalman appeared at our apartment around eight o'clock. Moholy looked white and his lips were bluish. In an attempt to keep him in bed, I warned him that I'd call the doctor.

"Never say that again," Moholy said with a voice that was so cold that it seemed to come from a strange person. "Never threaten me again, or I'll go away."

We carried the heavy sheets into the car, and when the students came to occupy the workshops, the three sculptures had been already cut. They were heated and bent during the following nights.

"Art must be forgotten—beauty must be realized,"

239

Fig. 81. Inverted curve,
1946. Molded Plexiglas
sheet on black wood base.

Mondrian had written to Moholy in 1939. The three sculptures were pieces of perfect beauty (Fig. 81).

In November the Museum of Modern Art in New York asked for Moholy's participation in a "Conference on Industrial Design as a New Profession." For a few days, following the completion of the sculptures and some intensified work for the Parker Pen Company, Moholy seemed willing to cancel this engagement. Coming home from the Institute, powdered with plaster dust and his noise-sensitive nerves tortured by the din of drills, hammers, saws, and the voices of a thousand students, he lay on his bed, unable to sleep but equally unable to do anything else. The trip to New York would be too much. On November 9 he attended a conference of some of the Board members, dealing with the remodeling of the school and the future enrollment policy. That night he came home late, but the deadly exhaustion was gone from his face.

"I'm going to New York," he said. "I'm leaving Monday."

"But you said yourself it would be too much of a strain."

"That was last week. I'm all right now, and I never knew as clearly as tonight that I have to go."

"What happened?"

"Nothing, nothing that hasn't happened before. They're all excellent men, these industrialists. They try to do the right thing by education, they say they understand it. But there is a basic misunderstanding; and I finally saw it. There's an insidious paternalism involved that strangles creative independence. 'Don't worry, we'll take care of you artists; you serve us and we'll earn money for you.' Industry as the Great White Father of the arts!"

"A trip to New York won't change that."

"I know, but it'll give me a chance to make one more statement about the place of art education. Somehow I have to make it clear that if there is such a relationship as guidance and being guided it is industry that follows vision, and not vision that follows industry."

Moholy didn't feel well the next day. I called his doctor, asking him to forbid the trip. But he didn't share my anxiety at all. He ordered a blood count, which showed no appreciable increase in the number of white blood corpuscles, and he shrugged off the slight temperature Moholy was running every night. When I balked at making plane reservations, Moholy lost his temper. He felt that any interference on my part was obstructive and presumptuous. I tried to subdue my fear, which had grown into an irrational anticipation of imminent disaster. We hardly talked to each other until he left for New York.

The "Conference on Industrial Design as a New Profession," under the chairmanship of Dean Joseph Hudnut of Harvard University, was divided into two groups. As Moholy had foreseen, there were the representatives of "Design for Industry," and the others who thought of industry as an instrument to realize design. Both groups prided themselves on their pragmatism, but the pragmatic results were measured in different terms. The artificial obsolescence policy found defenders who saw in an unending stream of design variations a beneficial stimulus for a free economy. They were the specialists who talked in terms of vocational aptitude as the goal of all design education. When one of them accused Moholy of "dabbling in design," Moholy smiled happily:

> I love to dabble. That is what made me what I am today. I was educated as a lawyer, but because I dared to dabble with plastics and wood and so on, I gained a wide experience. Almost every educator, if he is sincere, tries to influence students to try the things he himself missed in his life or in his education. I was educated at a university as a so-called academist. That is how I found out I had a right to educate *the senses* of people. Today I am 25% a scholar, and 75% an artist and a what-not.[7]

And in the closing session he found formulations which stand as a lasting credo:

> Some day we'll grasp the confusion of the Industrial Revolu-

[7] From the Minutes of the "Conference on Industrial Design as a New Profession," organized by the Department on Industrial Design, Edgar Kaufmann, Jr., Chairman, of the Museum of Modern Art in New York (Mimeographed edition, New York, 1947).

tion. On the one hand we make the people literate, and on the other hand we take this literacy away from them by means of advertising, radio, and other forms of propaganda which appeal to the lowest standards for profit's sake. . . .

Design is not a profession; it is an attitude—the attitude of the planner. Every high school in this country has better equipment than we have or Harvard has. It is simply prodigious. And what do they do with it? Nothing. It is the spirit that determines the whole thing. We have to develop, step by step, an educational procedure in which the creative abilities and capacities of young people are used. That would mean general education. When any human being works with his hands, whatever he does will be translated into the brain as knowledge. This knowledge, in turn, will react on his emotional self. That is how a higher level of personality is achieved.

On the last day of the Conference he wrote in a letter:

I feel excellent, better than I have in weeks. Although there were some nasty personal attacks at the conference, I knew that what I do in Chicago is right. And I loved—yes, Darling. I outrightly *loved*—my fellow men who "dabble" like me.

Bob and Elizabeth [Wolff] gave a nice party for me tonight. Bob has developed very much in his painting, another proof of the clarifying impact of teaching and being taught by one's students.

I know now that I'll weather the Chicago storm. I'm full of defiance and determination. . . .

And in a conversation with Wolff that same night he said: "I don't know yet about my paintings, but I'm proud of my life."

When he came back from New York he was running a temperature of 101 degrees and he went straight to bed. But he was up next morning to go to the Institute and to hold a faculty meeting. The doctor maintained his professional optimism. "Don't worry, he has at least another five or six years before him," he told me. "There are no alarming symptoms or changes."

The Chicago Society for Contemporary Art had invited him to a lecture by S. I. Hayakawa on "Semantics and Modern Art." Moholy felt that he was too tired to attend, but he changed his mind when the lecturer called up in the afternoon,

243

explaining that his talk would largely center around Moholy's work. His left leg dragged as we walked from the parking lot to the Art Institute, and his hands were ice-cold.

"Now watch me," he said as we paused for a moment before mounting the steps leading to the entrance. "The greatest transformation trick of the century."

He straightened his back, his gait became regular and youthfully elastic, and his face lighted up with a radiant smile. As we joined the crowd in the restaurant, there was no trace of sickness in Moholy's attitude. Only those who knew him closely wondered at the strange pallor of his skin. Hayakawa's lecture was a scholarly exposition of the common aim in the fundamental form-language of Constructivism and the search for a precise system of signs and symbols in general semantics. Moholy enjoyed it thoroughly. As we crossed the overpass above the tracks of the Illinois Central Railroad on our way to the parking lot, he suddenly leaned against the railing.

"There is an unconscious creativeness in the way modern man has lighted up the night," he said, looking out over the Chicago skyline. "How I've loved city lights!"

It was the past tense in his last sentence that remained fixed in my mind.

His painting class the following night met in the auditorium of the Institute of Design to look at slides Moholy had selected. When he came home he complained about a strong pain in his left side. "No, don't call the doctor," he insisted. "It's nothing at all. I lifted the projector to put it in the right place. I strained a muscle. It'll be gone by tomorrow."

When the doctor arrived in the morning, Moholy could no longer walk.

"He has strained his spleen," was the medical diagnosis. "Eight days rest on his back will heal it completely. A light diet and lots of sleep will have a beneficial influence on his whole condition."

An hour later Moholy had his first severe hemorrhage. By night he felt agonizing pain, radiating from his spine. No amount of morphine brought relief, and the injections to stop bleeding were without result. During the ride to the hospital I

244

held him in my arms because his inflamed nerves could not stand the jarring and swaying of the ambulance, careening through the afternoon traffic.

There was no single room available in the large private hospital to which he was taken, and there was no night nurse. The oxygen tent did not function and the blood transfusion clotted. A stream of relatives, doctors, and orderlies brushed by his bed in an emergency ward, while wide-open doors gave on a noisy corridor. It was like dying in Union Station. But Moholy was no longer aware of his surroundings. Breathing had become such a torture that it occupied all his attention. And there was an excruciating thirst after the heavy loss of blood. An old man brought a tray of food at regular intervals, and took it away, untouched, with equal regularity. Another old man wrapped the body of the patient in the next bed in paper strips and carted it away. An oxygen pump supplying the victim of an apoplectic stroke in another bed hammered on day and night. Over everything lay the stench of a menagerie.

Our children had been alone for two days. After a vigil of fifty hours I had to go home to look after them. When Moholy saw me in hat and coat he seemed to become wide awake.

"Glasses," he whispered. And as I looked uncomprehending, he repeated with a frown of impatience: "Glasses."

I lifted the cellophane curtains of the oxygen tent sufficiently to put them on.

"You go?"

His eyes were of a new color, a deep pure blue that had an unknown depth.

"I have to—just for one night."

His hand started to sweep slowly over the counterpane. "Work."

He closed his eyes, exhausted from the strain of speaking. Then he repeated: "Work."

I went down in the elevator, but I couldn't leave the building. When I returned to the room, his head had slipped from the pillow and his glasses had fallen to the floor

I came back early next morning. There was no one in attendance, and at first sight it looked as if Moholy had died. His face had changed completely—the bone structure showed through the yellowish skin, and his hair, which had been gray, had turned snow-white over night.

As I called his name he opened his eyes, and a smile of indescribable softness spread over his face. It was as if a myriad of small reflecting waves had shattered the surface of a very dark sea. For a moment all his features were liveliness and warmth.

"You're back!"

It was almost inaudible. And after a long pause, still smiling: "I'll make it. Don't go again."

His lips were dried out, with deep gashes.

"Are you thirsty?"

"Terribly thirsty."

No one had cared to ask him while I had been at home.

Unquestioned by anyone in the long, crowded corridors I took a tea-bag from a breakfast tray and found a pantry with a gas cooker. I made some tea, and from a straw dropped it into his mouth. It revived his breathing as if the hot liquid had refilled his empty veins.

"Hungarian—last night—lovely—" he whispered, referring to the visit of his Hungarian doctor. "Only Hungarian—"

He closed his eyes, and I thought back over many years to Sergei Eisenstein's words: "One dies in one's own language, they say," spoken to a young and powerful man who had had nothing but scorn for the death-awareness of his friend.

"Higher—"

Moholy breathed with tremendous difficulty, pushing air from his lips as if it were lead.

I raised the head end of the hospital bed as high as the mechanism would permit, but within minutes it increased the restlessness. Slowly I lowered his head, and for a few minutes it brought relief.

"Higher—"

With slow turns of the crank I followed his restless stirs, strangely aware that it was a cradling motion that rocked him to sleep.

"*Aludni—*"

246

With a last immense effort he turned his head away from the light.

"*Aludni*—"

The air around his bed filled with a tension that eclipsed my being. There was no sadness, no grief, no fear. When it was over and his jaw fell, there was total nothingness.

It was November the twenty-fourth, nineteen hundred and forty-six.

epilogue

Letter by
Robert Jay Wolff,
former dean of the Institute of Design in Chicago.

New York
May 2, 1949

SIBYL DEAR:

Finally this long delayed letter. You know I don't like writing it. The closer words get to an experience like Moholy's last week here the more I distrust them. I seem to be always missing the facts and I end with a feeble comment on it. Nobody who had any contact with Moholy that last visit to New York can ever forget the experience. To most people Moholy was simply being himself. To me and to others who knew he was dying and knew he knew, he was unbelievable. He was anxious to see as many of his friends as possible. I went with him to three or four gatherings, one of which was at my place. I watched him and it was hard to believe what I saw and heard. He led every discussion. He covered everything from painting and town planning to hilarious stories about his linguistic blunders when he first came to this country. He never referred to his illness except to joke about the array of pill bottles that he had to sample every now and then and which I know he considered pure hokus pokus. This was not the sort of thing you expect from a sick and dying man. You think of yourself in the same spot and you wonder. And you end by forgetting that Moholy is dying and you laugh like hell with him over the absurdity of a vigorous man carrying around a satchel full of medicine and submitting to a diet that couldn't be expected to keep a bird alive. And you realize suddenly that there aren't the usual vanities in this performance. Moholy always loved being the center of attention and this was no different. But you noticed something else here. There was no question of this not being a herculean effort. You had only to look closely at his face which he didn't give you much chance to do because you were most of the time listening to his stories and plans and ideas.

249

But when you did look at his face and stopped hearing his voice you saw that he was beyond vanity and you sensed that he was trying to tell his friends that he loved them and that he needed their love. To people who knew Moholy only as a fascinating performer and intellectual this might seem strange. The truth did not come clear to me actually until his last night when I went into our living room where he slept on the studio couch. The couch extended out into the room and one of my pictures hung on the opposite wall. Before I entered the room I stopped in the hall and watched him for a moment. He was lying on the couch with the covers over him, his hands propping up his head from behind, staring intently at my picture. I went in and without turning to look at me he said with that incredibly convincing enthusiasm that has made brilliant teachers out of self doubting neophytes, "Bob, it's a wonderful picture."

Written, those words seem innocuous enough. You have to hear Moholy speak them and have to have heard him that particular night a few days before he died to feel their impact. They made you feel suddenly not alone, I mean not alone in things that you finally resign yourself to never fully sharing with anyone. You have the feeling for an instant that this man is you and you are him. He had a rare, almost instinctual skill for dissolving ego barriers and bringing minds together in a common experience. No one I know could induce in others more fruitful and selfless collaboration. Yet what a target he set up for the eventually resentful ego, and I don't exclude my own. Somehow he seemed to take our weaknesses along with our positive gifts as part of his job and I've never known him to hold a grudge against any gifted person no matter how rough the circumstances got.

I started talking to him that night about his painting. I said I was beginning to understand the meaning of it more and more the longer I knew him. I told him that I had always admired the purely visual and material resourcefulness but that it was only recently that I had begun to realize the life content in his work, not exterior and objective, but interior and subjective. I told him that what he had been painting was his own life, his refusal to be motivated by conflict and tragedy, fear and disbelief, and that his work embodied his great faith in himself and the power of his own optimism. I said that if his paintings were without negative tensions, so was his life. And I told him that in this sense it seemed to me that his life and the way he lived it was the subject content of his painting and that he had expressed it well. . . .

You know Sibyl we have all said what an act of almost super-human courage those last weeks of Moholy's life constituted. But now that I look back I am sure that Moholy would not think of it as courageous and would, in fact, be annoyed at the thought. He had made of himself a creature so positive that I am sure he resented having to approach anything in life with calculated courage. He would be prouder to be seen as man who had achieved a power within himself that no longer needed recourse to courage. What you said about his last hours bears out the fact that Moholy refused to believe that he could die. I really believe he had brought himself to the point where his mind could not grasp the reality of a negative force. I wonder if at the very end he did not have to face the tragic antithesis of everything his life had stood for. I hope he was spared this.

BOB

Bibliography of English-language publications
by and about
Laszlo Moholy-Nagy

Books by L. Moholy-Nagy

Painting-Photography-Film, Bauhaus Bücher No. 8, Munich 1927, English
     translation London 1968, Cambridge, Mass., 1969
The New Vision, New York 1935
The New Vision and Abstract of An Artist, New York 1947
Vision in Motion, Chicago 1947
TELEHOR, Special issue L. Moholy-Nagy, Brno 1936

Some major articles by L. Moholy-Nagy

Confession, *The Little Review*, New York, Spring No., May 1929
New Approach to Fundamentals of Design, *More Business*, August 1938
Better than Before, Proposals for the Rehabilitation of the Handicapped.
     The Technology Review, November 1943
Photography and the Study of Design, *American Annual of Photography*,
     1945.

Some major articles about L. Moholy-Nagy

Herbert Read: A New Humanism, *The Architectural Review*, October 1935
Anon: Moholy-Nagy, Experimentalist, *Art and Industry*, London, March 1937
Siegfried Giedion: L. Moholy-Nagy, *Institute of Design Catalogue*, Chicago
     1941
Sibyl Moholy-Nagy: The Making of a Constructivist, *Copy*, San Francisco,
     January 1950
Sibyl Moholy-Nagy: Documented Seeing, *Art and Photography*, Chicago 1949
Thomas Hess: Moholy-Nagy Memorial, *Art News*, June 1947
Alexander Dorner: In Memoriam Moholy-Nagy, *Art Institute*, Chicago, Nov.
     1947
Sibyl Moholy-Nagy: Constructivism from Malevitch to Moholy-Nagy, *Arts
     and Architecture*, June 1966

Books with relevant references to L. Moholy-Nagy

H. Bayer and W. Gropius: Bauhaus 1919 to 1928, The Museum of Modern
     Art, New York, 1938
Reyner Banham: Theory and Design in the First Machine Age, London and
     New York 1960
Sibyl Moholy-Nagy: Moholy-Nagy, Experiment in Totality, New York 1950,
     Cambridge, Mass., 1969
Hans Maria Wingler, Das Bauhaus, Bramsche 1962, second edition 1968,
     English translation Cambridge, Mass., 1969

253

index

(*Italicized numerals refer to illustrations.*)

257

258